IMAGES
of America

WASATCH MOUNTAINS

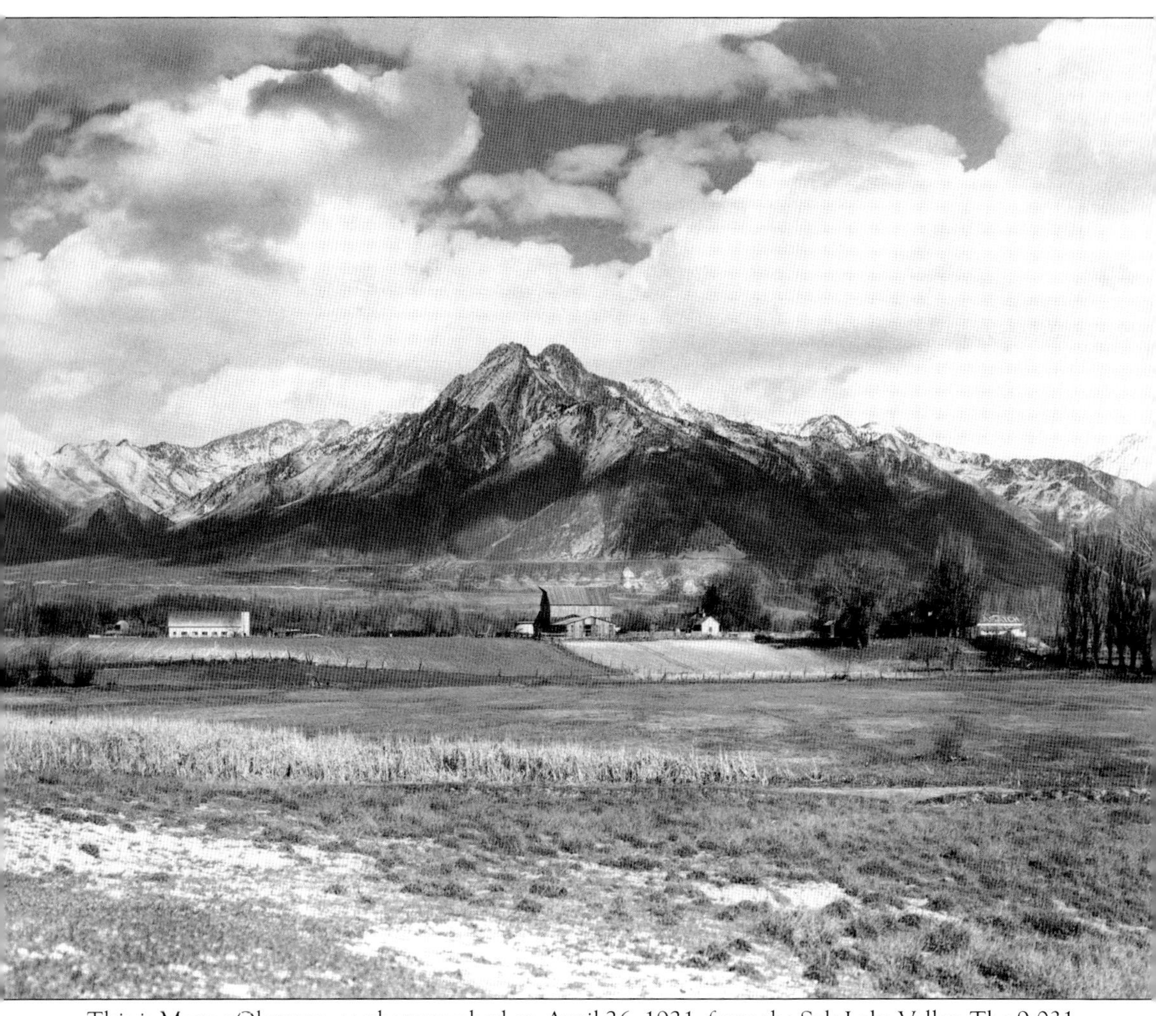

This is Mount Olympus, as photographed on April 26, 1921, from the Salt Lake Valley. The 9,031-foot peak is not the highest peak in the area by more than 2,000 feet in elevation. However, its sharp, pinnacle top appeared to resemble the legendary home of the Greek gods, hence its fabled name. The peak is also more visible and accessible to downtown Salt Lake City than the taller peaks to the southeast. A steep, 3.1-mile, one-way hike, plus a scramble in the last few hundred yards, is required to reach the south summit. (Courtesy of Utah State Historical Society.)

On the Cover: Mount Timpanogos doubled as a dancing platform in the sky more than a century ago. This photograph from the morning of July 28, 1923, shows four couples from the Wasatch Mountain Club dancing at sunrise atop the 11,750 feet above sea level summit. The hikers climbed the popular peak by moonlight overnight so they could dance at sunrise in celebration of the strenuous feat. (Courtesy of J. Willard Marriott Digital Library, the University of Utah.)

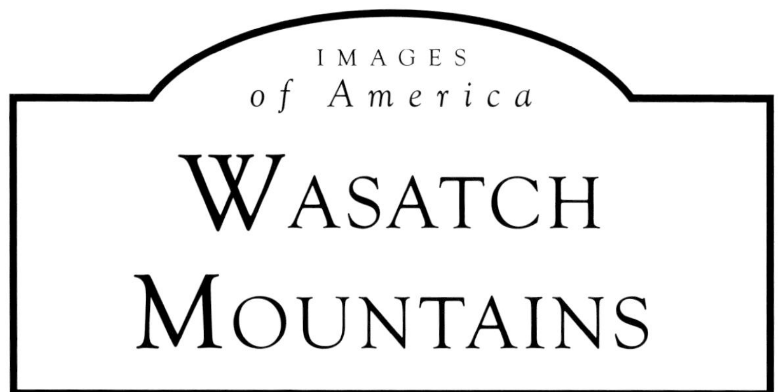

Lynn Arave

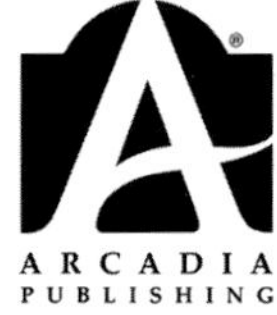

ISBN 978-1-4671-6243-2

Published by Arcadia Publishing
Charleston, South Carolina

Printed in the United States of America

Library of Congress Control Number: 2024952086

For all general information, please contact Arcadia Publishing:
Telephone 843-853-2070
Fax 843-853-0044
E-mail sales@arcadiapublishing.com

Visit us on the Internet at www.arcadiapublishing.com

To the Wasatch Mountain Club, past and present, whose century-plus-old legacy not only promoted recreation in the Wasatch Mountains, but also preserved many vintage photographs of their mountainous exploits of old—some of which grace this book

Contents

ACKNOWLEDGMENTS

Special thanks to all the sources that allowed the use of their historical images for this book.

These include the Utah State Historical Society, the J. Willard Marriott Digital Library at the University of Utah, Uintah County Library Regional History Center, the Library of Congress, and the *Deseret News* archives.

Friends and family who supplied pictures for this book are Ravell Call, Ray Boren, Scott Winterton, Harris Adams, Roger Arave, LeAnn Arave, Steven Arave, Taylor Arave, Liz Arave Hafen, Whitney Arave, and Wayne Arave.

Also, a special thanks goes to the Wasatch Mountain Club for making sure that its historic photographs were preserved from the early 20th century.

Note that there is a significant amount of the author's family photographs in this book, a necessity, since Wikipedia pictures could not be used here.

Note, too, that the history of skiing and ski resorts along the Wasatch Front is only briefly explored in this book. Space will not permit otherwise, and ski history is already expounded on in other works. This book is but a sampling of what numerous features and businesses are available in and near the Wasatch Mountains.

Finally, note that sometimes the names of all persons in a photograph could not be listed due to a lack of information available. Also, at times, the last name—or a full name—of all persons listed in photographic captions could not always be found. Sadly, records from more than a century ago often failed to list the full names of everyone in a particular photograph.

INTRODUCTION

The Wasatch Mountains have religious as well as practical significance.

The first local peak the Mormon pioneers climbed was not nearly one of the tallest, but it was a strategic and sacred mound. This was Utah's own version of Mount Sinai, alias Ensign Peak, in the Wasatch Mountains, just north of the center of downtown Salt Lake City. At an elevation of 5,414 feet, this mound-shaped peak, located behind the Utah State Capitol, is only about 1,100 feet above the city streets.

According to Pres. George A. Smith, the first counselor in the first presidency, Brigham Young had a vision of Joseph Smith and Mount Ensign while in the Nauvoo Temple prior to leaving the East:

> President Young had a vision of Joseph Smith, who showed him the mountain that we now call Ensign Peak, immediately north of Salt Lake City, and there was an ensign that fell upon that peak, and Joseph said, "Build under that point where the colors fall and you will prosper and have peace."

The Mormon pioneers arrived in Utah on Saturday, July 24, 1847. They spent all of the next day, Sunday, resting and worshiping God. However, on July 26, one of the first tasks attempted was to climb what is now known as Ensign Peak to get a better look at the valley and probably also to see firsthand the mountain in President Young's vision.

Among those pioneers who made that first climb were Brigham Young, Heber C. Kimball, Willard Richards, Wilford Woodruff, George A. Smith, Ezra T. Benson, Albert Carrington, and William Clayton. (The party used horses to make the first two-thirds of the climb, then dismounted and went on foot.)

Elder Woodruff was the first to reach the summit. President Young was ill (and barely able to make it to the top with help) and was likely the slowest climber. On top of the peak, President Young said, "Here is a proper place to raise an ensign to the nations." This is a reference to the scriptures that mention an "ensign." These scriptural references are likely the inspiration for the peak's name. Not long after the pioneers arrived in the Salt Lake Valley, Ensign Peak was also used for a brief period as an outdoor temple until the Endowment House was constructed.

Today, there is an 18-foot-tall monument on Ensign Peak, placed there on July 26, 1934, by the Salt Lake Ensign Stake Mutual Improvement Associations. Stones gathered from all along the Mormon Trail are incorporated into the rock monument.

Coincidentally, it took 40 years for members of the Church of Jesus Christ of Latter-day Saints (Mormons) to build the Salt Lake Temple, but it is composed of actual granite rocks from the Wasatch Mountains in Little Cottonwood Canyon, 20 miles away. (Originally, they tried using the sandstone rock from the nearby Red Butte Canyon, but it proved to be too soft.) Essentially, the Salt Lake Temple is a downtown symbol/monument to the Wasatch Mountains as well as a religious shrine.

Moving to the south end of the Wasatch Mountains is its tallest summit, Mount Nebo.

Perhaps the first published account of a climb to the top of Mount Nebo, the tallest summit in the Wasatch Mountains, was in the *Deseret News* of August 3, 1887—and it was mostly done on horseback.

"Mount Nebo. An interesting account of the ascent of this majestic peak" was the headline. Dr. Park and J.H. Paul, both of Salt Lake, and F.W. Chappell, T.L. Foote, a Mr. Noble, and a Mr. Field, all of Nephi, were the climbers.

This early trek, on July 22, 1887, started at Mona, on the west side of Mount Nebo, in contrast to modern climbs beginning on the east side. The group rode horses up Willow Canyon. They went to about the 6,700-foot level and then rested for the night and continued the morning of July 23. With horses, they were able to easily carry many supplies.

"Ascending over gravel beds, rocks and drifted soil, through oak-brush, maples . . . and groves of quaking aspens, past witches' rocks and over fields of broken, shifting slate; along narrow trails facing a steep descent of a thousand feet, past great precipitous ledges, and tolling up the last cone-like steep, we reached the apex of Mt. Nebo—the giant of the Wasatch Range. A cold wind from over several snowbanks saluted and chilled us," the story stated.

"The light atmosphere made the smallest amount of clambering around the mountain very laborious and most of the party complained of headache or dizziness and cold feet."

While the writer agreed that Mount Nebo did not have the religious history of the original peak in the Old Testament, "it far surpasses it in physical grandeur," he wrote.

On the summit, the story stated, "We could see Fountain Green, Moroni, Ephraim, part of Manti, Mount Pleasant, Nephi, Leamington, Moria, Deseret, Goshen, the west fields of Santaquin, Provo, American Fork, Lehi and the cemetery of Salt Lake City." (Note that the cemetery view seems unlikely, though.)

The group measured the temperature at 24 degrees and saw six-foot-deep snowbanks near the summit.

The story ended with "Altogether, Mt. Nebo is not difficult of ascent, but is not safe to those unaccustomed to the saddle and far too rough and hazardous for ladies. Our train of seven horseman [*sic*] made a pretty sight along the steep serpentine trail."

Mount Nebo was mentioned in the *Salt Lake Telegram* newspaper of March 25, 1920, as being urged to have an observatory atop its summit. This was to be a "Yankee Memorial" to honor the soldiers, sailors, and marines of all wars that the United States had been involved in.

It was also noted that a radio station could be housed on its lofty summit. Having a searchlight powered by the streams around the huge mountain was another proposal.

Of course, none of that ever happened, but it had been a dream of George B. Hobbs, a Nephi, Utah, resident. (Nephi is just southwest of Mount Nebo.)

Hobbs felt that the searchlight atop Nebo would be beneficial to aviators flying through Utah.

"Aloft on Mount Nebo" was a March 1, 1920, headline in the *Salt Lake Herald* newspaper. "Utah peak has beauty of Alps; Grandeur in view," the story stated.

After the completion of an official trail to the top of Mount Nebo, 82 hikers made it to the summit on August 6, 1919.

The story reported that Nephi residents wanted to make the Salt Creek trailhead and area "a playground" for all to enjoy.

"Gov. Dern leads party to the top of Mount Nebo" was an August 19, 1927, headline in the *Mount Pleasant Pyramid* newspaper.

The five tallest peaks in the Wasatch Mountain range are as follows: 1) Mount Nebo North Peak, 11,928 feet above sea level; 2) Mount Nebo South Peak, 11,877; 3) Mount Nebo Middle Peak, 11,824; 4) Mount Timpanogos North Peak, 11,752; and 5) Mount Timpanogos South Peak, 11,722.

Today, the majority of Utah's population, more than 80 percent, live in proximity to the Wasatch Mountains and enjoy its watersheds, beauty, and related recreational activities.

One

Early Exploration

The Shoshone and Ute Native Americans hunted and fished in the Wasatch Mountains. The Utes particularly liked the Utah County area and Utah Lake. The Utes were hunters and gatherers. Their contact with the Spanish provided them with horses and greater mobility.

The Spanish expedition from Santa Fe of 1776, headed by Francisco Atanasio Dominquez and Silvestre Velez de Escalante, included the first known Europeans to see the Wasatch Mountains. This group was likely to have at least seen Mount Nebo and Mount Timpanogos, plus the southern end of the Wasatch.

Next came the era of the trappers and mountain men. First, it was probably Jim Bridger, a trapper and explorer. Bridger had tromped through the north end of the Wasatch Mountains as early as 1824 in today's Cache County. By 1825, he had seen the Great Salt Lake.

Peter Skene Ogden, with the Hudson's Bay Company, led a brigade of 131, and by the spring of 1925, he had entered Cache Valley and eventually to Ogden Valley and to today's Mountain Green. Although he may have never seen the Wasatch Front (except in Cache Valley), he was very familiar with the Wasatch Mountains per se.

There may have been others, too. In fact, when the Mormon pioneers arrived in the Salt Lake Valley in July 1847, there were at least five white men living in the Ogden area and a sixth white man residing on Antelope Island. Miles Goodyear was the most well-known of these men, and the Mormons purchased the Ogden area land from him. (Plus, the Donner Party had crossed the Wasatch Mountains in the summer of 1846 on the way to California.)

The Mormon pioneers settled Salt Lake City first. Then, they expanded north into the Ogden area and then south into Provo. The Wasatch Mountains were the backbone of early Mormon settlements. The mountains offered a sense of protection and invaluable water resources and timber.

Wasatch is a Ute Indian word meaning "mountain pass" or "low place in a high mountain." The word was originally spelled "Wahsatch," but the "h" was eventually dropped, as it was deemed unnecessary to its usage.

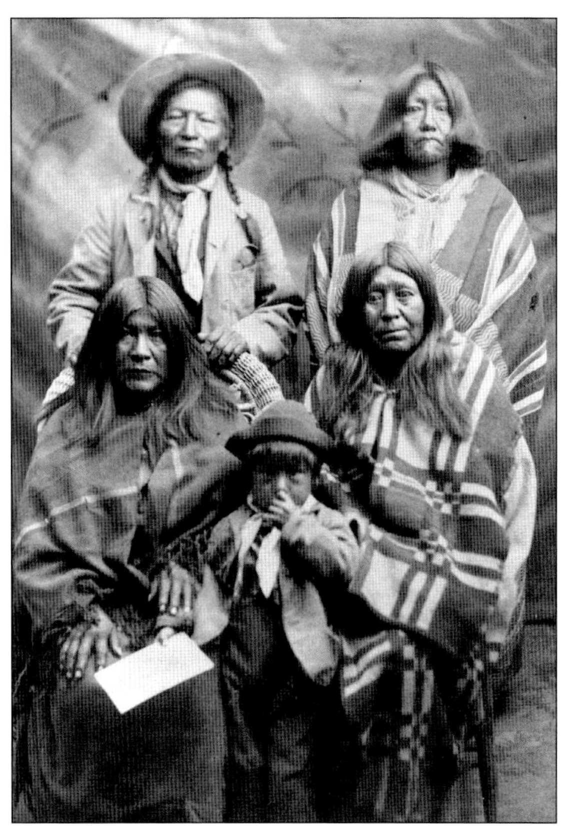

This is a typical Ute family from 1902 living in western Colorado, just east of the Uinta Mountains. In their pre-reservation days, the Utes would hunt and fish in the Wasatch Mountains (as well as the Uinta Mountains) during the warmer months of the year since the harsh winters there made the lower valleys more hospitable. (Courtesy of Library of Congress.)

From left to right, a Mr. Brockbank, Mrs. Jack Hosmer, Mrs. M.K. Parsons, and Spanish Fork mayor Hansen stand next to a new city marker in the 1920s. This one highlights Atanasio Dominguez and Silvestre Velez de Escalante and their expedition of 1776. The two Franciscan priests from Spain explored the early American Southwest and followed the stream down Spanish Fork Canyon; they were possibly the first Europeans to see the Wasatch Mountains. (Courtesy of Utah State Historical Society.)

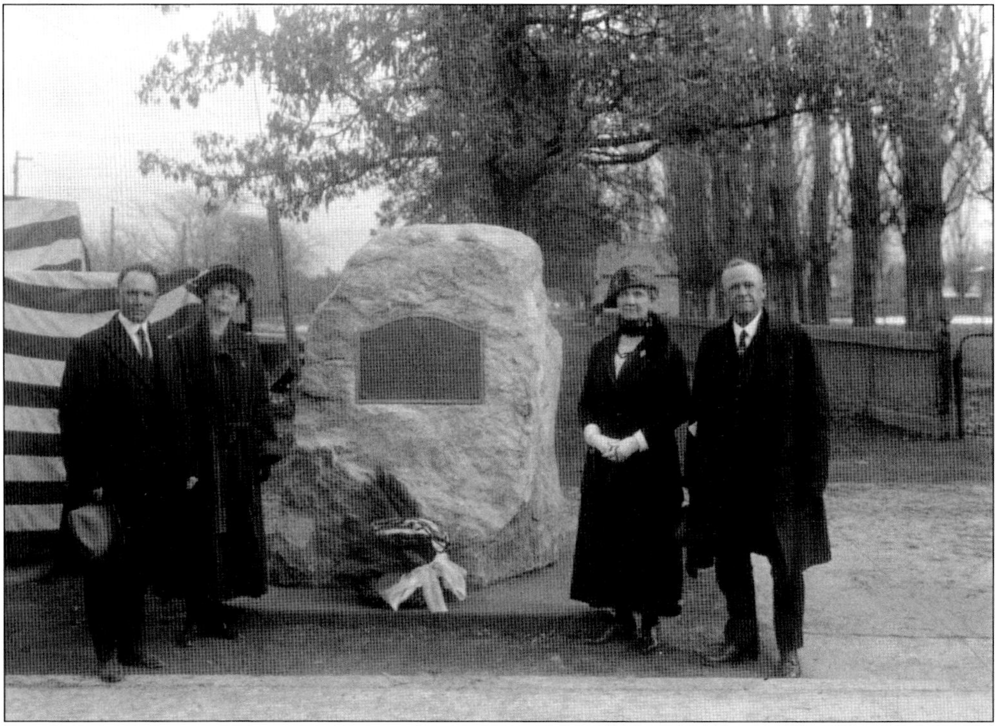

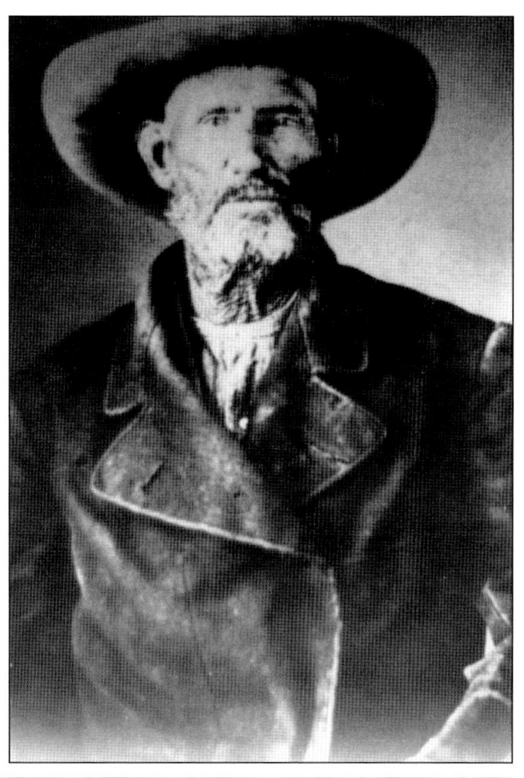

Jim Bridger was an American mountain man, explorer, and trapper in the early 19th century. He explored the Wasatch Mountains and the Great Salt Lake, first in 1824. He was living at Fort Bridger in southwestern Wyoming in 1847, when the Mormon pioneers passed by. He is considered one of the foremost frontiersmen in the American West. (Courtesy of Uintah County Library Regional History Center.)

This 1870s picture shows the rugged nature of Devil's Gate in Weber Canyon. This narrow gorge detoured the Mormon pioneers in 1847 to travel through Emigration Canyon instead. More than a century later, Devil's Gate became "Scrambled Egg Curve," a rough bottleneck in lower Weber Canyon that caused numerous traffic accidents and delays. This obstacle was finally conquered in the 1960s when the interstate road through the canyon was constructed. (Courtesy of Utah State Historical Society.)

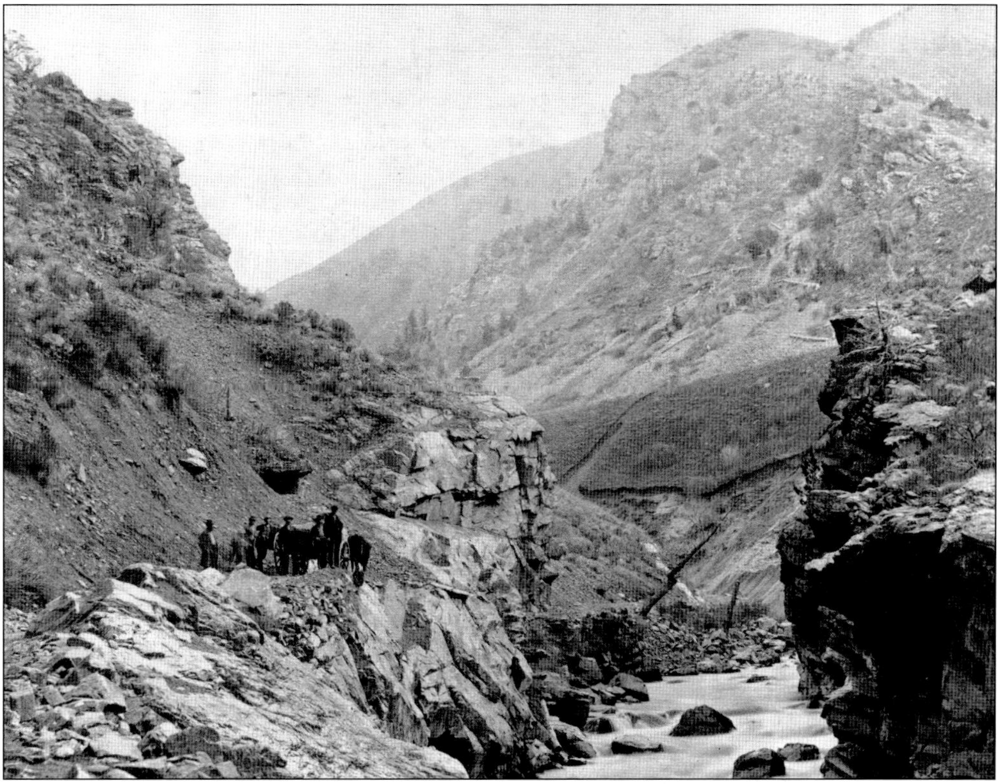

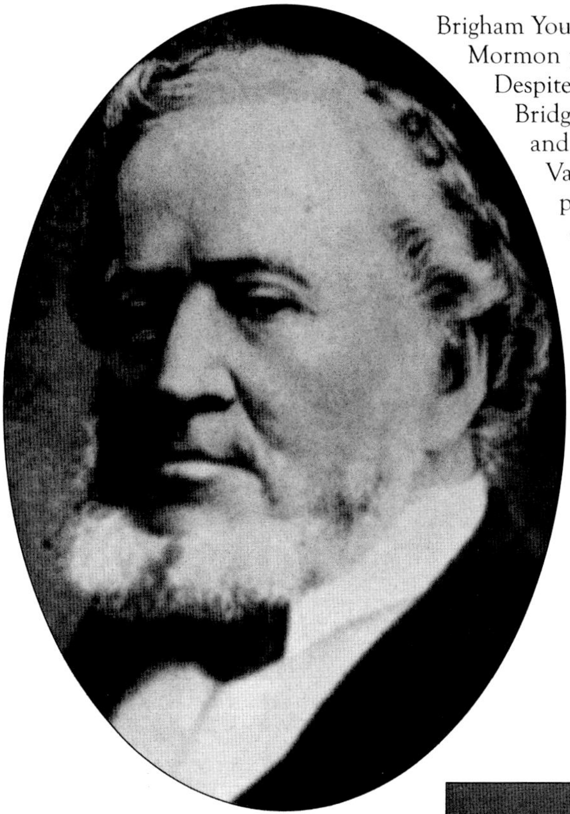

Brigham Young, acting as an American Moses, led the Mormon pioneers to the Salt Lake Valley in 1847. Despite being advised by mountain man Jim Bridger that it was a poor place to settle, Young and the other pioneers made the Salt Lake Valley "blossom like a rose." Young, also president of the Church of Jesus Christ of Latter-day Saints (LDS), directed the colonization of the entire Wasatch Front and much of the Great Basin and surrounding area. (Courtesy of Library of Congress.)

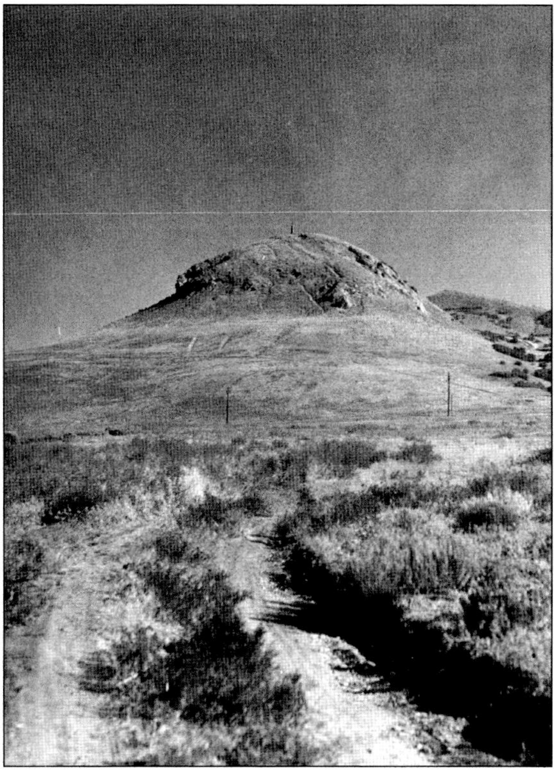

This is a c. 1940 photograph of Ensign Peak, directly north of downtown Salt Lake City. This summit was the first Wasatch Mountain peak officially climbed by the Mormon pioneers, just two days after arriving in the Salt Lake Valley. Ensign Peak sits at an elevation of 5,414 feet above sea level, or about 1,100 feet above the valley floor. The 18-foot-tall monument seen atop Ensign Peak was placed there in 1934. (Courtesy of Utah State Historical Society.)

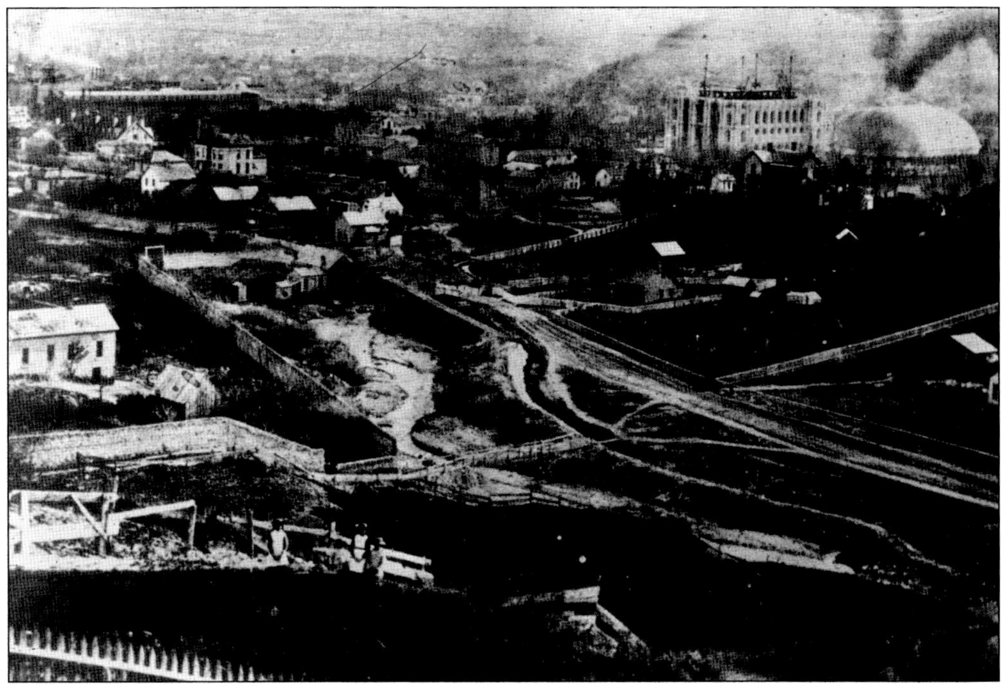

The bottom of City Creek Canyon looks pretty rugged in this 1880 photograph. The creek has made some deep cuts in the landscape. Note the half-completed Salt Lake Temple as well as the absence of any tall buildings yet to be constructed. The Salt Lake Temple, being composed of granite blocks from Little Cottonwood Canyon, technically means a portion of the Wasatch Mountains stands downtown. (Courtesy of J. Willard Marriott Digital Library, the University of Utah.)

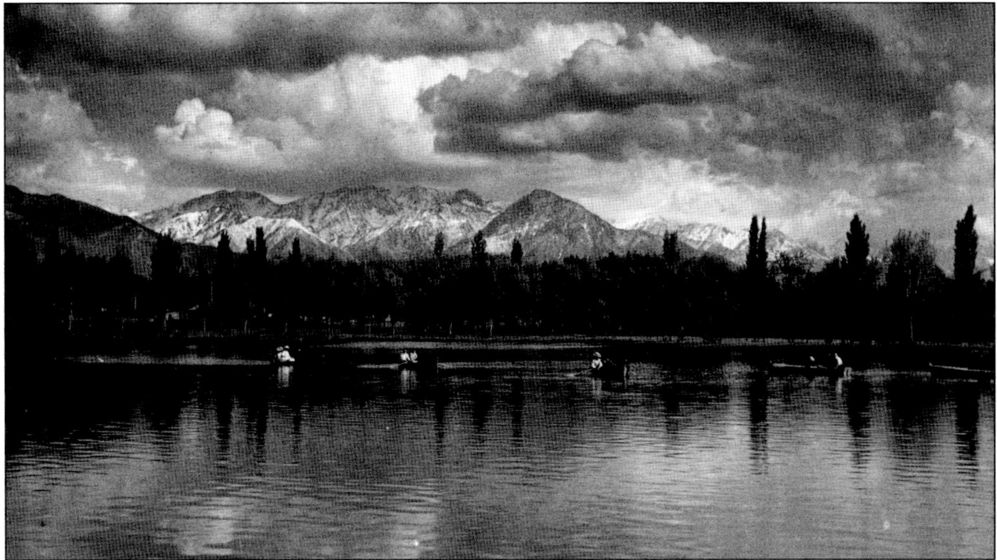

This 1920s view of the Wasatch Mountains from Liberty Park highlights their Rocky Mountain beauty. Likely taken in the spring, the mountains still contain ample snow. Note the extra tall trees at the east end of the park that almost obscure the mountains. The large size of the pond in Liberty Park easily makes it big enough for pleasure boating. (Courtesy of J. Willard Marriott Digital Library, the University of Utah.)

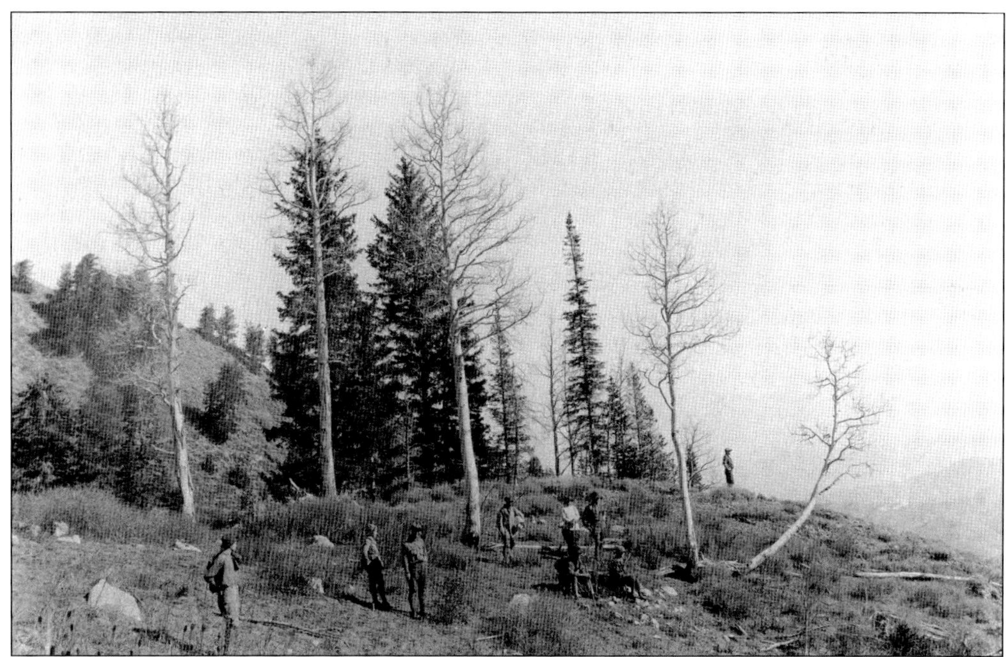

Hikers stop to enjoy the view on the way to the top of Mount Nebo in this October 15, 1921, picture. Nebo is such a mammoth mountain that it is one of the few in the Wasatch Range that rated so highly that it received a Biblical name. (Courtesy of J. Willard Marriott Digital Library, the University of Utah.)

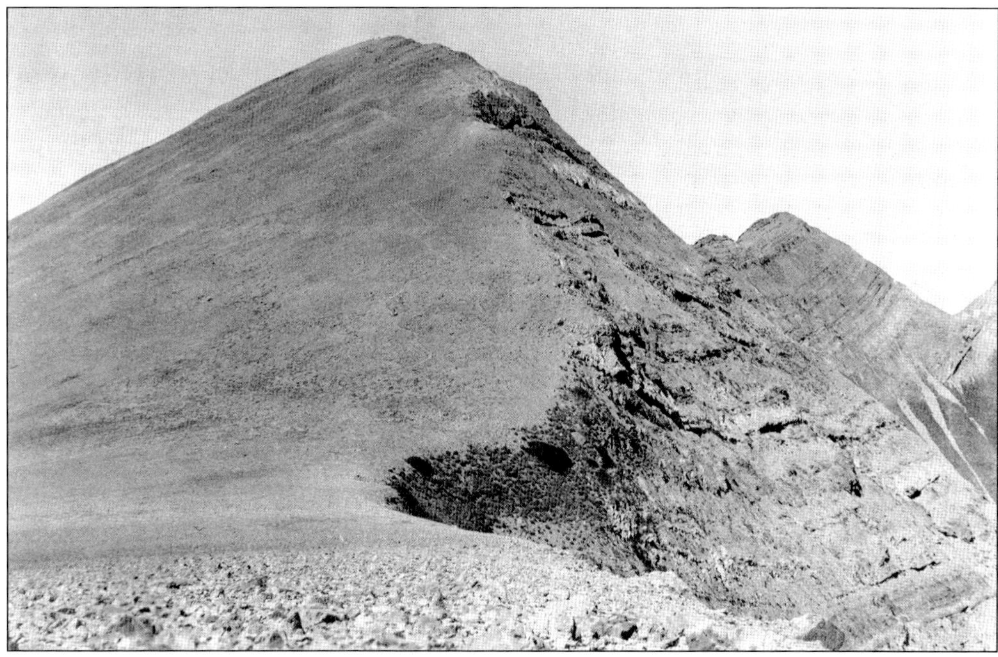

This is a photograph taken in the late summer of 1934 or 1935 that highlights the rugged nature of the peaks of Mount Nebo. The South and Middle Peaks are readily visible here in this Wasatch Mountain Club picture. Nebo boasts the tallest summits in the Wasatch Range. (Courtesy of J. Willard Marriott Digital Library, the University of Utah.)

Two

Mount Nebo

"Cold, austere, a triple pyramid of limestone, Mount Nebo rises under the central Utah sky, the final exclamation point in stone of the Wasatch Mountains."

Still appropriate today, that was an accurate description of Mount Nebo by Harrison R. Merrill, a *Deseret News* reporter, on July 4, 1930. Merrill went along with 33 Brigham Young University students and faculty members on a Nebo hike, back then a nine-mile trek to Nebo's southern summit.

Merrill noted how much drier the terrain was along the Nebo route compared to Timpanogos Peak's water-blessed trails. That is, until a big rainstorm hit and drenched the hikers. The group also reported seeing elk.

Twenty-seven hikers reached the summit, and Merrill described his feelings while on top: "Eleven-thousand feet above sea level, like specks along the ridge pole of the world, we sat down and feasted," he wrote. "While our eyes gorged, we ate our lunches beside a little fire that sent its pinion pine smoke toward heaven. It was a huge altar."

Other peaks along the Wasatch Range may be more legendary (Mount Timpanogos), more classically elegant (Mount Olympus), and simply more imposing because they loom so dramatically over metropolitan and suburban enclaves (Ben Lomond and Lone Peak).

But Nebo—the Wasatch's "final exclamation point in stone"—is actually the highest Wasatch Peak of them all, at 11,928 feet above sea level.

Yes, there are actually three different Nebo peaks, though, to the casual observer below on Interstate 15, it often looks more like just a single summit.

Nebo, like many a Utah village and eminence, is a Biblical namesake. As mentioned in the Old Testament (Deuteronomy 34:1), the original Mount Nebo was the peak from which Moses saw the promised land.

Perhaps the first Mormon settlers who caught sight of the peak in the late 1840s thought it was a great example of their promised land, and so they named it after a prominent scriptural landmark.

Who was the first person to climb Utah's Mount Nebo? Other than perhaps some Native Americans, William W. Phelps, a Mormon pioneer songwriter and editor, was the first known person, back on August 24, 1849.

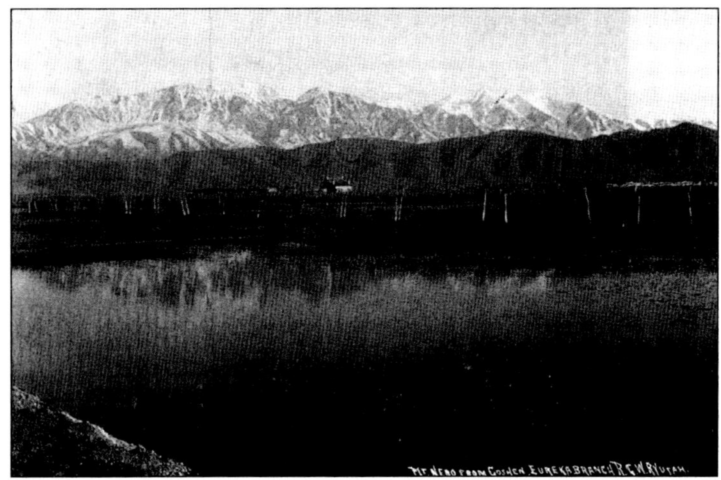

Seen here are Mount Nebo and some of the southern Wasatch Mountains in an 1870s photograph taken from westward, in the town of Goshen. First settled in 1857, this town surprisingly had some 600 residents in the 1870s. The town had four earlier names, including Sodom and Sandtown. (Courtesy of Utah State Historical Society.)

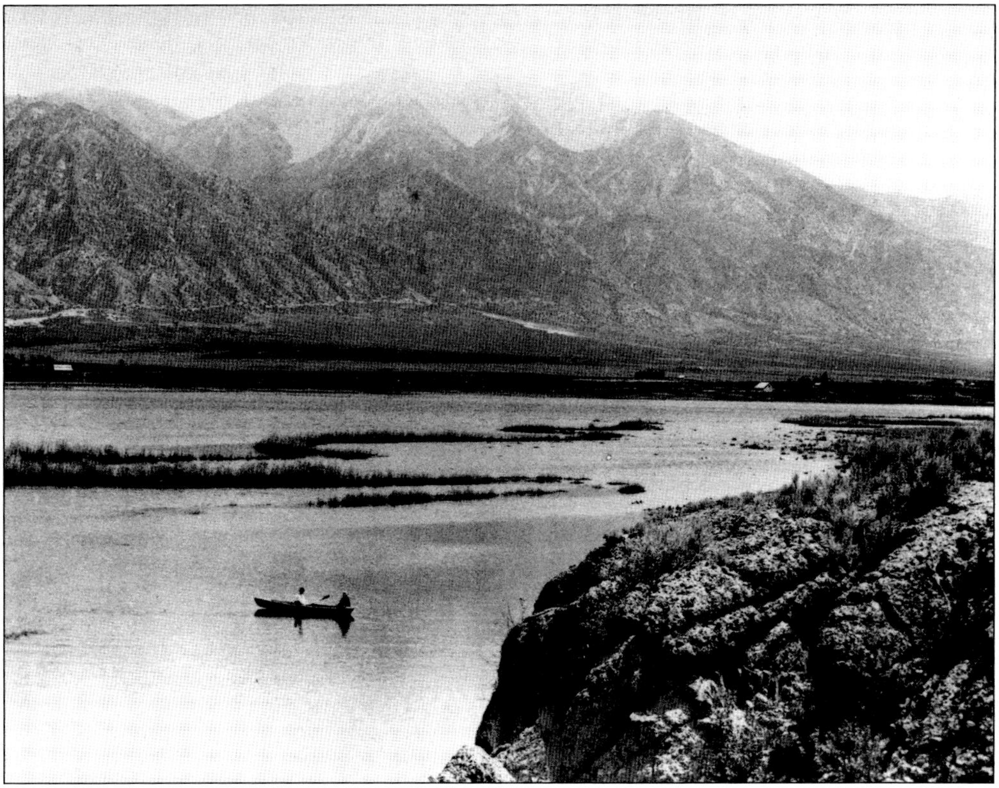

The triple peaks of Mount Nebo are still abounding in snow in this 1896 photograph from Mona Reservoir. This earthen dam was new then, having just been built in 1895. The town of Mona, to the southeast of here, has one of the state's latest morning sunrises because of Mount Nebo, which rises almost 7,000 feet above the town and delays the sun's appearance. (Courtesy of Utah State Historical Society.)

“They all went to the top!” is the title of this photograph from the summer of 1921, showing hikers in progress of climbing up the backside of Mount Nebo. Information on the picture states that even the two children in the foreground successfully made the climb. Note that the group of adults in the background are all carrying a tree limb as a hiking pole. (Courtesy of J. Willard Marriott Digital Library, the University of Utah.)

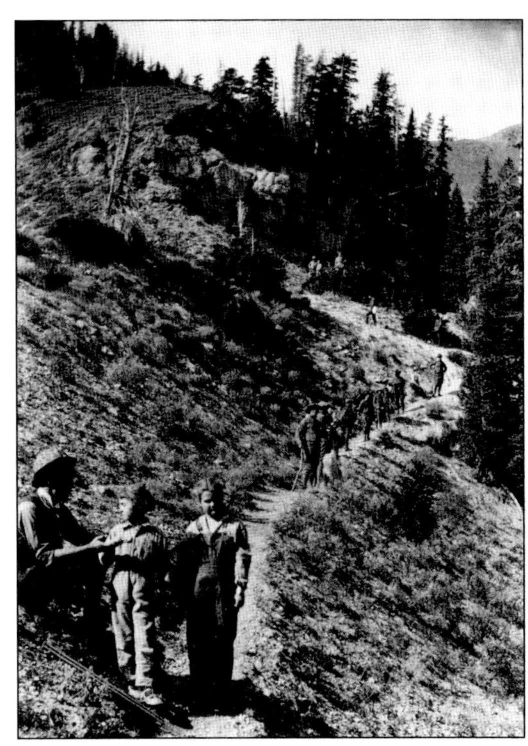

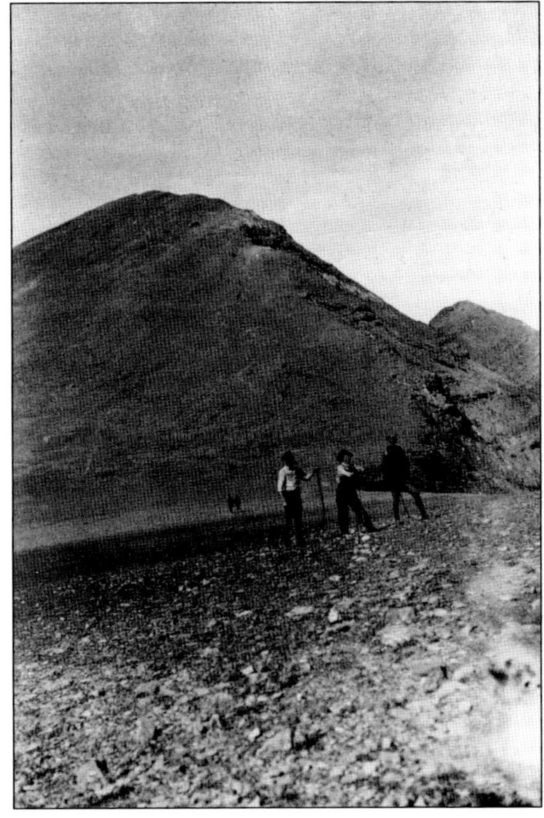

This photograph, from August or September 1921, shows three men posing at the base of the final ascent to the top of Mount Nebo’s South Peak, elevation 11,877 feet above sea level. There are other hikers already climbing up the last mound along the well-worn, switchback path, which can be seen on the mountainside. (Courtesy of J. Willard Marriott Digital Library, the University of Utah.)

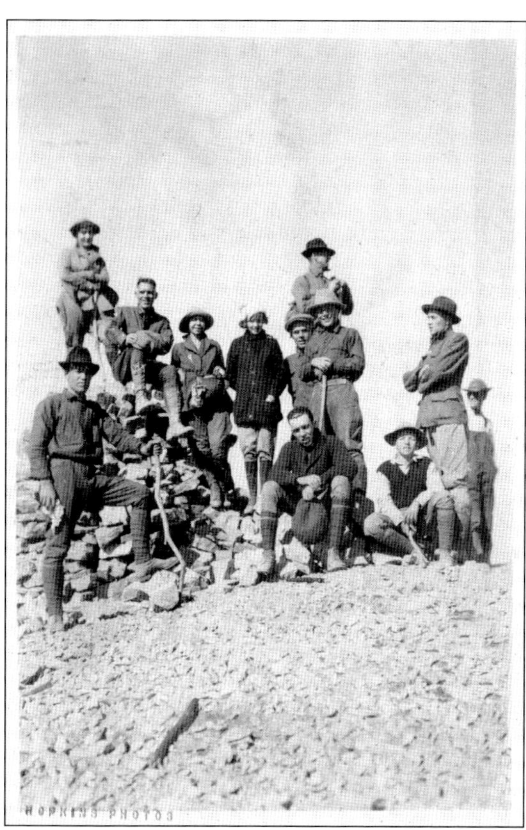

This is another late summer of 1921 Mount Nebo photograph, showing a dozen-large group of adults posing on the lofty summit. Writing with the photograph states, "Up on top, Forest Service says, 11,860 ft., sure, we're happy." This picture was taken by William H. Hopkins of the Wasatch Mountain Club. (Courtesy of J. Willard Marriott Digital Library, the University of Utah.)

A large group of more than three dozen hikers pose at some point on their hike to the top of Mount Nebo in the summer of 1921. This picture was not taken anywhere near the summit, given the trees in the background. The established path to the Mount Nebo South Peak was developed in 1919. (Courtesy of J. Willard Marriott Digital Library, the University of Utah.)

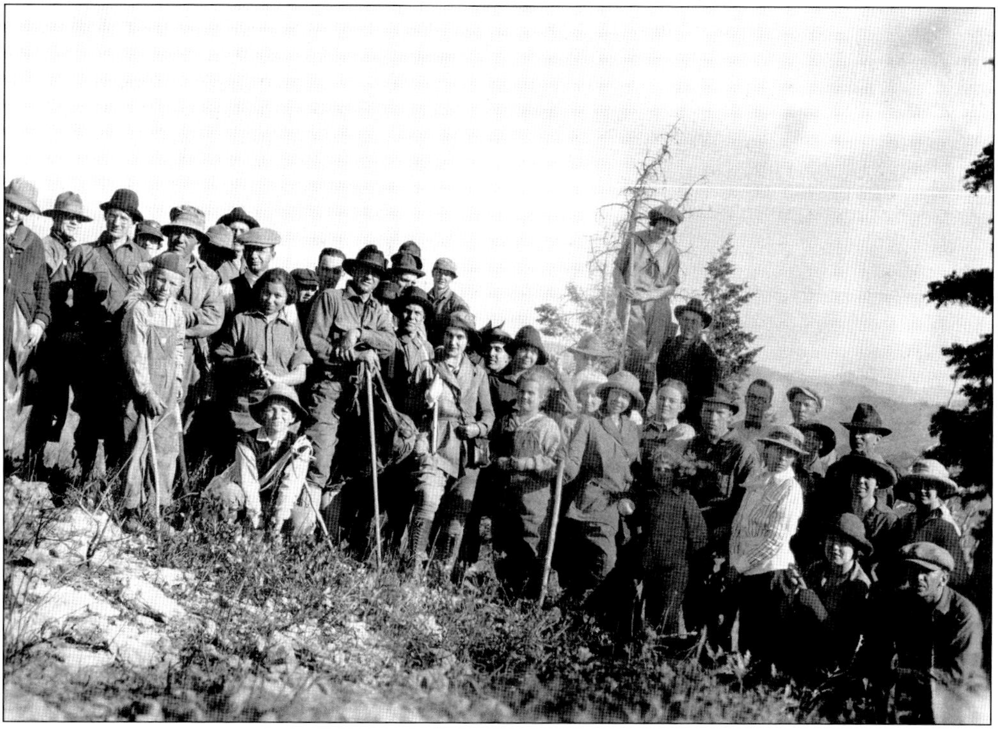

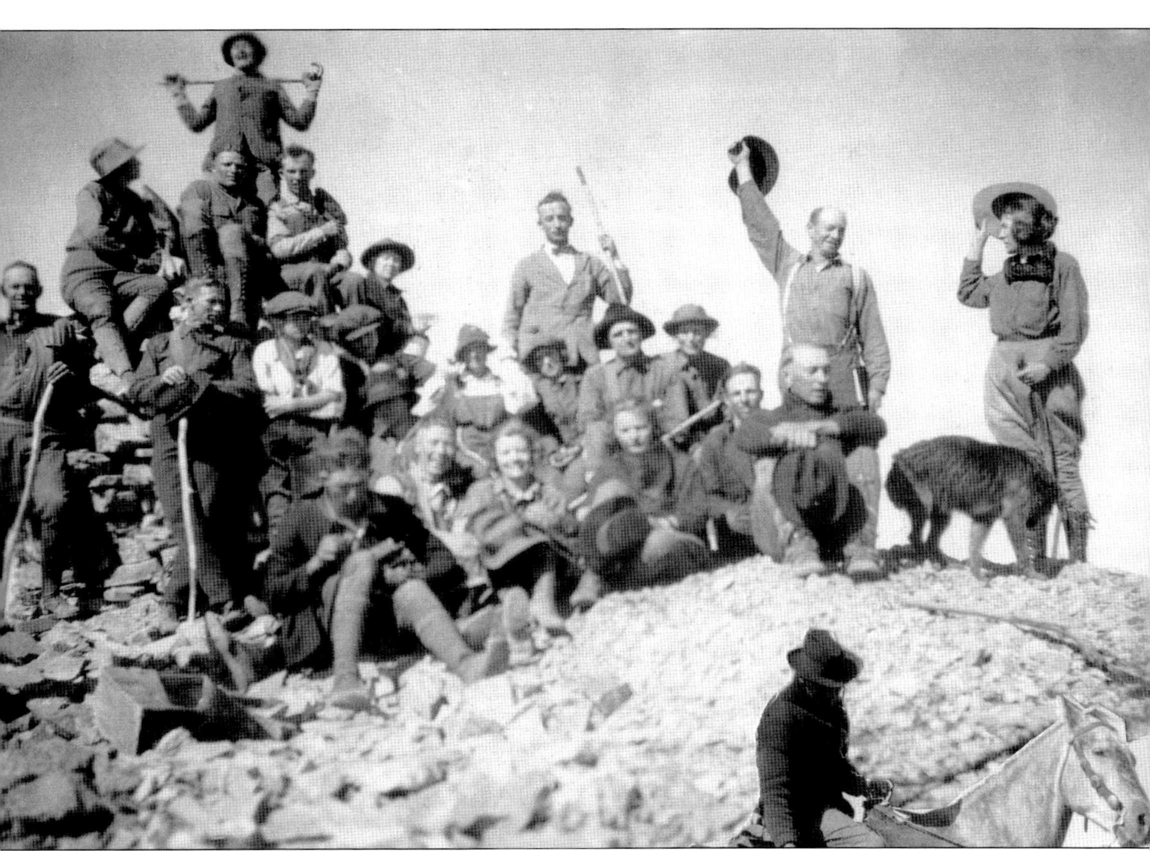

This is yet another group that posed in the summer of 1921 atop the South Peak of Mount Nebo. There was likely an annual group hike each August and for some years afterward. Note the dog, who also successfully made the climb. A man on a horse appears to have been superimposed at the bottom of this picture. That begs the question, did the man on the horse not fit in the group picture, or did he and the horse not even make it to the summit? (Courtesy of J. Willard Marriott Digital Library, the University of Utah.)

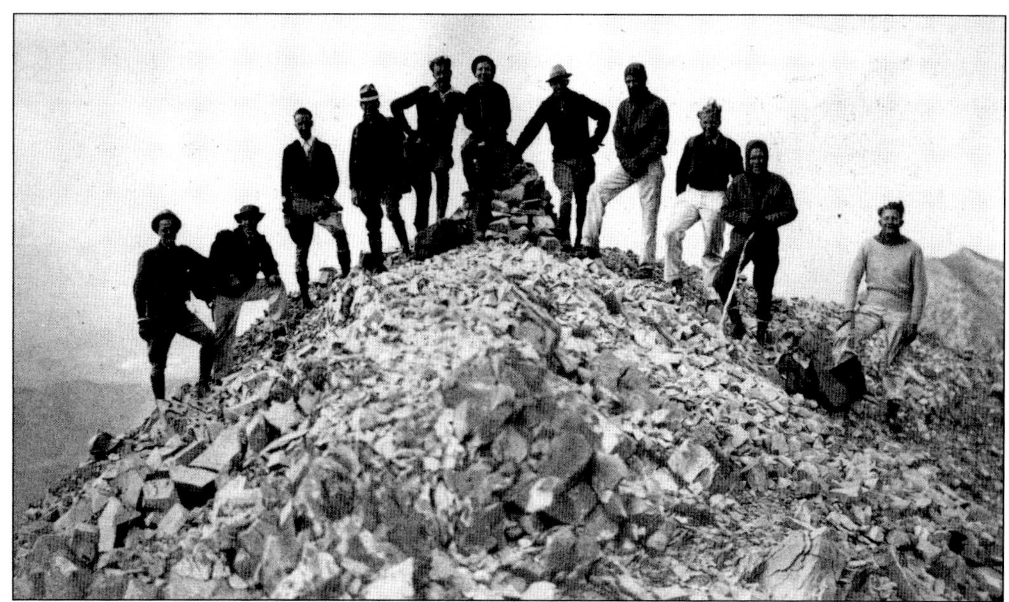

Eleven hikers pose on top of Mount Nebo after a successful summer climb there in 1930. Because of a lack of waterfalls and isolation, the hike to Nebo never took off in popularity like its Timpanogos Peak counterpart to the north. William W. Phelps, a Mormon pioneer songwriter and editor, was the first known person to climb Mount Nebo, back on August 24, 1849. (Courtesy of J. Willard Marriott Digital Library, the University of Utah.)

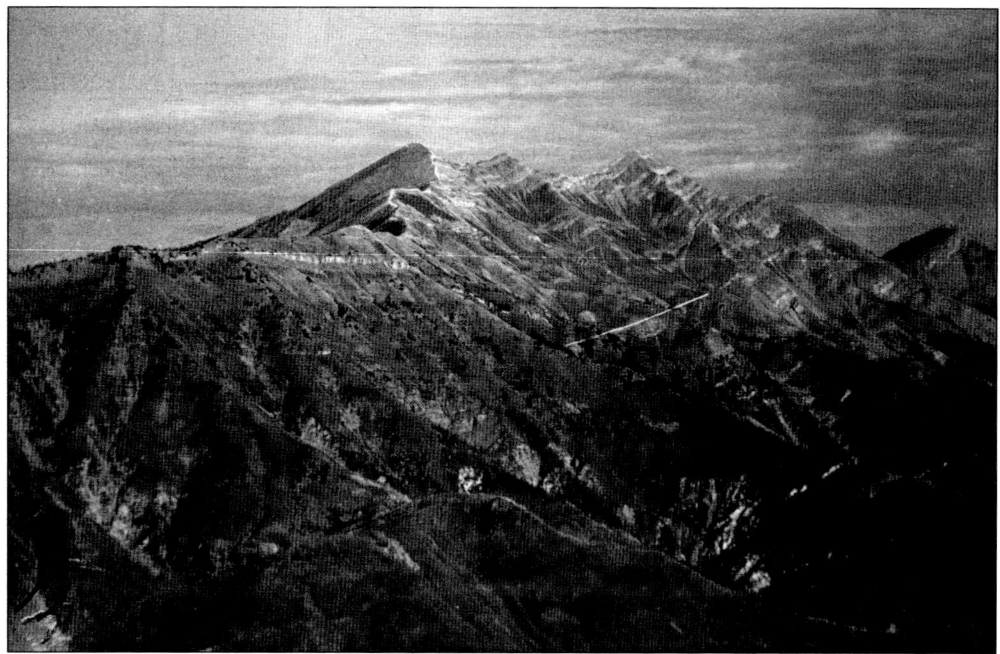

This is an aerial photograph taken in 1945 from the southeast side of Mount Nebo. Note the straight line, or scratch, across the backside of the mountain. Some Utahns had hoped to put an observatory and "Yankee Memorial," complete with a searchlight, atop Mount Nebo in 1920, but that feat never took place. Yet today, a 35-mile paved road travels across the eastern backside of Mount Nebo as a scenic byway. (Courtesy of Utah State Historical Society.)

Three

Mount Timpanogos

Mount Timpanogos is the second-highest peak in the Wasatch Mountain range at 11,752 feet. It is also the most prominent peak in Utah County and is climbed by thousands of people each year. In the past, it became a victim of its own popularity, as an almost six-decade-long annual mass hike to the summit had to be discontinued.

Eugene L. Roberts, the director of physical education at Brigham Young University, started a new school tradition in July 1912 by sponsoring a hike to the "Timp" summit. He led a combined group of 22 students and teachers on a three-day expedition to the top of that lofty peak.

Yes, many others had already hiked the Timpanogos summit before that, but it was Roberts who envisioned it as a "Wonder Mountain" that made it more than merely a lofty place. This was a religious place, too.

The idea for the mass hike came from Roberts's service as a full-time missionary for the Church of Jesus Christ of Latter-day Saints. Serving in Switzerland, he watched some 5,000 Catholics in 1908 hike in a religious pilgrimage to worship at a shrine high in the Swiss Alps.

This annual Timp hike became more popular each year, and by the end of the tradition in 1970, the one-day event was attracting thousands of hikers. And that is what killed the tradition—too many hikers on the mountain at once, creating not only unsafe conditions (with rolling boulders and rock), but also ecological damage to the trail and mountain itself.

Today, the designated Timpanogos Wilderness Area has a 15-person per group limit to avoid mistakes of the past.

With an abundance of small waterfalls, blooming flowers, and alpine scenery unparalleled in the Beehive State (and more akin to Switzerland), there is no reason to not understand why a Timp hike is so appealing.

There are also mountain goats living in the Timp region, and an old metal hut stands atop the summit. Hikers mainly hike to Timp from Aspen Grove, and many still slide down the glacier to the south of the peak, taking this shortcut back to Emerald Lake.

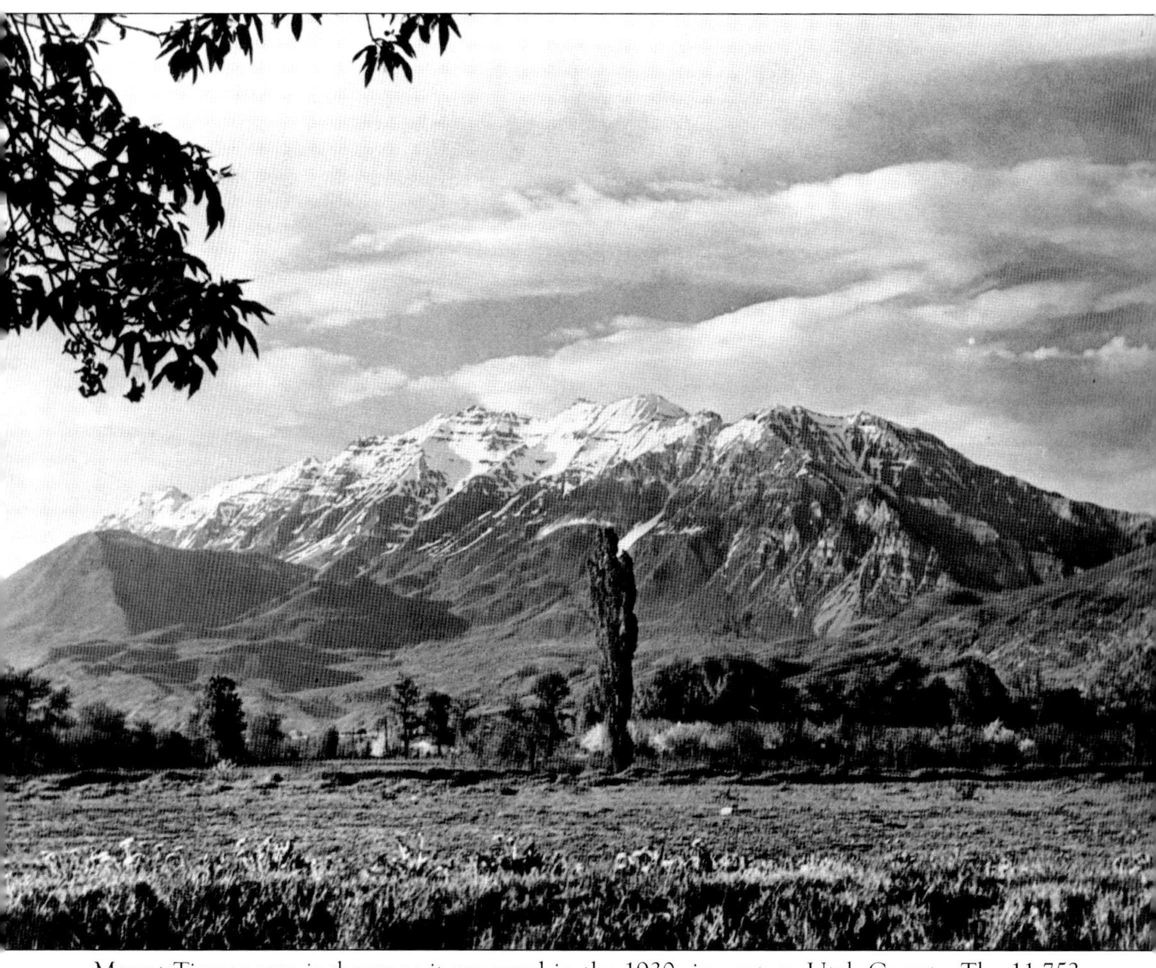

Mount Timpanogos is shown as it appeared in the 1930s in western Utah County. The 11,752-foot peak has long been a scenic wonder for the Wasatch Range. The peak is named after a Piute Indian name for the Provo River, Timpanogos, which refers to rock and running water. (The "Timp" name does not refer to a legendary sleeping Native American princess, as some claim.) (Courtesy of Utah State Historical Society.)

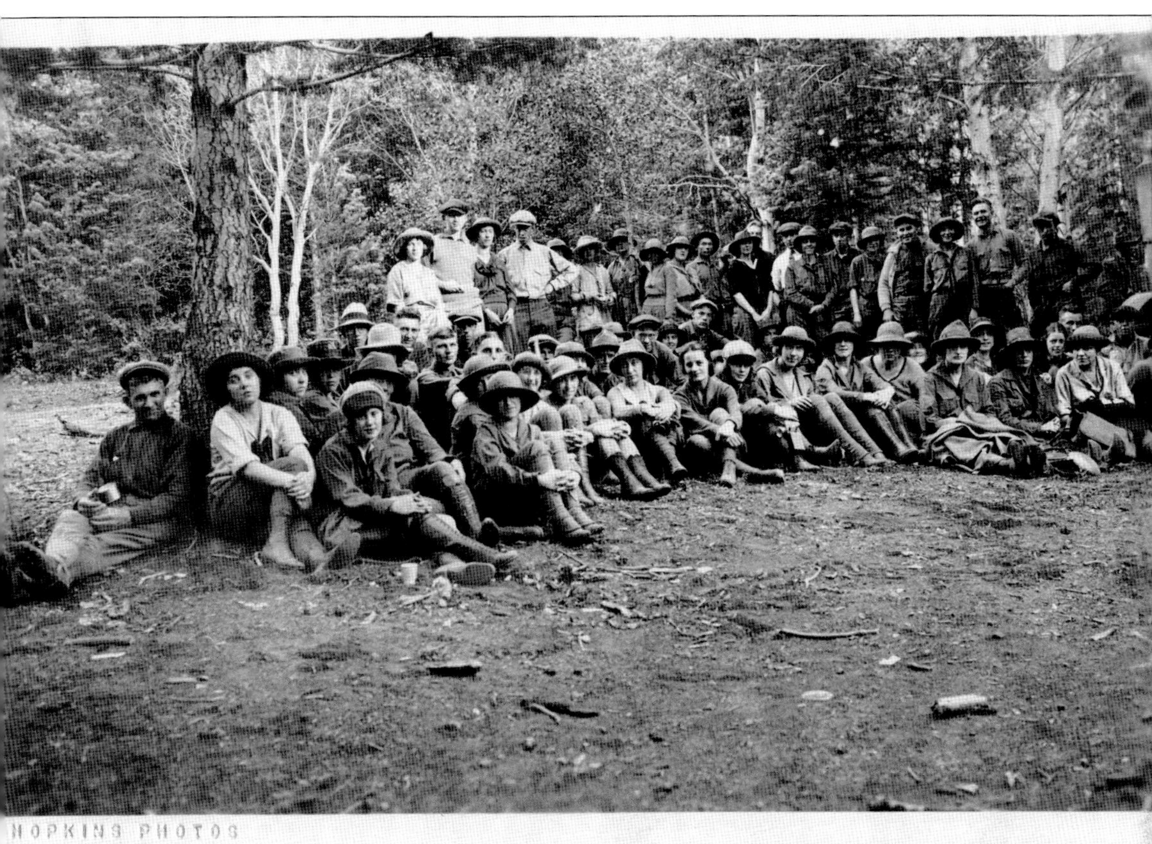

A large group poses at Aspen Grove either before or after a moonlight hike to the top of Mount Timpanogos in the 1920s. Note that, surprisingly, most of the group is composed of women. The goal of such hikes was to see the trail with a full moon shining and then enjoy the sunrise on top of the summit. (Courtesy of J. Willard Marriott Digital Library, the University of Utah.)

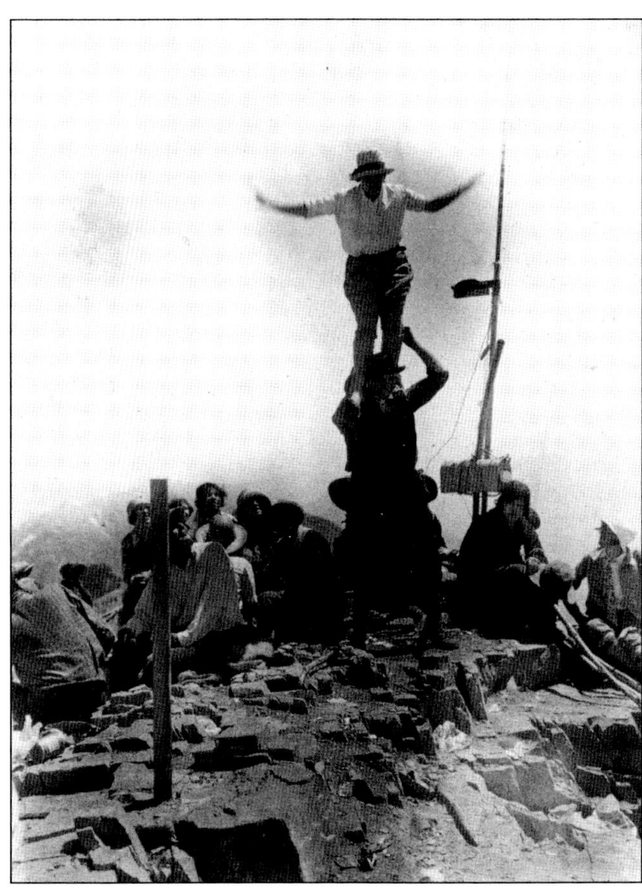

The University of Utah Hiking Club and perhaps Wasatch Mountain Club members savor the summit of Mount Timpanogos on July 15, 1927, after a successful hike there. An unidentified woman stands on the shoulders of Dr. William H. Hopkins to attain an even higher elevation than 11,752 feet. (Courtesy of J. Willard Marriott Digital Library, the University of Utah.)

Several groups of hikers rest and picnic at Emerald Lake, situated below the east side of Mount Timpanogos. The year is 1920. Emerald Lake sits at an approximate elevation of 10,000 feet. Snow often persists in this basin well into late summer. The lake is often a turnaround point for those without the stamina or desire to climb to the Timp summit. (Courtesy of J. Willard Marriott Digital Library, the University of Utah.)

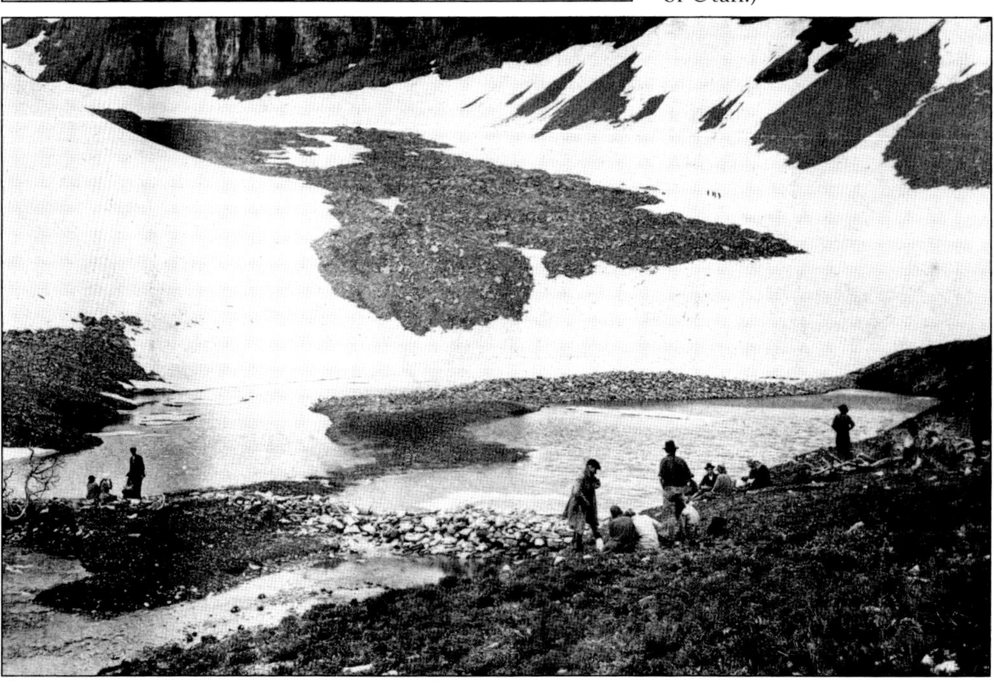

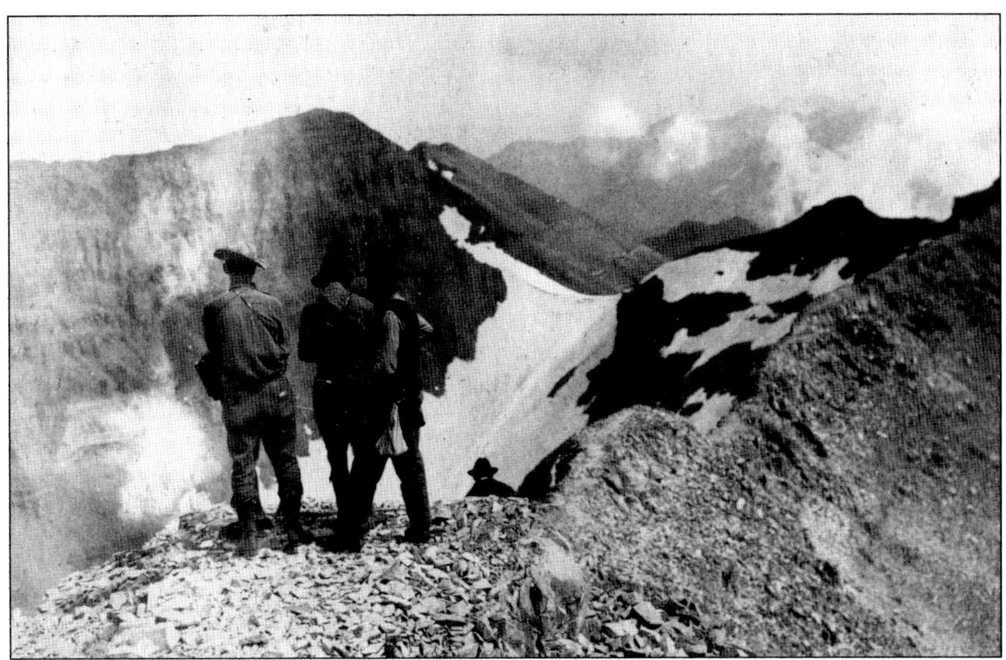

Three men stand atop Mount Timpanogos, apparently watching all the clouds float by around them in the summer of 1920. The picture's inscription states, "The top of the world, 12,000 feet, up midst the clouds." A fourth man is seen just below the summit, possibly pondering a shortcut to descend to Emerald Lake. (Courtesy of J. Willard Marriott Digital Library, the University of Utah.)

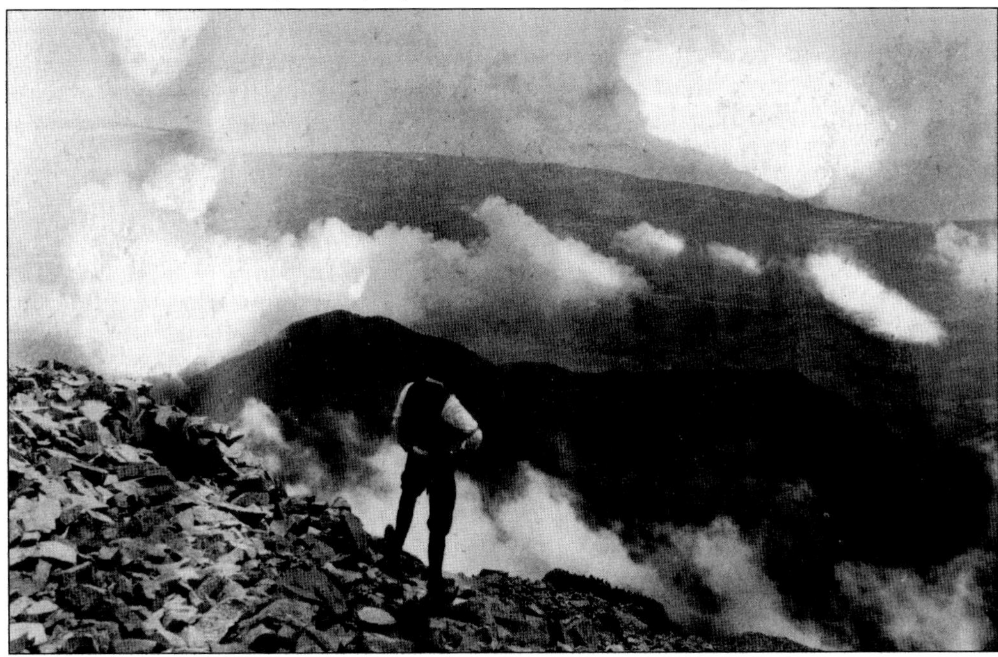

A solitary hiker stands on the side of Mount Timpanogos in 1920, enjoying all the puffy clouds that are moving like low-hanging fog amidst the highest peaks in Utah County. Note all the loose, broken rocks that are piled atop this mountain, the second-highest behind Mount Nebo in the Wasatch Mountains. (Courtesy of J. Willard Marriott Digital Library, the University of Utah.)

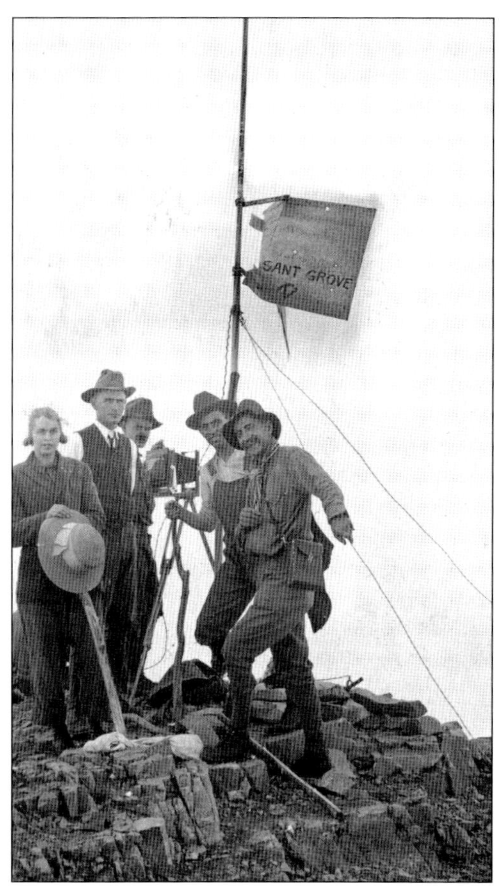

Five hikers, possibly members of the Wasatch Mountain Club, pose after climbing Timp in the summer of 1920. All the hikers appear to have at least one hiking stick. Also, one man has a formal camera sitting on a tripod that he hauled to the summit. "At the flag, where the winds plays, elevation 12,008 feet," is an inscription on the picture. Note that a battered cardboard sign is attached to the peak pole and likely originally stated, "Pleasant Grove," before being damaged by the elements. (Courtesy of J. Willard Marriott Digital Library, the University of Utah.)

This is a 1920s view of the Mount Timpanogos glacier, located southeast of the summit. A man is shown pondering the rocky, cliffy route over to the glacier. Many hikers often slide down this glacier to complete a Timp loop as well as a quick shortcut back down to Emerald Lake. (Courtesy of J. Willard Marriott Digital Library, the University of Utah.)

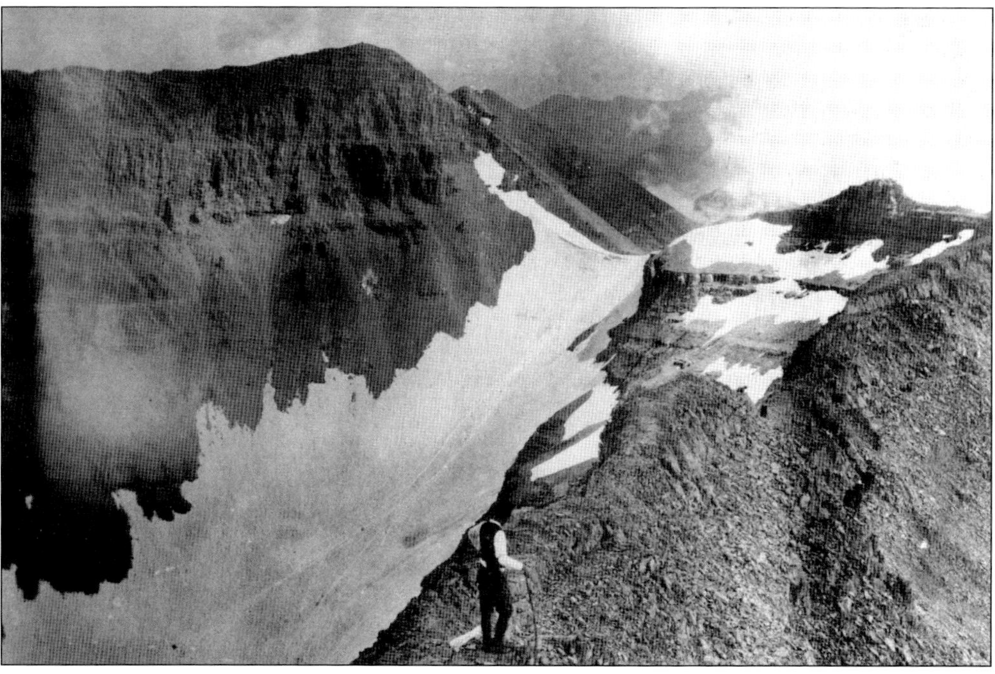

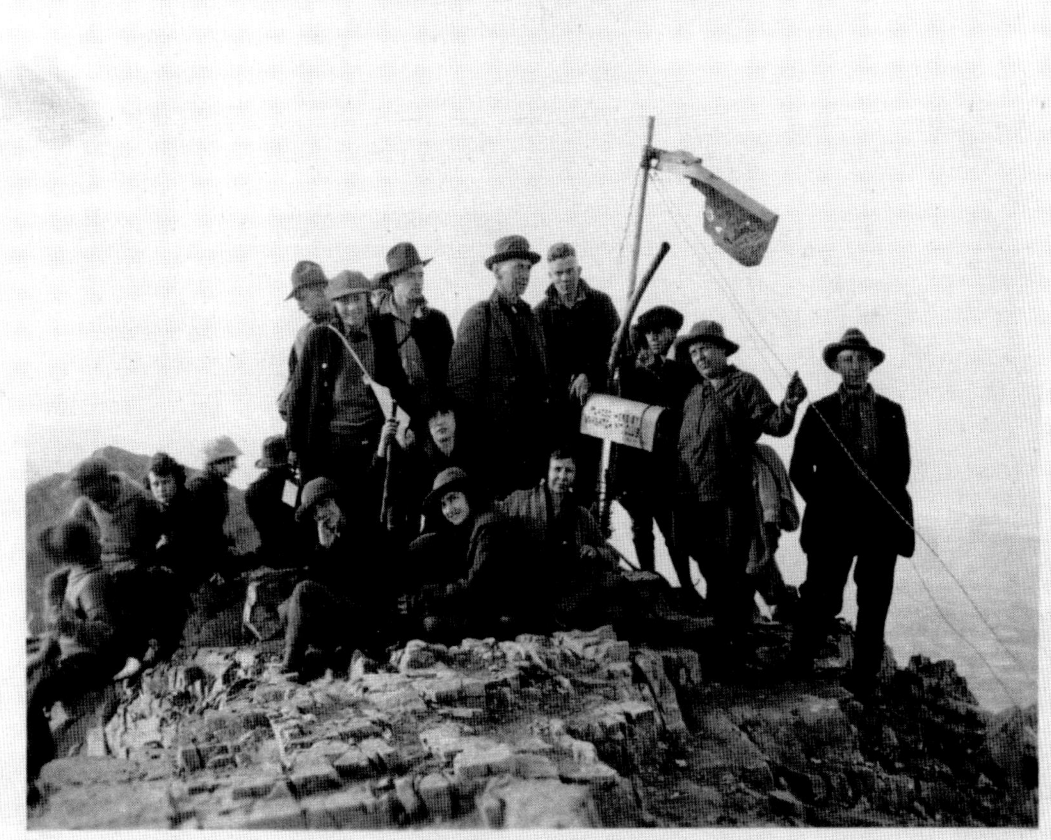

A group of 17 hikers pose atop Mount Timpanogos in the summer of 1920. They may be members of the Wasatch Mountain Club, who were very active with strenuous outings in that era. Today, the Timpanogos Peak area is a designated wilderness. Although Timp is rated a strenuous hike, it is one of the most popular, with many traveling from Aspen Grove. (Courtesy of J. Willard Marriott Digital Library, the University of Utah.)

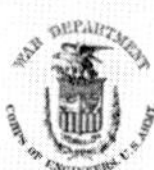

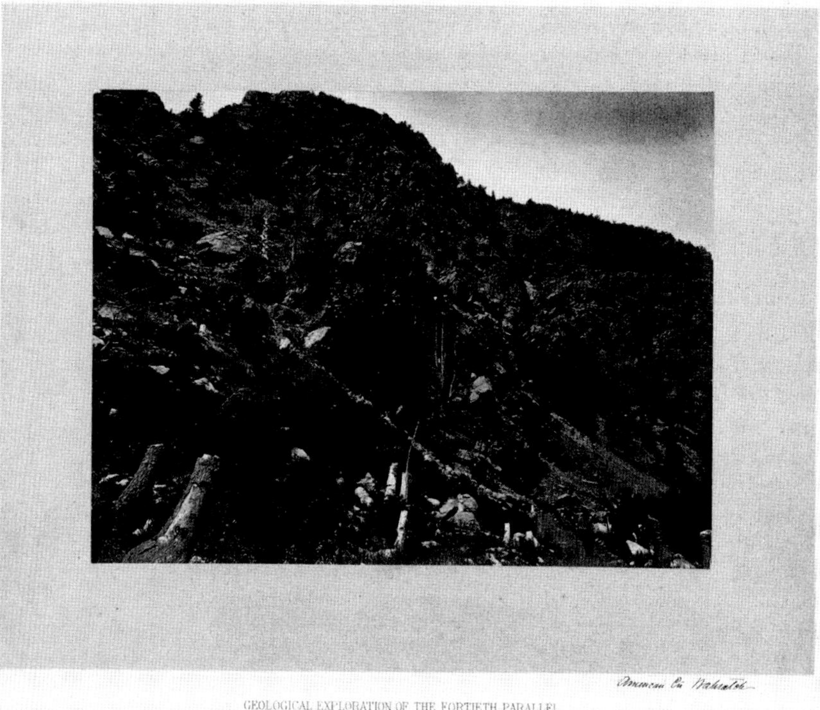

This is a US Government Survey photograph of somewhere in the Wasatch Mountains in 1869. Note that some of the trees shown have already been chopped down. There is also an unidentified man standing on a trail in the canyon. Almost all the lumber in early Wasatch Front history came from the Wasatch Mountains. (Courtesy of Library of Congress.)

A muscular hiker lifts a woman atop his shoulders on the summit of Mount Timpanogos on July 29, 1923. Other hikers rest on the opposite side of the peak. This group hike was part of a "Moonlight" event, where hikers traditionally start moving up the mountain around midnight from Aspen Grove and arrive at the peak by sunrise. (Courtesy of J. Willard Marriott Digital Library, the University of Utah.)

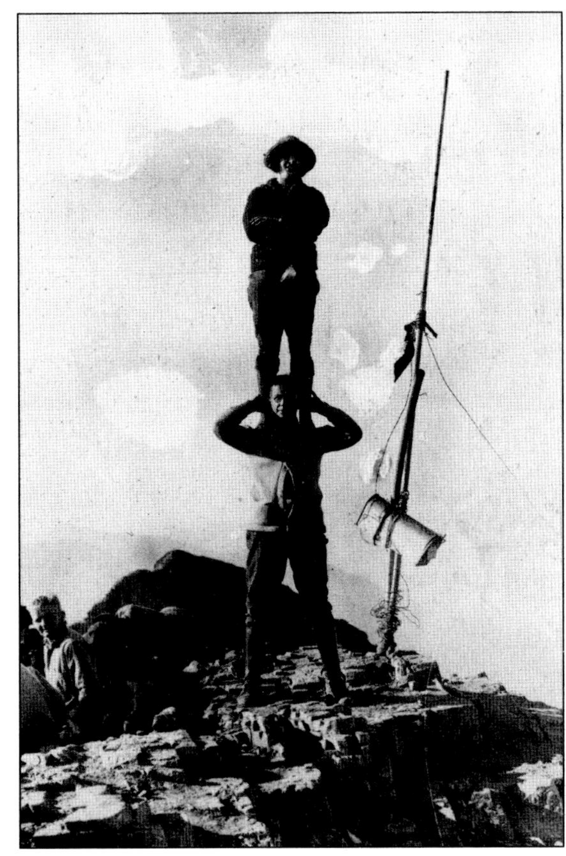

"Dancing on the top—when the sun comes up" is the title of this photograph from the Wasatch Mountain Club's picture collection. These four couples hiked through the moonlit night on July 28, 1923, to reach the Mount Timpanogos summit at sunrise so they could dance on the summit. From left to right, Cornell and Eloise, Roberts and Polly, and Hopkins and Rhea Cazier are three of the couples dancing. The fourth couple is unidentified. (Courtesy of J. Willard Marriott Digital Library, the University of Utah.)

"DANCING ON THE TOP--WHEN THE SUN COMES UP." [Cornell Eloise] [Roberts and Polly] [Hopkins and Rhea Cazier] [???]
Wasatch Mountain Club Collection Book VII p 89.

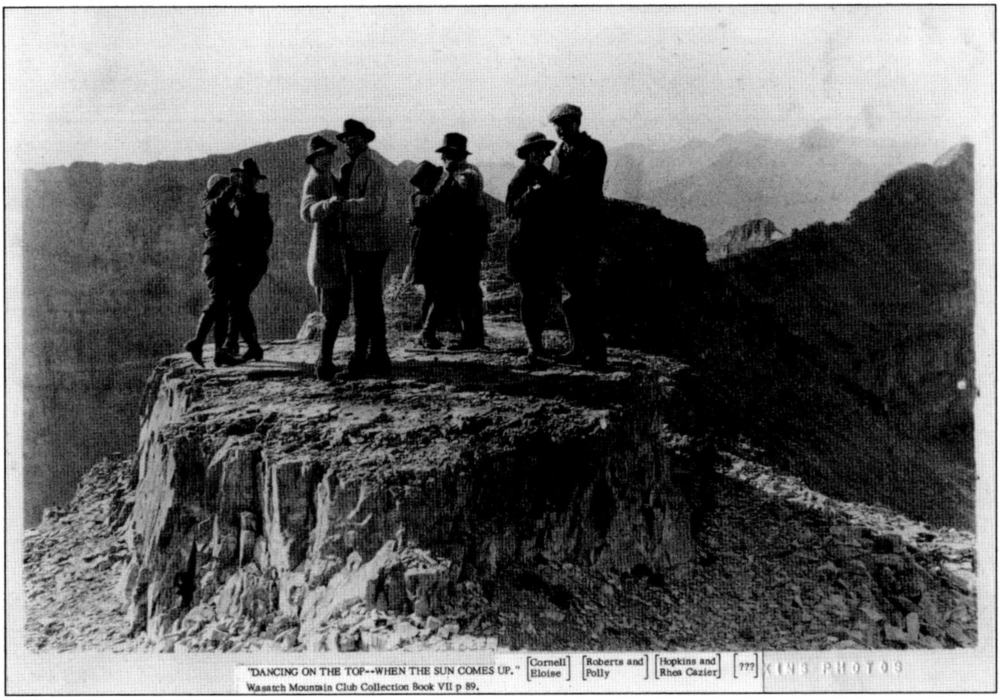

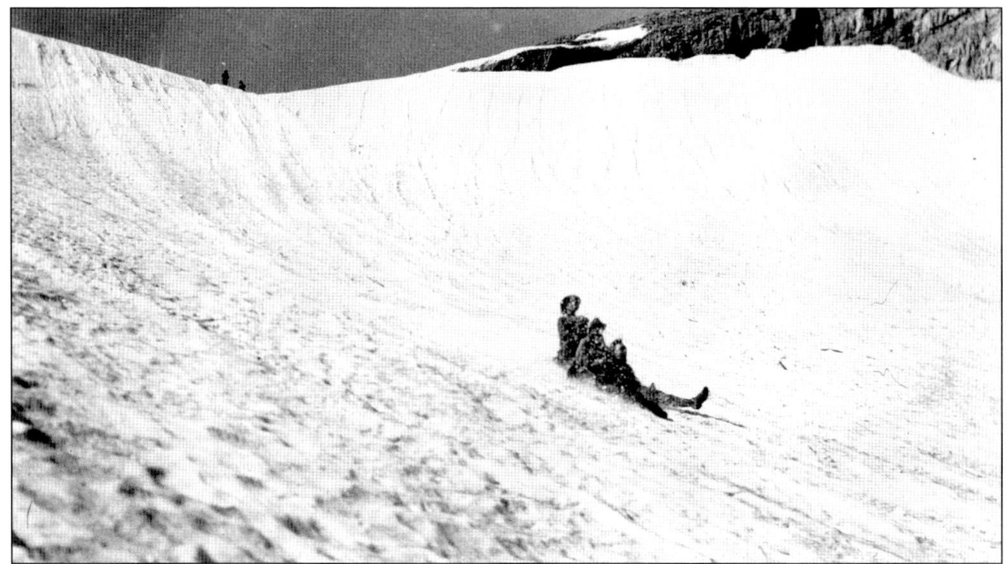

A trio slides down the glacier near Mount Timpanogos and heads toward the rocks around Emerald Lake on July 28, 1923. At least two hikers watch from above. These are all likely members of the Wasatch Mountain Club. Sadly, this practice of glacier sliding has resulted in injuries over the decades, from people being unable to stop their sliding and crashing into the rugged rocks below the glacier. (Courtesy of J. Willard Marriott Digital Library, the University of Utah.)

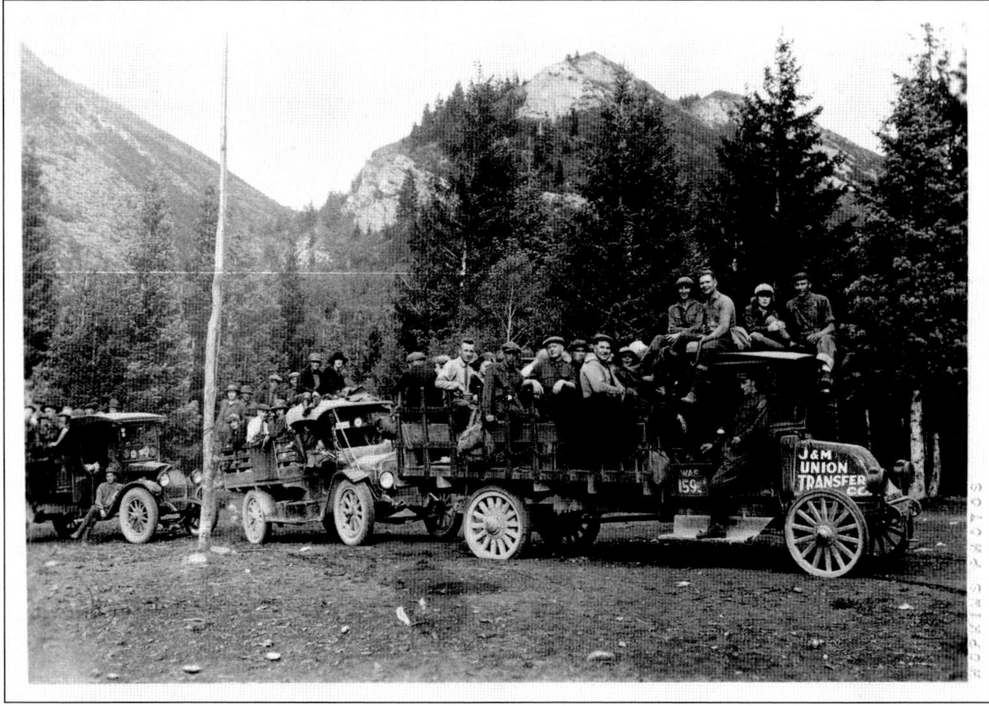

Three vehicles are shown at Aspen Grove after transporting dozens of anxious hikers to the trailhead of Mount Timpanogos sometime in the 1920s. One of the trucks states J&M Union Transfer Company and that the business excels in long-distance trips. Note how crowded all the vehicles appear to be. (Courtesy of J. Willard Marriott Digital Library, the University of Utah.)

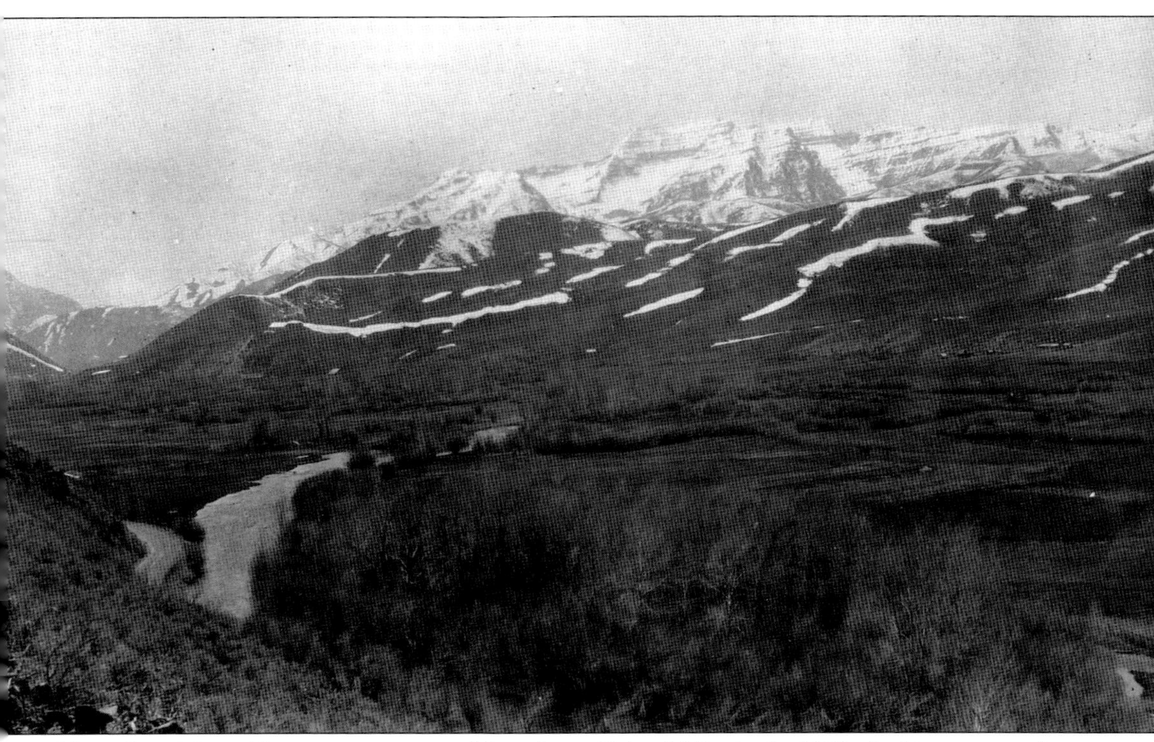

This is how Mount Timpanogos appeared from lower Heber Valley in the 1920s, looking westward. The lingering patches of snow on the mountainside likely mean it is late spring. The view shows lots of open ground and few buildings. The stream in the picture may be the Provo River. (Courtesy of J. Willard Marriott Digital Library, the University of Utah.)

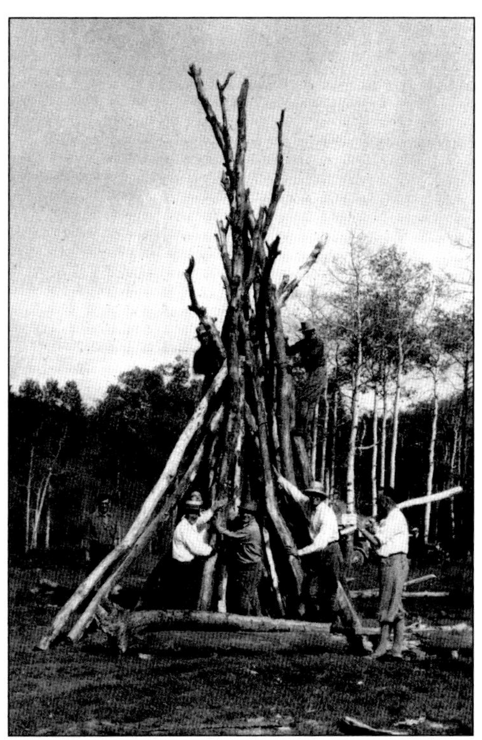

A large group of people hiked to Mount Timpanogos one summer day in 1929. Here, a group of men are assembling what will eventually be a large bonfire as part of the hiking festivities. This is being prepared in a large clearing, likely at Aspen Grove. (Courtesy of J. Willard Marriott Digital Library, the University of Utah.)

This is a group of skiers assembling for a race on the glacier below Mount Timpanogos in July 1948. "Here's terrain over which ski wizard Alf Engen will set course for Timpanogos Glacier Giant Slalom July 24" is the information listed on the picture. Why this event did not continue annually over the years is unclear. (Courtesy of J. Willard Marriott Digital Library, the University of Utah.)

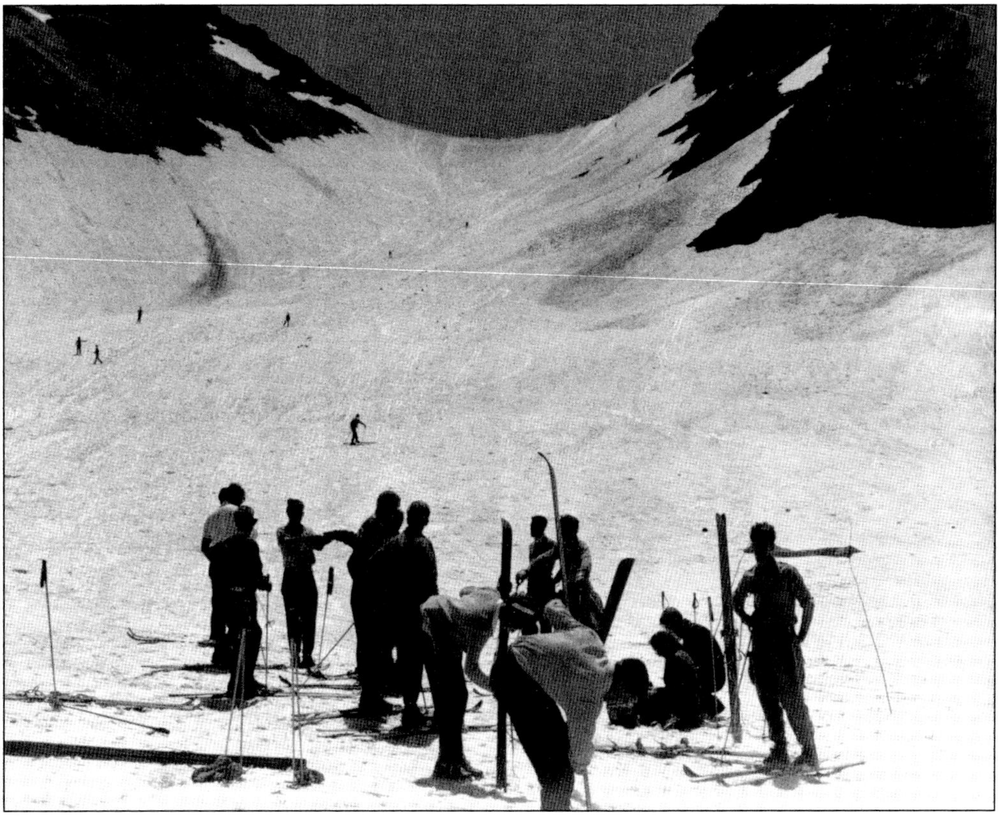

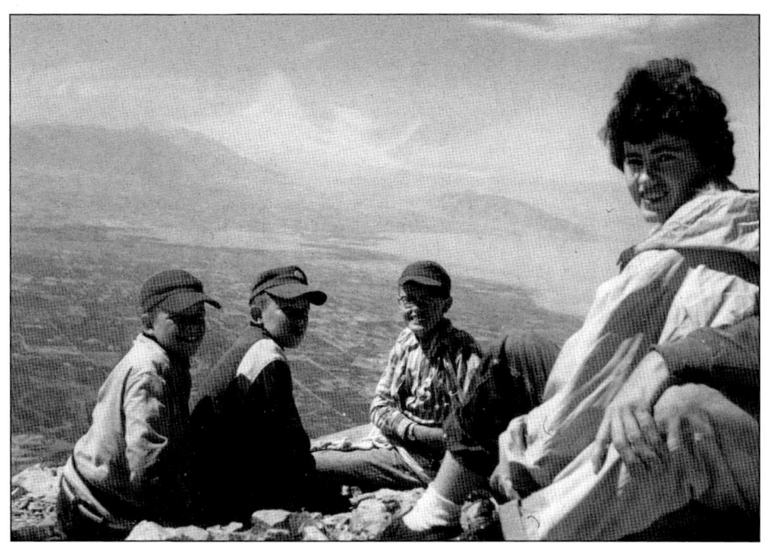

This photograph from the summer of 1957 shows a group of young teenagers enjoying the view of Utah Valley, Provo, and Utah Lake from near the Timpanogos ridge down to the glacier. From left to right are Terry, R.V., Craig, JoAnn, and Bryan (obscured). (Courtesy of J. Willard Marriott Digital Library, the University of Utah.)

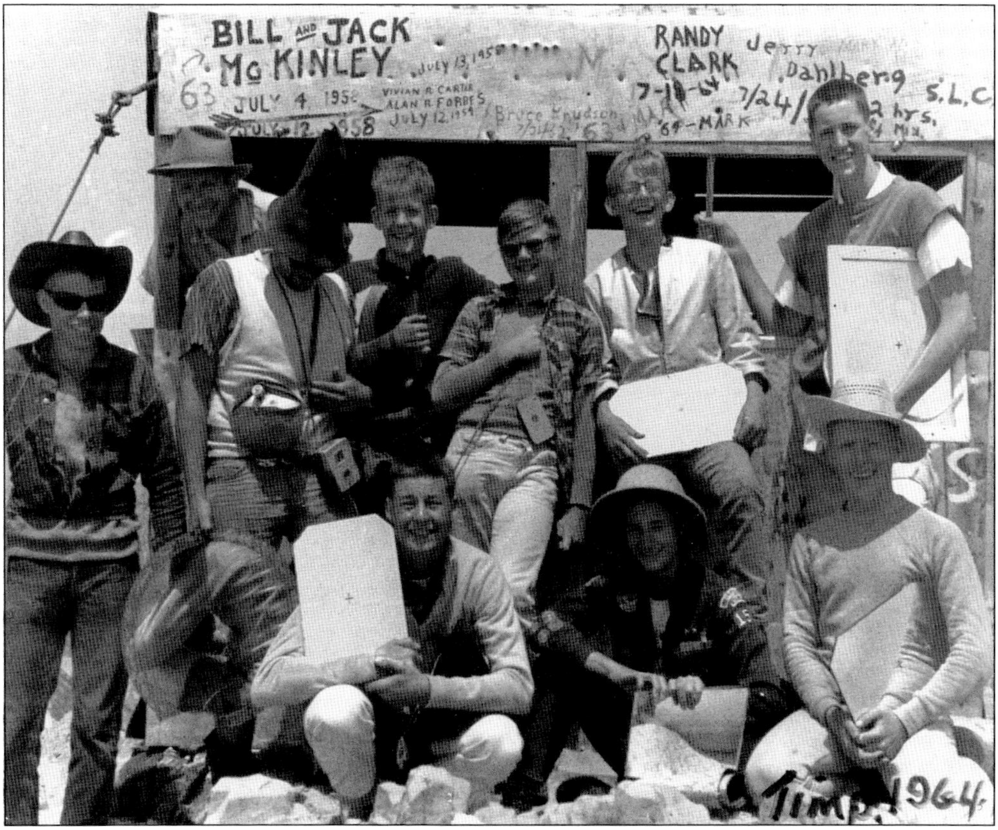

This photograph from the summer of 1964 shows a group of 10 Explorer-age Boy Scouts, Post 156, from Clearfield, Utah, atop Mount Timpanogos. The young men used signal mirrors in a communications exercise. How long has the old metal hut, seen behind the Scouts, been atop Timp? Vintage photographs show it as being there as early as 1930. The hut was also originally entirely enclosed. (Courtesy of J. Willard Marriott Digital Library, the University of Utah.)

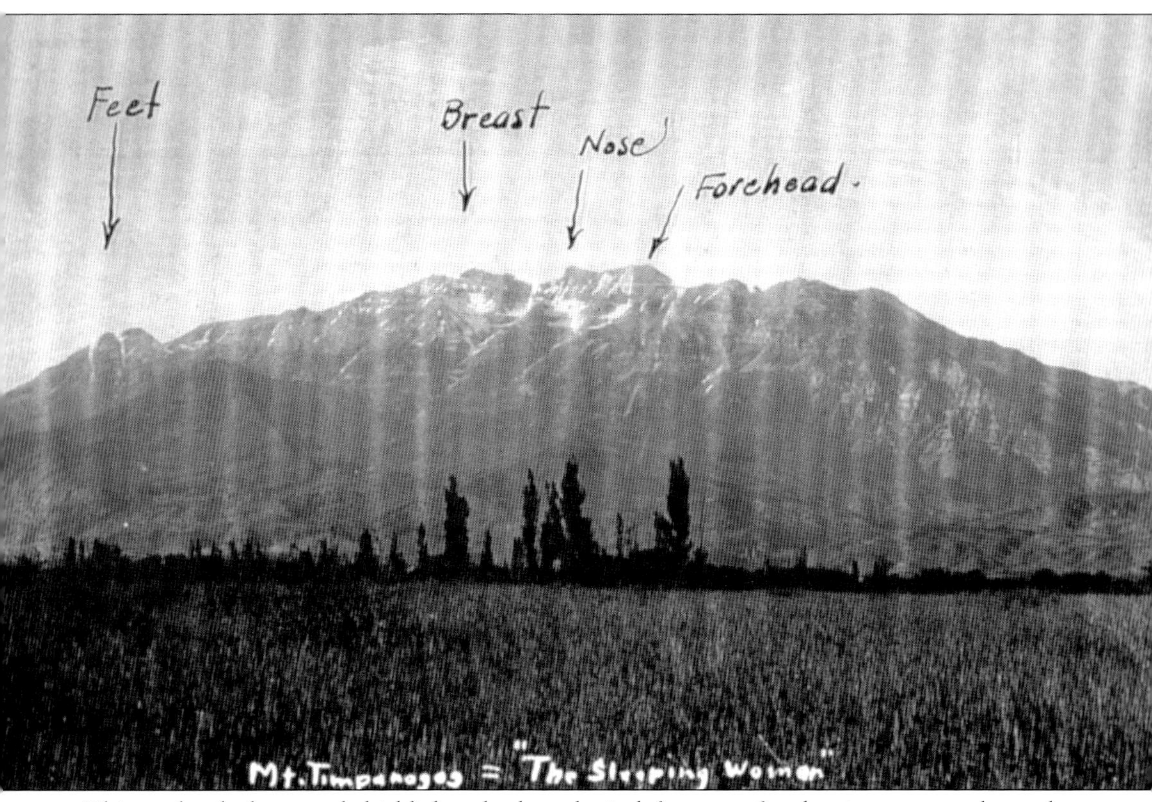

This undated photograph highlights the key physical features of a sleeping woman shape that the top outline of the entire Mount Timpanogos mountain saddle resembles. This picture was taken from the west of the mountain. However, oftentimes, this legend is best seen when traveling northbound on Interstate 15, from just north of Nephi and just when Timp comes into view. A sleeping Native American princess is oftentimes part of this legend, which sometimes ties into Timpanogos Cave as well. (Courtesy of J. Willard Marriott Digital Library, the University of Utah.)

Four

Other Key Summits

The most striking geographical features in Salt Lake County are the Wasatch Mountains on the east side of the valley. Rising sharply up to a maximum of 7,000 feet above the valley floor, the Wasatch Mountains create natural landmarks for the area.

These mountains are home to many animals, offer year-round recreational activities, and are important watersheds.

The easternmost Twin Peaks (11,489 and 11,433 feet above sea level) are the tallest summits in Salt Lake County. (One of the most surprising things about the names of Salt Lake County mountain peaks is the repetition of the Twin Peaks name. There are no less than three sets of Twin Peaks in the Salt Lake section of the Wasatch Mountains listed on maps.)

In Davis and Morgan Counties, Thurston Peak is highest at 9,706 feet above sea level. However, nearby Francis Peak is lower but has two radar domes on its summit and, thus, captures the most attention.

For Weber County, Ben Lomond Peak at 9,712 feet above sea level does not even rank among the 250 tallest named mountain summits in Utah. Ironically, Ben Lomond is not even the tallest summit in Weber County—nearby Willard Peak is 52 feet higher. However, Ben Lomond may still be the state's most famous mountain. William Wadsworth Hodkinson started some theaters in Ogden and later Paramount Pictures Corporation. He designed the famous mountain logo for the company back in 1914.

He grew up in Ogden, and from his home, a majestic mountain—Ben Lomond Peak—dominated the northern skyline, rising a vertical mile above the valley floor. That mountain inspired his logo, though like all things Hollywood, the peak in the logo is very exaggerated.

In Box Elder County, there are few standout peaks other than the Wellsville Cone. For Cache County, Mount Naomi is the tallest, but there is a shorter Mount Logan.

Going north into Idaho, the Wasatch Peaks are shorter there than anywhere else.

In Utah County, although Timp gains the most attention, a hike to the "Y" lettering on the mountain above Brigham Young University is perhaps the second-most popular mountain venture in the Wasatch there.

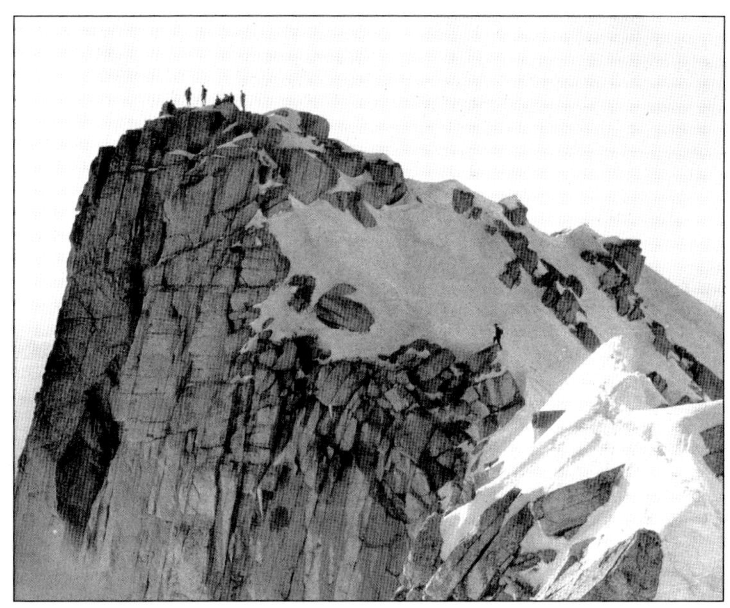

This is a 1930 picture of Lone Peak, an 11,260-foot summit at the southern edge of Salt Lake County. The peak's name comes from being a significant stand-alone summit, apart from other peaks. Note all the snow still around the peak despite the summer season. Even with its cliffy status, more hikers have died from lightning strikes on Lone Peak than falls. (Courtesy of J. Willard Marriott Digital Library, the University of Utah.)

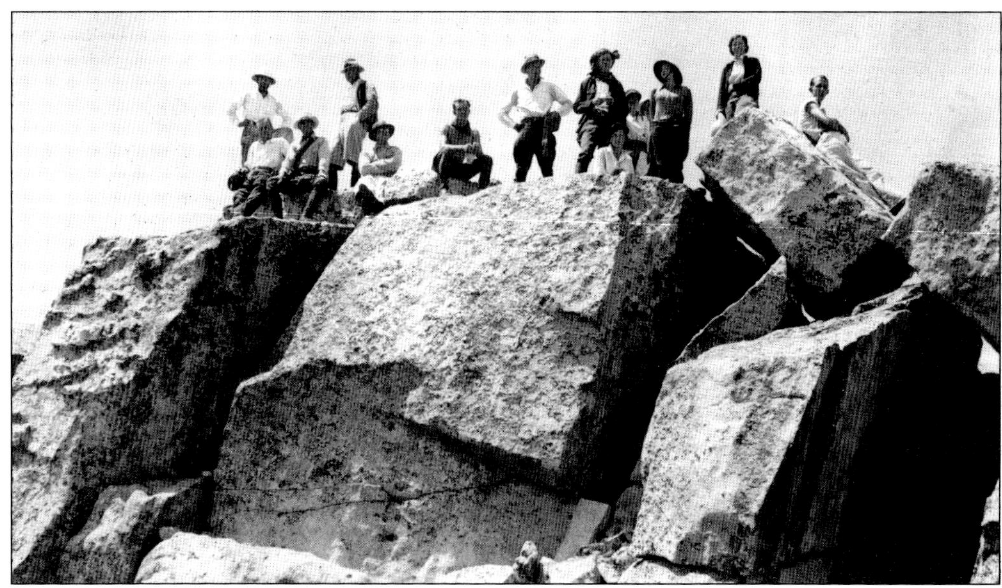

This is another 1930s photograph of the top of Lone Peak. Thirteen hikers, members of the Wasatch Mountain Club, are shown posing on July 13, 1935, atop the cliffy summit. Obviously, the likely photographer, Homer A. Collins, is probably situated on an even more precarious ledge to take this picture. Yet, like Angels Landing in Zion National Park and its perilous nature, such dangerous places have a sort of magnetic attraction for daring hikers. (Courtesy of J. Willard Marriott Digital Library, the University of Utah.)

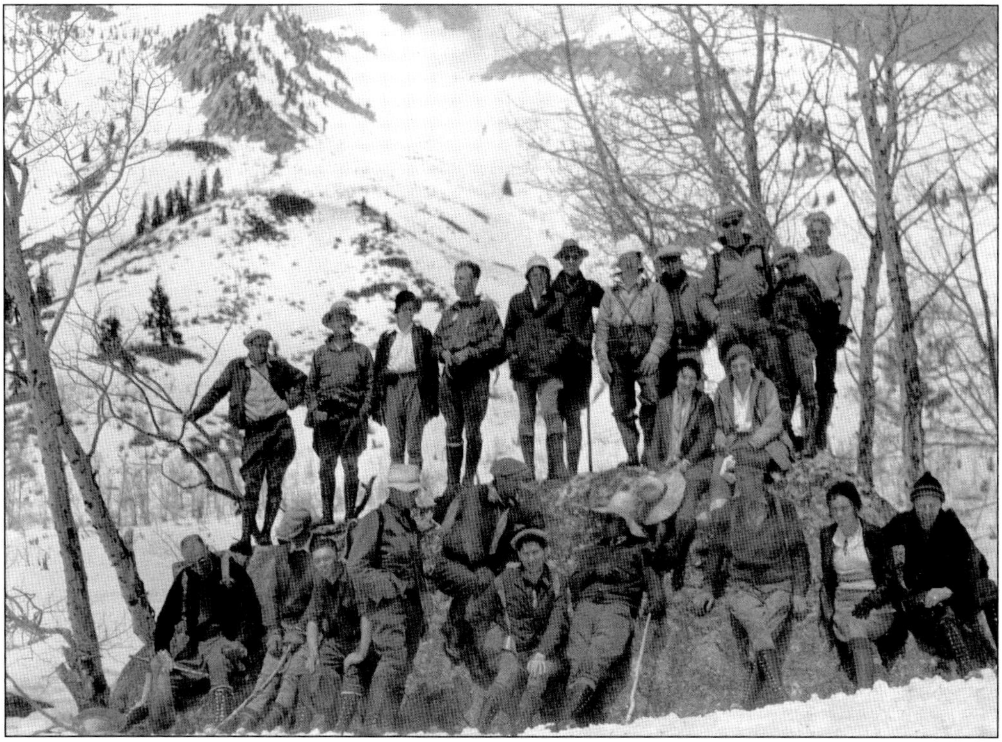

Lone Peak in springtime could be the title of this picture. Twenty-three Wasatch Mountain Club members pose on May 8, 1932, along the Alpine Canyon approach. These hikers appear to be not even halfway up the snow-covered mountain, and no special climbing equipment is shown. So, it is unclear if they actually summited that day. (Courtesy of J. Willard Marriott Digital Library, the University of Utah.)

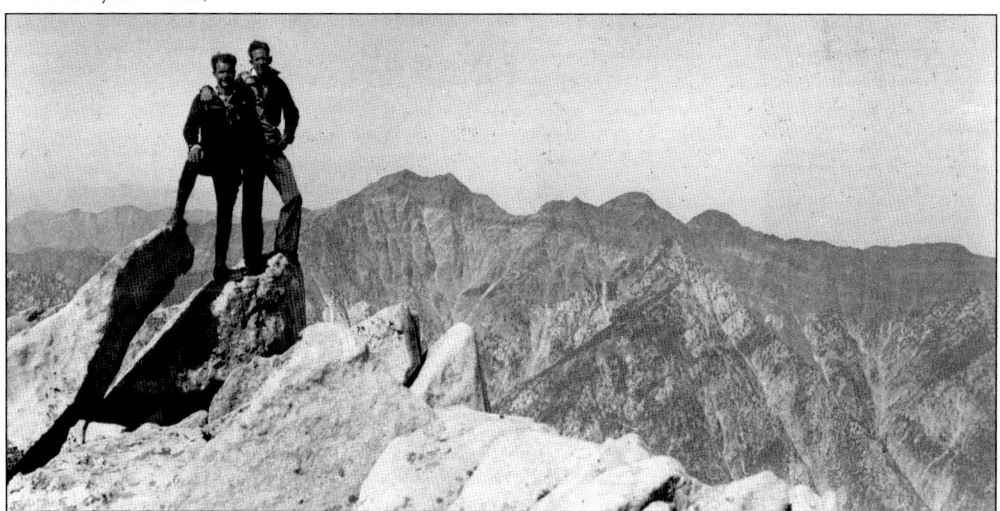

Bill Kamp (left) and Ephraim Odell "Pete" Peterson (right) were described as "peerless partners" in the Wasatch Mountain Club. Here, they are shown in the mid-1930s atop Lone Peak. The view behind them is north across Little Cottonwood Canyon to Snowbird's Twin Peaks and Dromedary Peak. The picture was taken by Homer A. Collins. (Courtesy of J. Willard Marriott Digital Library, the University of Utah.)

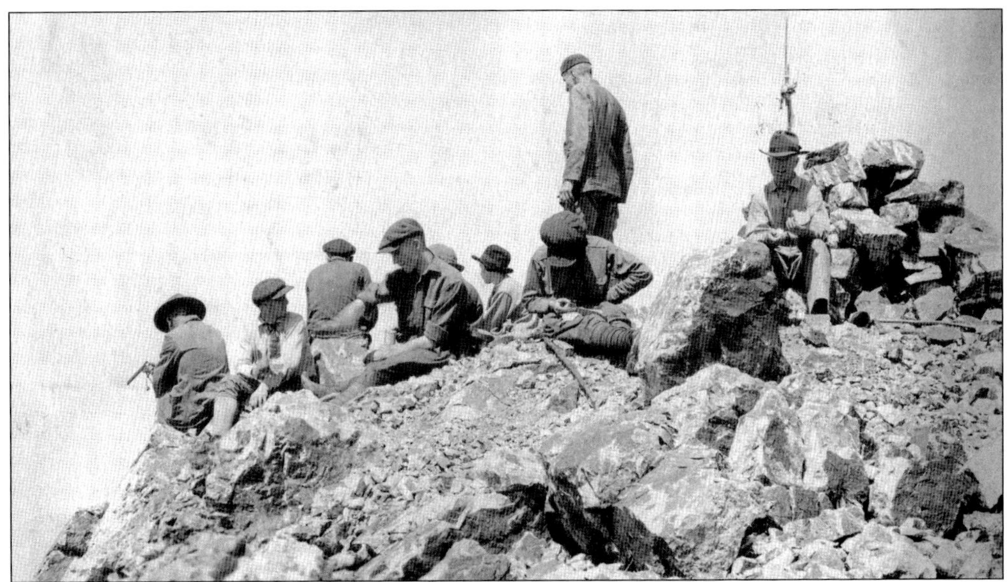

Members of the Wasatch Mountain Club, who are also University of Utah students, sit atop one of the Broad Fork Twin Peaks in Salt Lake County in the summer of the early 1920s. Although the picture lists a 12,000-foot elevation, the actual number is 11,330 feet for the eastern summit. These "Twin Peaks" are in between the two Cottonwood Canyons and are separate from the slightly higher but different Twin Peaks above today's Snowbird Ski Resort. (Courtesy of J. Willard Marriott Digital Library, the University of Utah.)

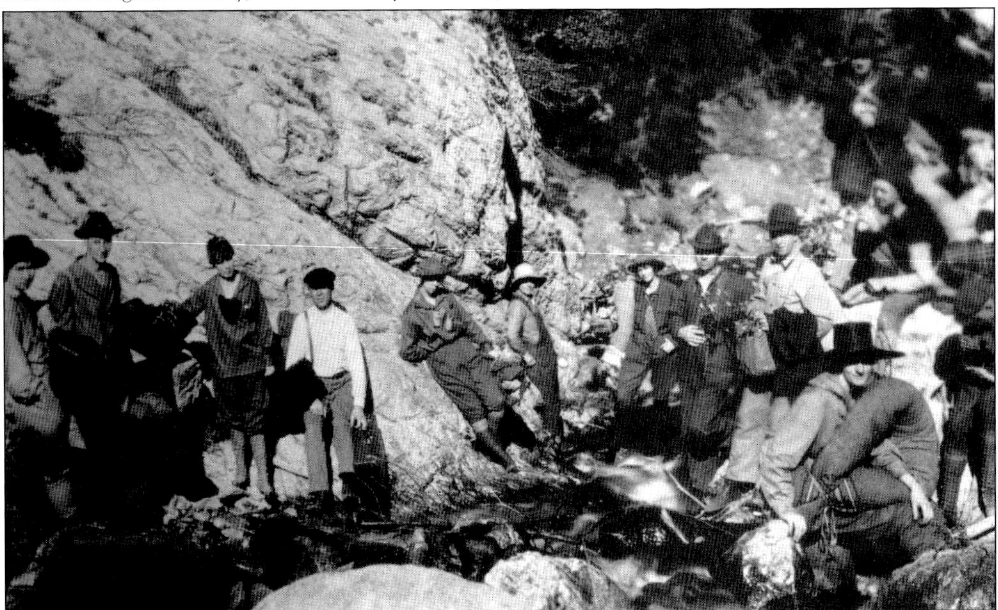

This is another picture of a Wasatch Mountain Club/University of Utah expedition to the top of the Broad Fork Twin Peaks in the 1920s. This photograph shows a large group along the trail with a stream of water likely bisecting the path. Today, the trail to Twin Peaks is about nine miles round trip and is a challenging route that climbs nearly 5,000 feet from Big Cottonwood Canyon and does require some scrambling. (Courtesy of J. Willard Marriott Digital Library, the University of Utah.)

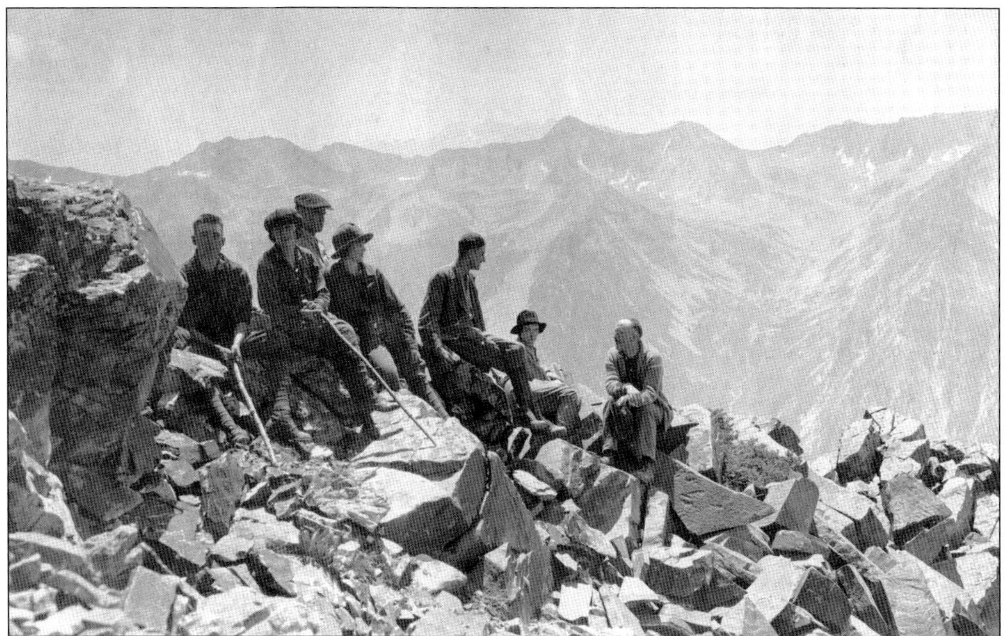

This photograph shows the top of Broad Fork Twin Peaks between the Cottonwood Canyons. Only seven hikers are pictured in this 1920s University of Utah/Wasatch Mountain Club adventure. These might be the few of a larger group where only they summited. Note that the other, slightly taller, Twin Peaks in the area are in the center background as two noticeable mounds. There was no Snowbird resort back in this era, and so these taller "Twins" were climbed less often then. (Courtesy of J. Willard Marriott Digital Library, the University of Utah.)

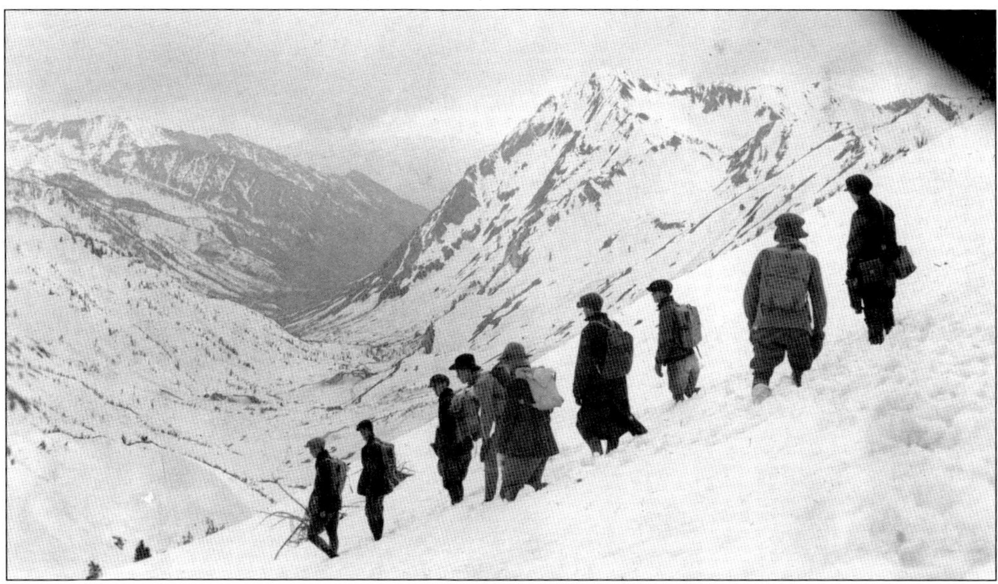

Forget avalanche danger or knee-deep snow—Wasatch Mountain Club members are shown in a winter of the early 1920s descending down to Alta during a long trek. The group traveled from Brighton to Alta. Mount Superior is shown in the background. Some of the club members have backpacks that identify their club membership. (Courtesy of J. Willard Marriott Digital Library, the University of Utah.)

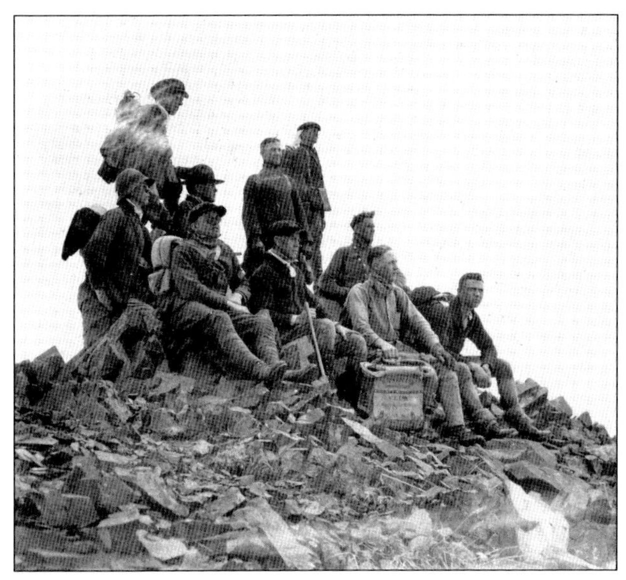

Ten members of the Wasatch Mountain Club are shown atop what is referred to as "Mount Blanc" after a summer hike in the early 1920s. The men were hiking in the Lake Blanche area, so it is possible that the summit shown is actually today's Sundial Peak, a distinctive 10,300-foot summit in that area. (In fact, Sundial Peak is the symbol for today's Wasatch Mountain Club.) While several approaches to the peak are technical climbs, the trail from Lake Blanche is not, though it does include a knife-edge scramble to the summit. (Courtesy of J. Willard Marriott Digital Library, the University of Utah.)

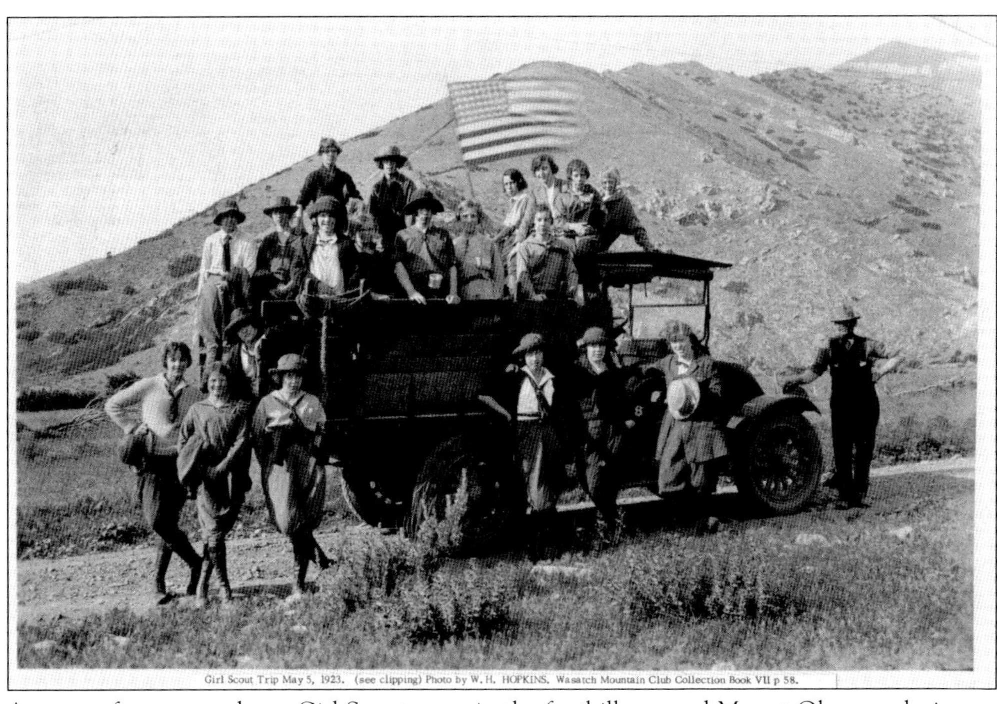

A group of some two dozen Girl Scouts pose in the foothills around Mount Olympus during an outing in the Wasatch Mountains on May 5, 1923. The picture was taken by William H. Hopkins of the Wasatch Mountain Club, so the trip may have had some connection to the club. Note the American flag flying on the truck that was transporting all the girls. (Courtesy of J. Willard Marriott Digital Library, the University of Utah.)

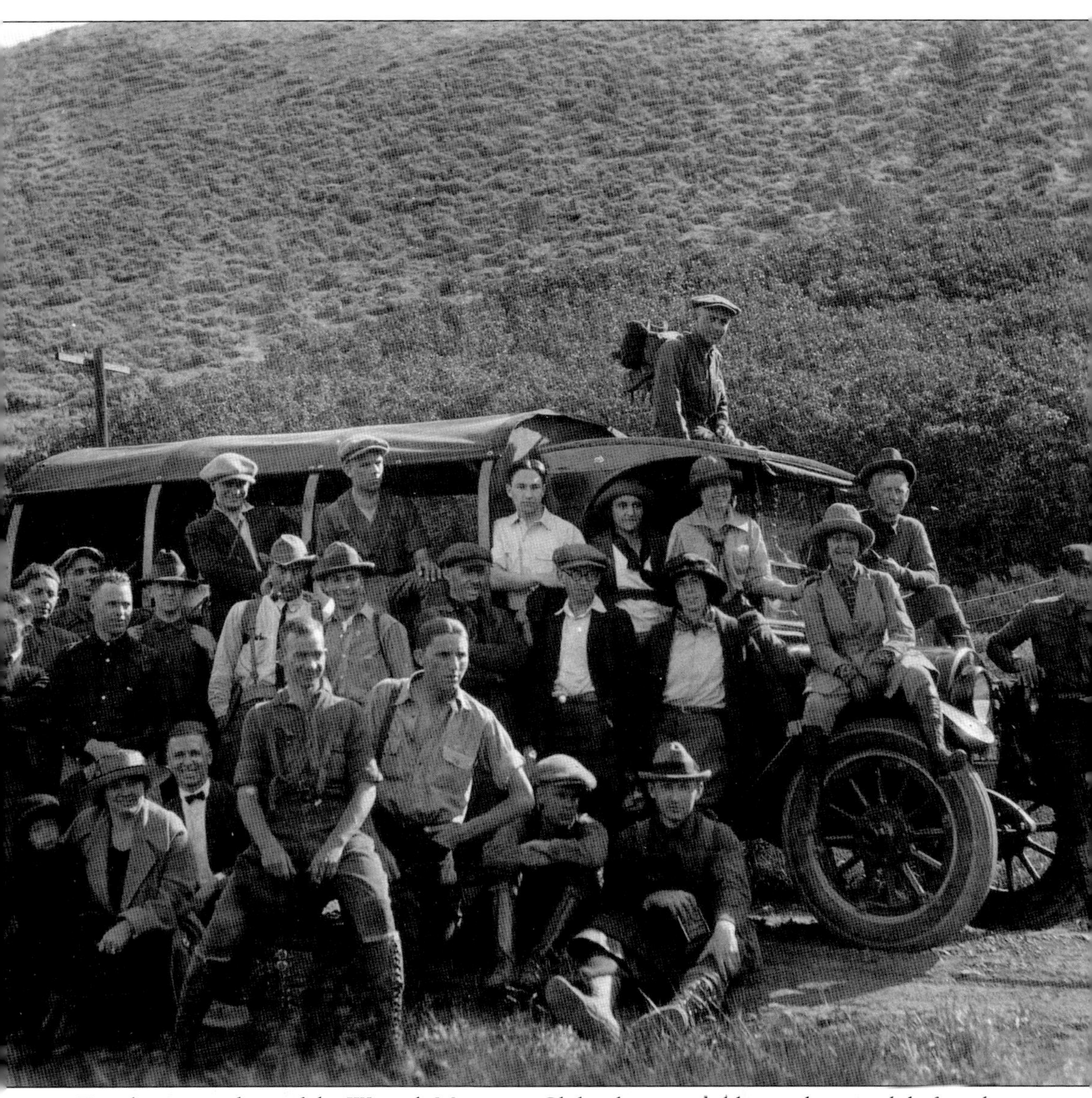

Two dozen members of the Wasatch Mountain Club, plus one child, pose by a truck before they begin a hike up Mount Olympus in the summer of 1923. (Mount Olympus is a very majestic 9,026-foot elevation peak.) Note that the couple with the child in the lower left-hand corner of the picture strangely appears way overdressed for such a rugged hike. The narrow dirt road where this picture was taken may well be the predecessor to today's Wasatch Boulevard. (Courtesy of J. Willard Marriott Digital Library, the University of Utah.)

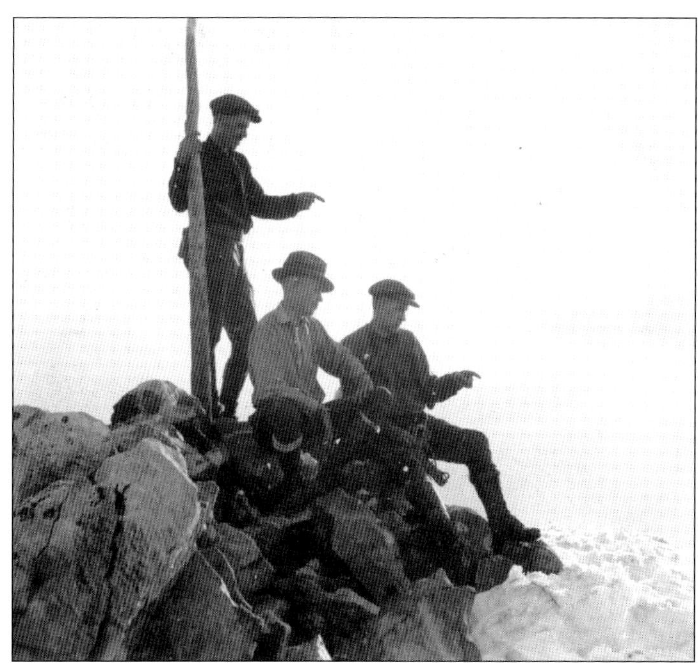

Three climbers rest on top of Mount Olympus after a successful spring assent. They are, from left to right, Reynold Gordon, Clarence Parry, and an unidentified man. William H. Hopkins took the picture. The four are members of the Wasatch Mountain Club. Note the snow in the photograph and that the unidentified hiker has some climbing rope in his hand. Mount Olympus was an often-climbed mountain and, with its lower elevation, was free of deep snow more often. (Courtesy of J. Willard Marriott Digital Library, the University of Utah.)

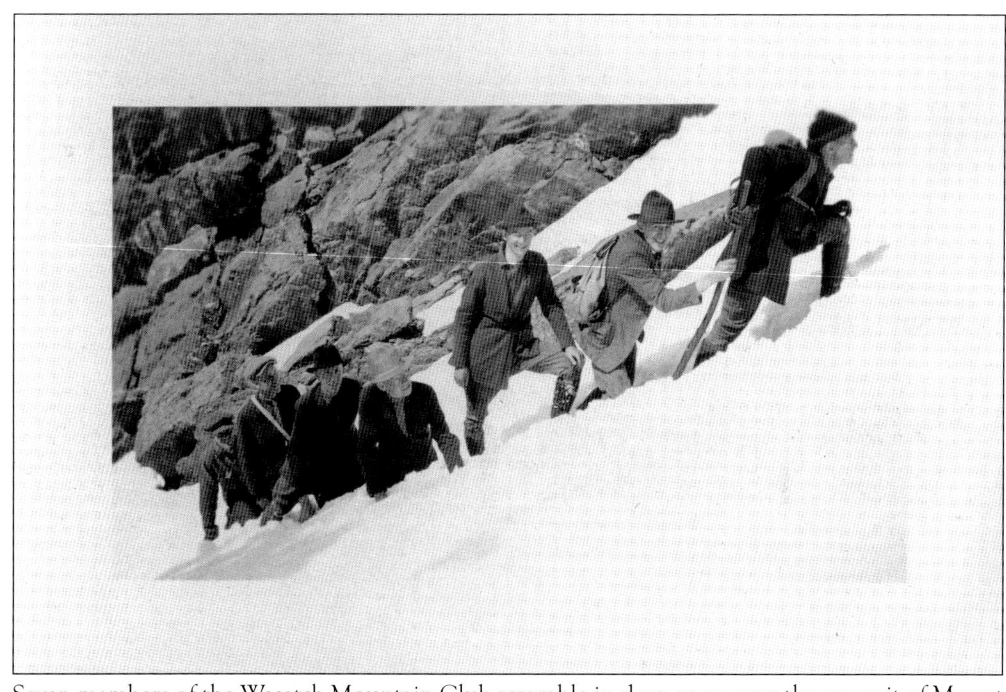

Seven members of the Wasatch Mountain Club scramble in deep snow near the summit of Mount Olympus in an early-1920s hiking photograph. Mount Olympus is named for the ancient peak in northeast Greece, fabled to be home to the Greek gods. In Utah, the mountain is east of Holladay in Salt Lake County. Tolcats Canyon is the traditional access to it. (Courtesy of J. Willard Marriott Digital Library, the University of Utah.)

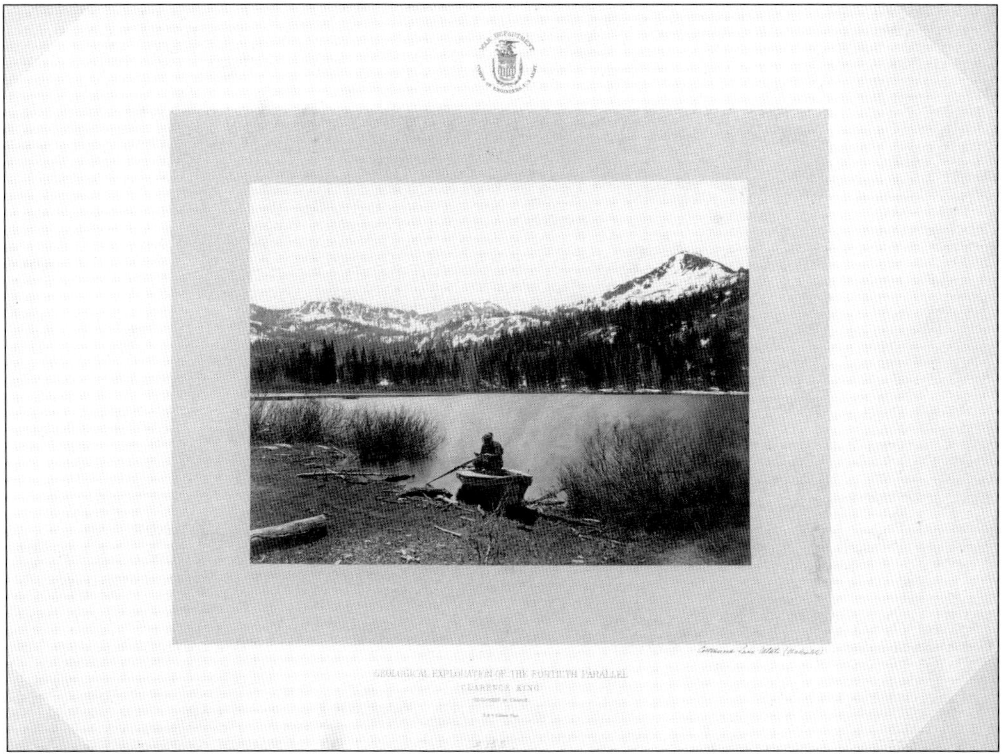

Famed Utah photographer Charles Savage is shown sitting in a small boat on Cottonwood Lake in the late spring of 1869. Savage appears to be reading or writing. Where was this lake? No such named lake exists in the area today. Perhaps it is Silver Lake, or Lake Blanche, near Big Cottonwood Canyon? (Courtesy of Library of Congress.)

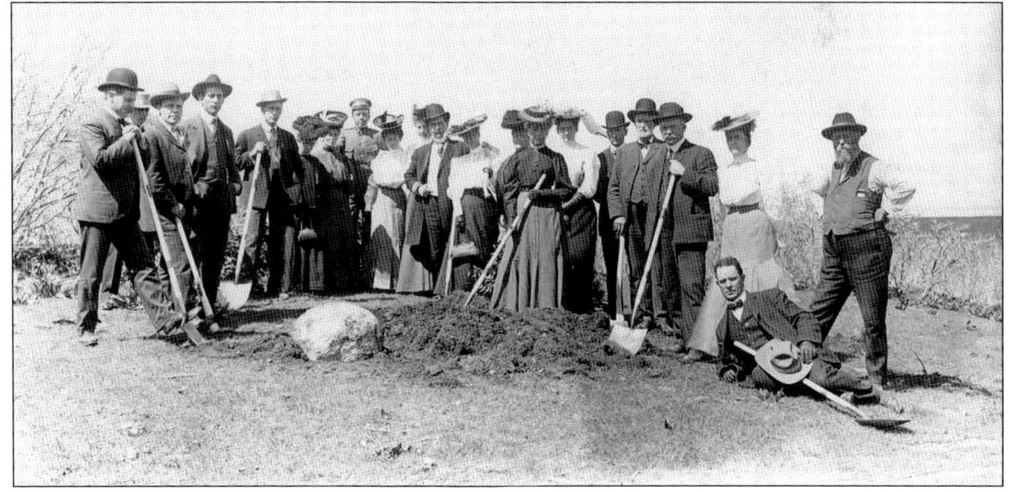

An unidentified, large group of dignitaries—all of them dressed in formal attire—dig holes to plant some trees atop Bountiful Peak on May 14, 1906. At an elevation of 9,259 feet above sea level, this summit is easily accessed by the Skyline Drive scenic backway road today. However, in the early 20th century, how this group traveled that high in the middle of spring—without such a dirt road—is unknown. Bountiful Peak is actually located in central Davis County, east of Farmington, and is not near the city of Bountiful. (Courtesy of Utah State Historical Society.)

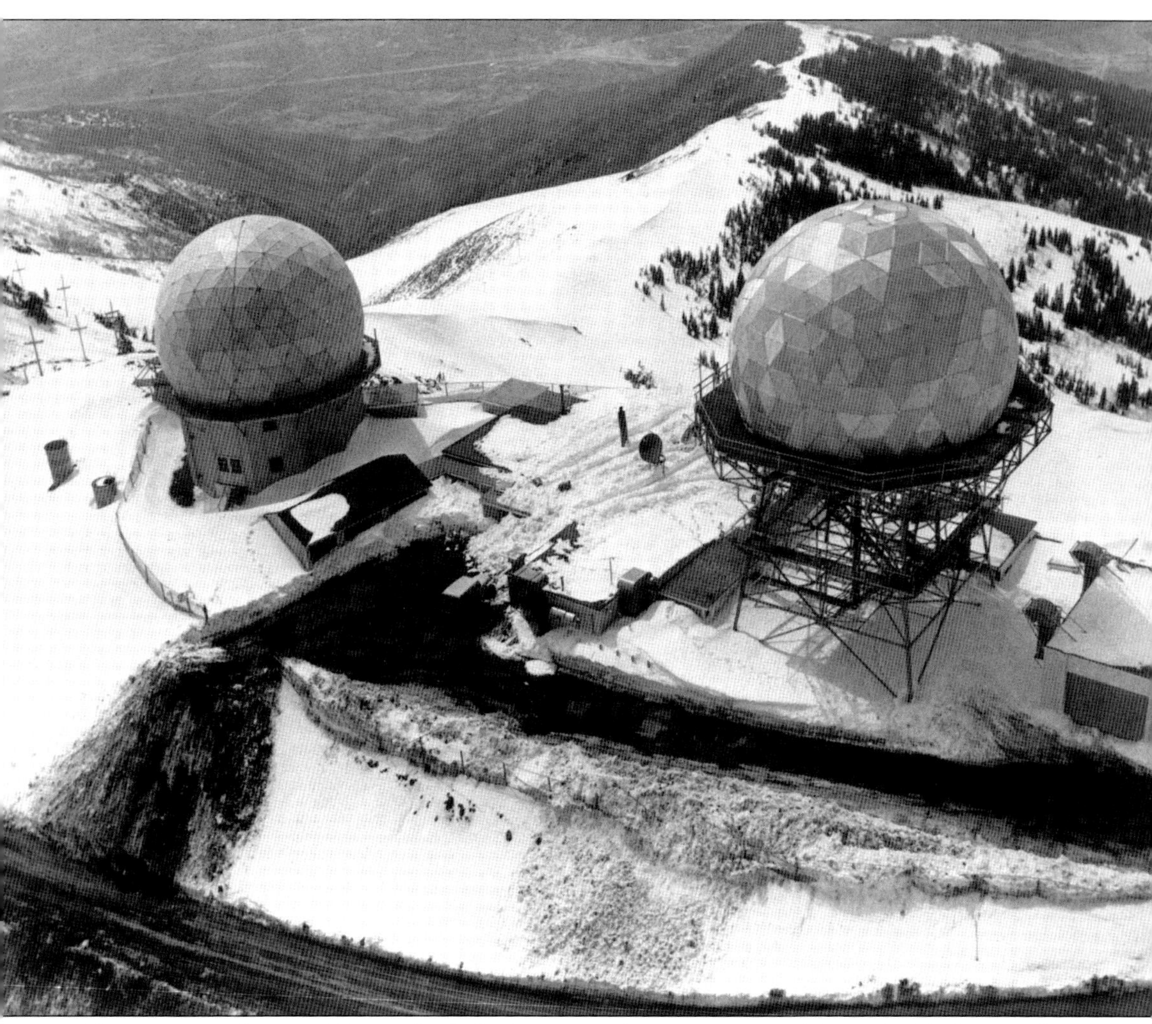

This is an aerial view of Francis Peak, looking west during a winter of the early 1970s, complete with its two geodesic radar domes on top. At a natural elevation of just under 9,500 feet above sea level, the domes raise the total elevation to about 9,515 feet. Built in the late 1950s, this Federal Aviation Administration outpost is accessible by a dirt road up Farmington Canyon. Note Interstate 15 crossing the valley below. (Courtesy of Utah State Historical Society.)

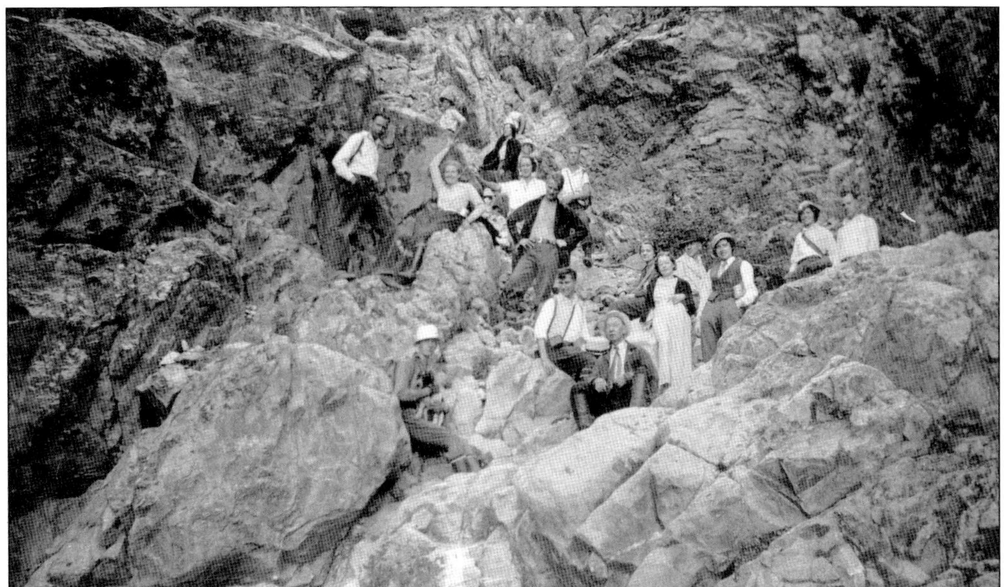

Seventeen members of the Wasatch Mountain Club pose on some rocks during their climb of Mount Ogden in Weber County sometime during the 1930s. This picture, taken by Homer A. Collins, was either shot on the east side of the peak, just below the summit, or it is in the upper reaches of Waterfall Canyon—far below the 9,572-foot elevation summit. (Courtesy of Utah State Historical Society.)

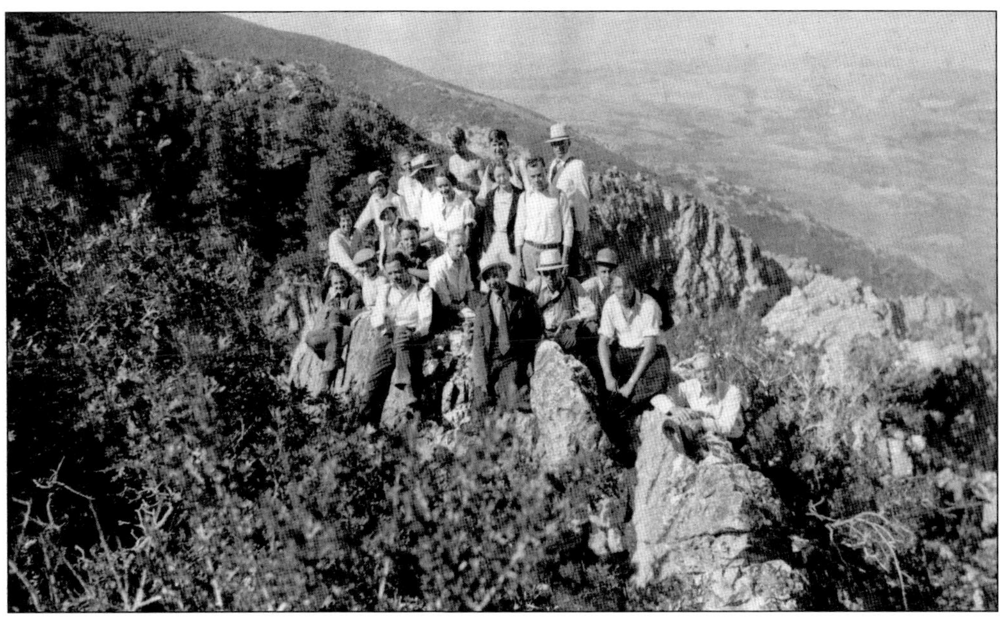

This is another Wasatch Mountain Club hiking group below Mount Ogden Peak, Weber County, in the 1930s. This picture was taken partway up the mountain, from Malan's Basin and not yet above the tree line. As the tallest summit around Weber State University, Mount Ogden has always been a popular hike. (Courtesy of J. Willard Marriott Digital Library, the University of Utah.)

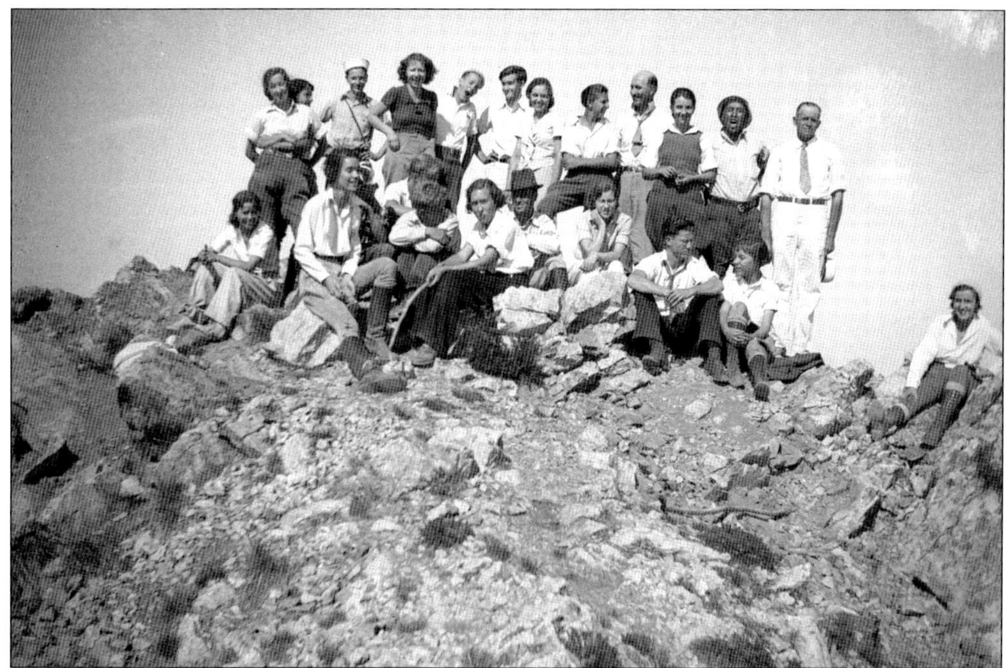

Almost two dozen successful hikers pose atop Ben Lomond Peak, elevation 9,712 feet, in Weber County on August 26, 1937. This picture was taken by Ray King, a *Salt Lake Tribune* photographer. (King may have set his camera on automatic, as he appears to be standing second from the right in the second row of the picture.) Ben Lomond is not the tallest summit in the area (Willard Peak is), but it is the most majestic summit in the region. (Courtesy of Utah State Historical Society.)

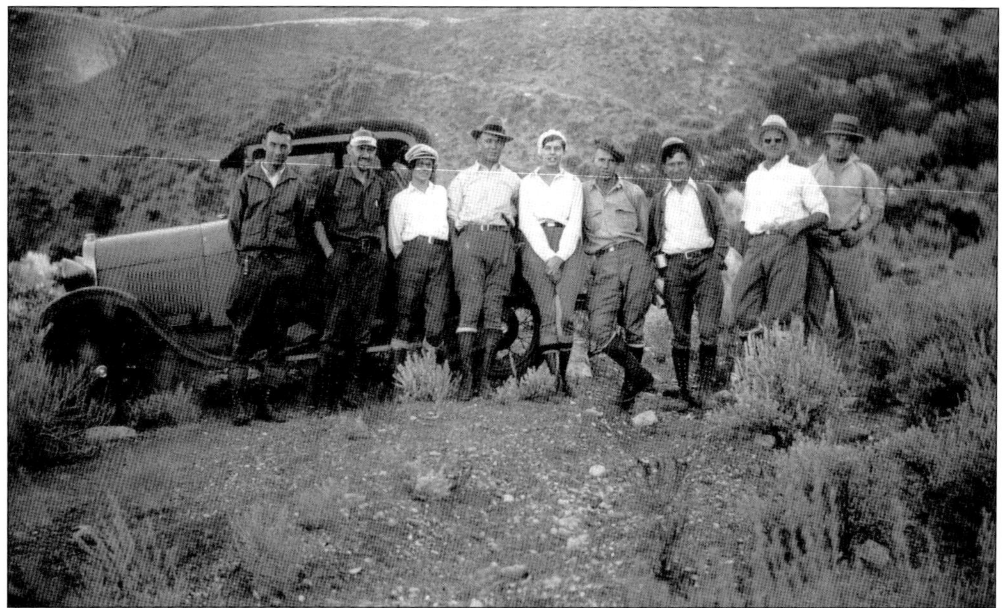

Nine members of the Wasatch Mountain Club pose by their vehicle near the top of Willard Canyon on July 19, 1931. This area had much easier access after the late 1920s when the Willard Basin dirt road was constructed to allow terraces to be built to try and halt future flash floods to the valley below. (Courtesy of J. Willard Marriott Digital Library, the University of Utah.)

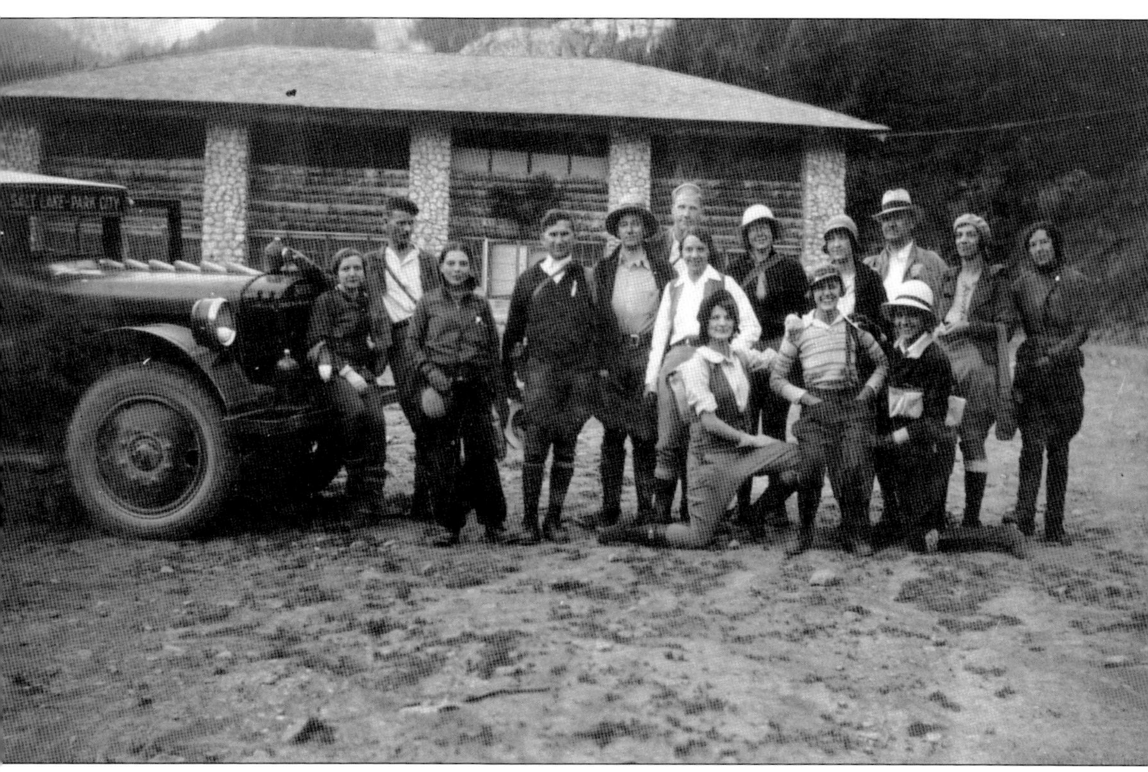

Fifteen Wasatch Mountain Club members pose somewhere in Logan Canyon before or after a climb up Mount Logan (9,710-foot elevation) in the 1930s. Today, a rugged road leads to the peak since a telecommunications relay sits atop its summit. These club members had to hike there back in the day. And true to their club's name, members hiked all over the Wasatch Front. (Courtesy of J. Willard Marriott Digital Library, the University of Utah.)

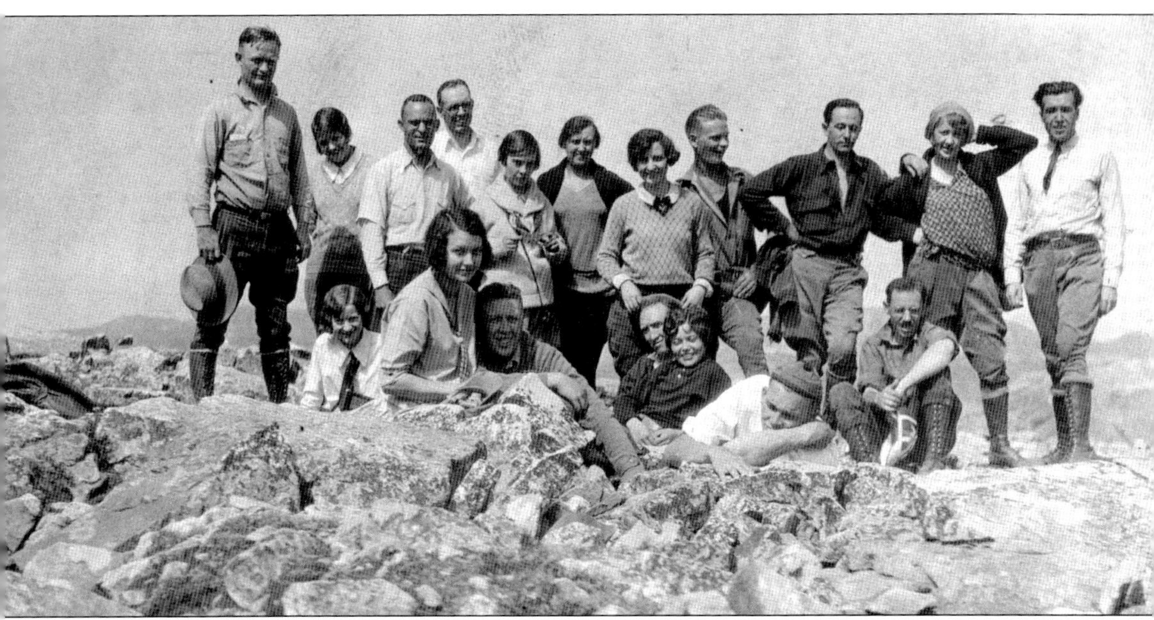

This is one of the best close-up, vintage pictures of a Wasatch Mountain Club hiking group from around the 1920s. Posing atop an unidentified peak, there appear to be taller mountains in the background. Common to most of the men are tall boots with almost endless laces. At least one man on the far right is even wearing a necktie. None of the hikers seem to have any backpacks or canteens. (Courtesy of J. Willard Marriott Digital Library, the University of Utah.)

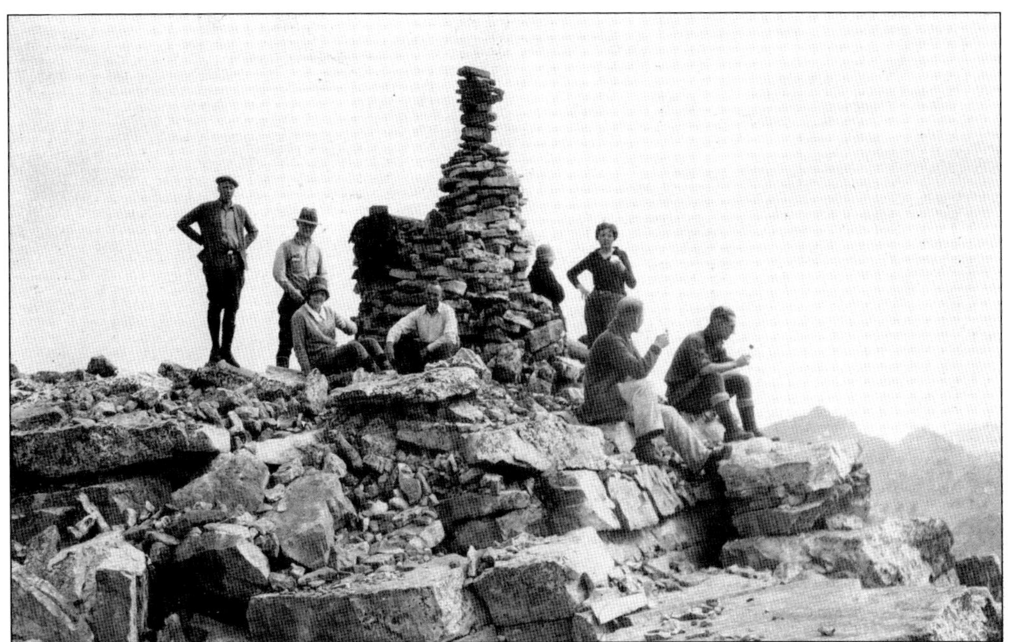

This is yet another Wasatch Mountain Club group picture on an unidentified summit. This peak has a tall rock cairn marking the top. Although the picture states it is probably in the Wasatch Mountains, the slabs of square rock and background peaks suggest it might well be in the Uinta Mountains instead. None of the hikers appear to have any backpacks, and several of the men are licking suckers. (Courtesy of J. Willard Marriott Digital Library, the University of Utah.)

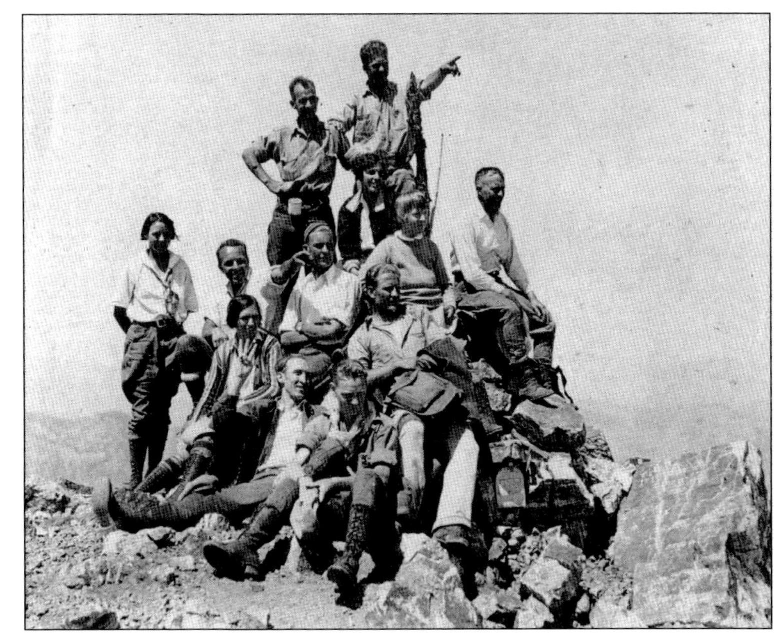

A smiling group of Wasatch Mountain Club hikers crowd the summit of an unidentified mountaintop in the 1920s. This peak also has a metal mailbox encased in rock. Strangely, only one of the 12 hikers appears to have any kind of hat, an unusual situation for the early 20th century. (Courtesy of J. Willard Marriott Digital Library, the University of Utah.)

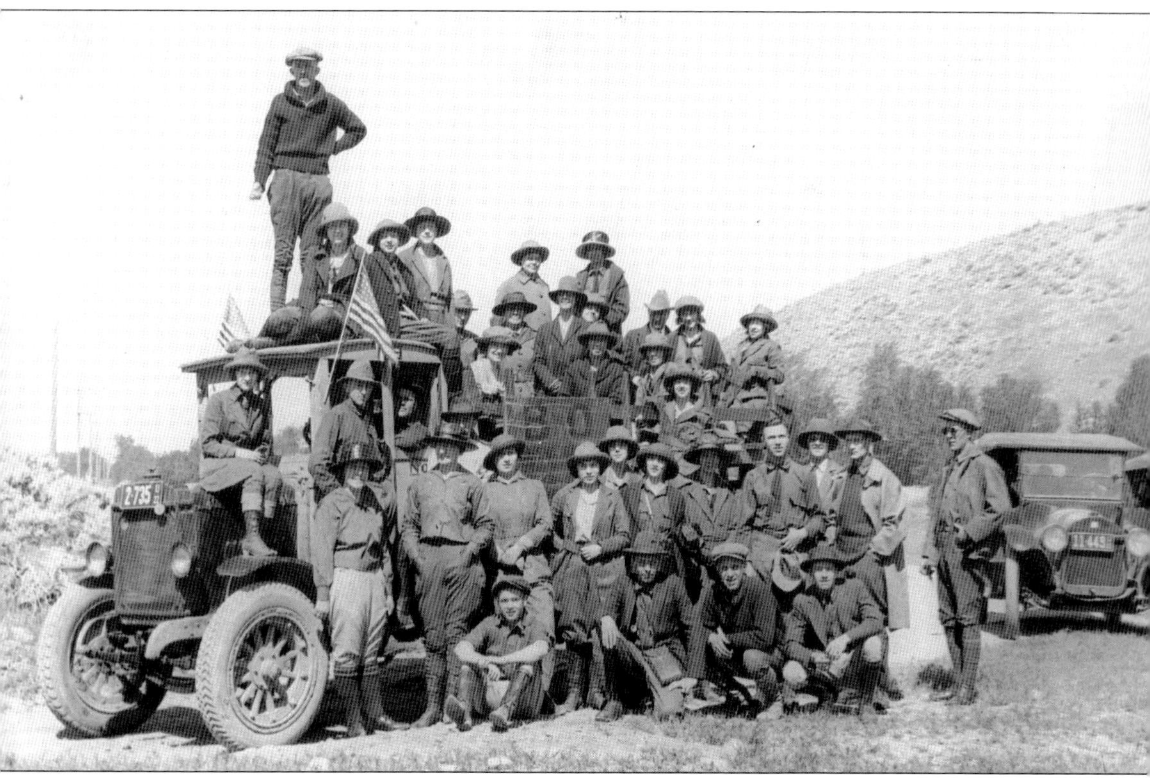

A large group of Wasatch Mountain Club members pose next to their vehicles after a 1920s outing in the Wasatch Mountains. This club was formed in 1920 and still sponsors a variety of outdoor activities in the Wasatch Mountains and beyond today. These days, the club even has mountain biking, kayaking, river rafting, skiing, snowshoeing, canyoneering activities, and more, besides traditional hiking, climbing, and camping activities. (Courtesy of J. Willard Marriott Digital Library, the University of Utah.)

Five

Key Canyons and Points

The Wasatch Mountains contain dozens of canyons, numerous ski resorts, and hundreds of miles of hiking and biking trails. There are also many campgrounds, scenic roads, and other amenities.

Which is the most scenic canyon in the Wasatch Mountains? The answer would spark many debates and is more of a subjective judgment. Historically, Emigration Canyon might be the most important mountain portal since the Mormon pioneers came to the Salt Lake Valley through it in July 1847.

Yet, today, it is Weber Canyon and Parley's Canyon that contain interstate freeways, with Interstates 84 and 80 respectively, making them the most critical in transportation needs.

Still, Logan Canyon has to be one of the leading contenders for pure beauty and natural eye candy since US Highway 89, a major thoroughfare, runs right through it.

Ogden Canyon, American Fork Canyon, and Provo Canyon can also make claims of high-ranking natural beauty.

Sardine Canyon is another segment of Highway 89 and traverses through the Wasatch and along the east side of the Wellsville Mountains, a spur of the Wasatch Mountains.

Little Cottonwood Canyon is home to the Alta Ski area, one of the oldest and snowiest ski locations in the United States. Snowbird Ski Resort is also in Little Cottonwood, while Big Cottonwood Canyon boasts Solitude and Brighton Ski areas. (Morgan County even has an exclusive, private ski resort.)

Utah's skiing is world famous—especially in the Wasatch Mountains, since they were the backbone of the 2002 Winter Olympic Games—and will be again in the 2034 Winter Olympics. The mountains also boast other blockbuster attractions. Timpanogos Cave is found in lower American Fork Canyon and is so popular that reservations have to be made long in advance. The Bear River segment of the mountains in Idaho has its own deep cave, too: Minnetonka.

Ogden Canyon hosted the Hermitage Inn for decades, feeding many hungry travelers and catering to large groups. Up the canyon was the Oaks, which began in 1902 as a "resort," though it became a restaurant until closing in 2023 and then reopening in 2025 under new ownership. Log Haven restaurant in Salt Lake's Millcreek Canyon was built in 1930, and Ruth's Diner opened in Emigration Canyon in 1949.

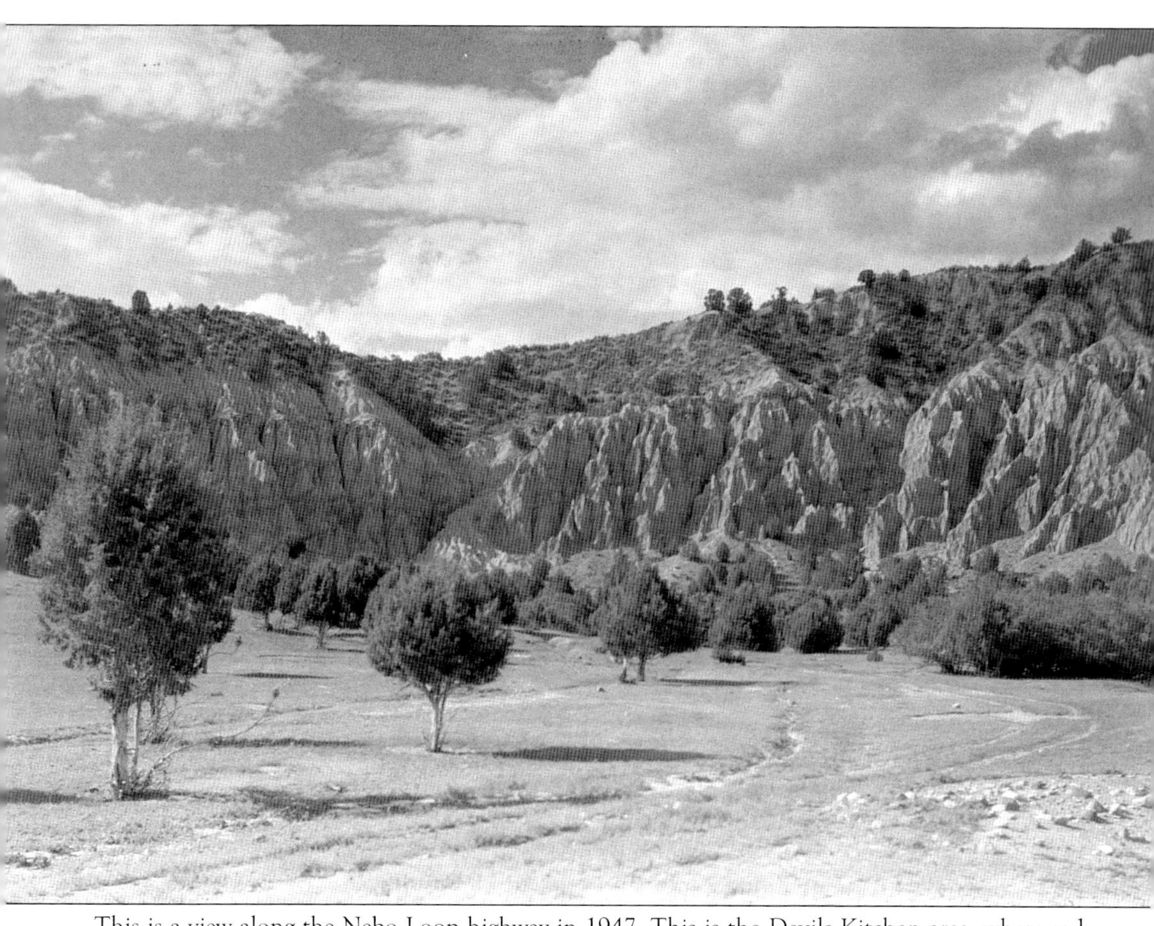

This is a view along the Nebo Loop highway in 1947. This is the Devils Kitchen area, where red rock, reminiscent of southern Utah, actually exists in the northern portion of the state. The road was first a scenic US Forest Service road, and today, it is a paved scenic byway and covers 38 miles from Payson to Nephi. (Courtesy of Utah State Historical Society.)

Two Deer Creek Scenic Railroad trains race past Deer Creek Reservoir in Provo Canyon in 1974. The railroad was nicknamed the "Heber Creeper" and then renamed the Heber Valley Railroad. The Denver & Rio Grande Western Railroad first rolled through this area in 1935, carrying livestock and people. The modern railroad only goes from Heber City to Vivan Park. (Courtesy of Utah State Historical Society.)

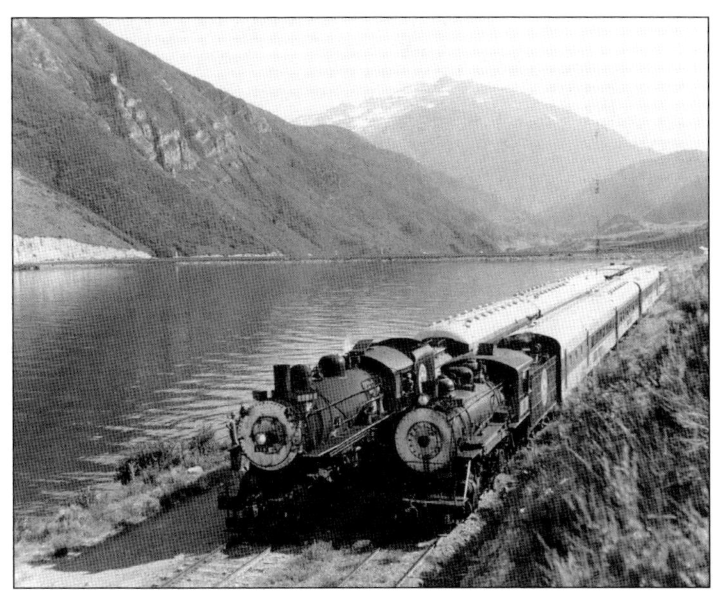

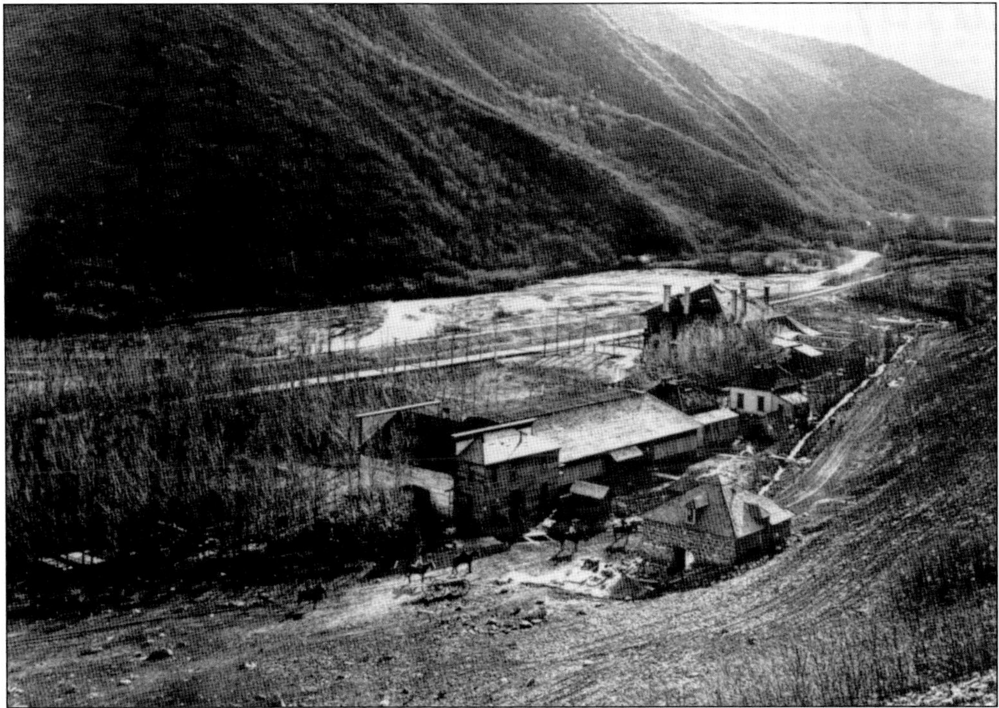

Castilla Hot Springs resort in Spanish Fork Canyon is shown in a 1917 photograph. The resort opened in 1889 and boasted of its hot mineral baths, which were thought to be very healthful. It closed in the early 1930s, and a fire around 1940 destroyed the main hotel building. Today, only a few cement vaults remain along Highway 6. The Wasatch Mountains still contain many other hot springs, though. (Courtesy of Utah State Historical Society.)

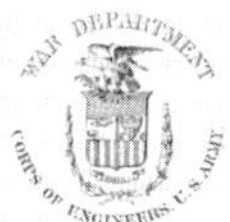

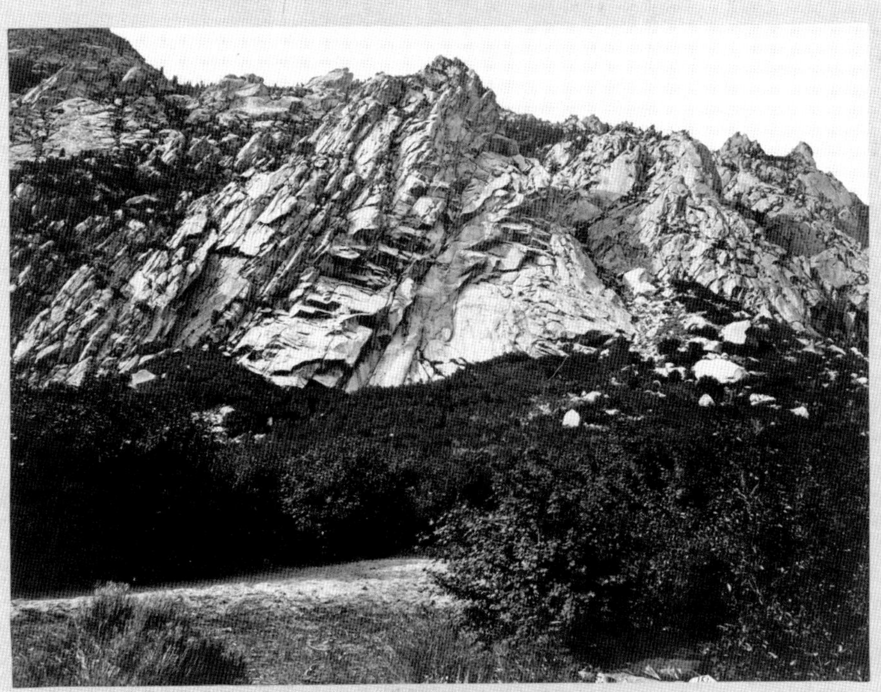

This is an 1869 photograph taken somewhere in the Wasatch Mountains, possibly in Little Cottonwood Canyon. Note the many rugged rocks in the canyon and that the picture itself is titled "Granite Rocks." There appears to be a road or trail at the bottom of the picture. (Courtesy of Library of Congress.)

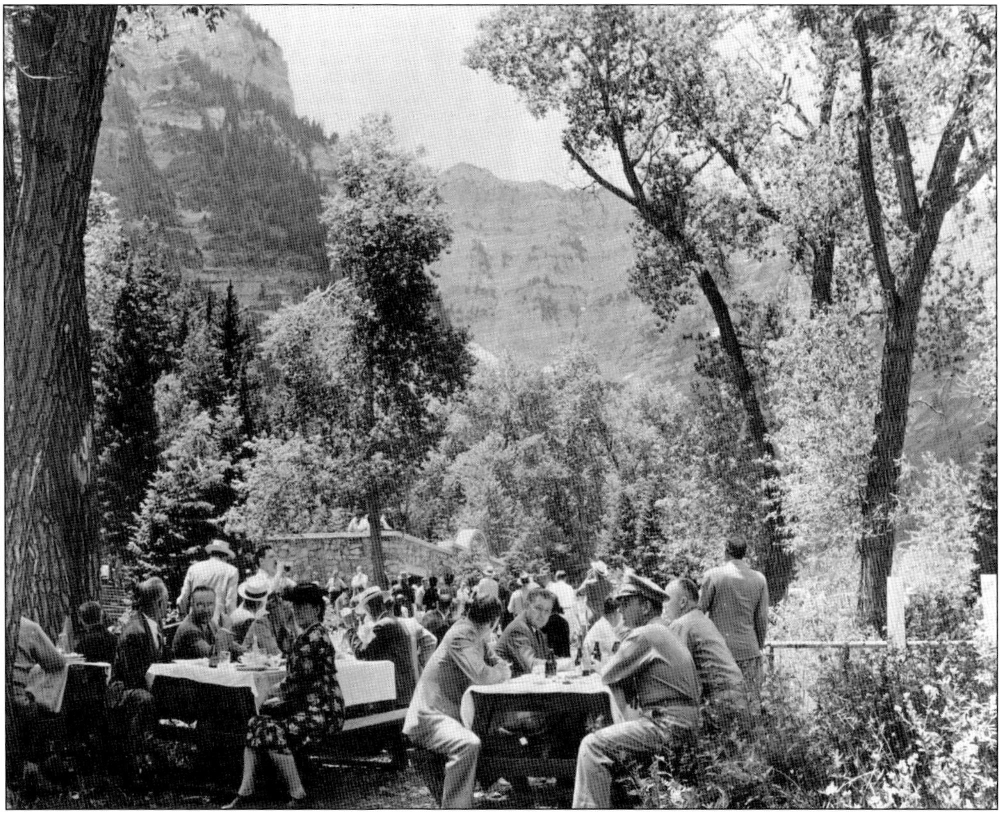

A large group of people enjoy a summer picnic in 1947 at Aspen Grove. This may be some sort of professional group, but there are a few military servicemen there, too. Aspen Grove has long been a summer resort since Brigham Young University (BYU) started using it in 1911 as a starting point for annual hikes to Timpanogos Peak. BYU also held summer school there from 1924 until 1942. Starting in 1962, Aspen Grove was expanded with cabins, kitchens, and facilities to host even larger groups comfortably. (Courtesy of Utah State Historical Society.)

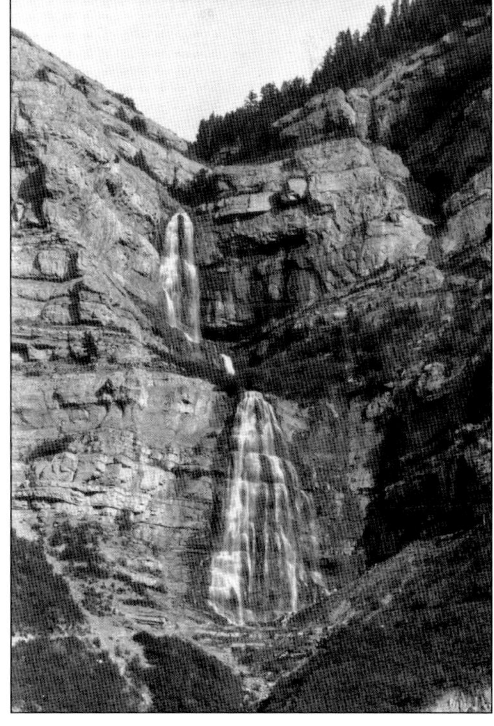

This is Bridal Veil Falls in Provo Canyon, sometime during the 1950s. The falls are located on US Highway 189 between Springdell and Vivian Park. They were originally named Beautiful Cascade in 1859 during a US government survey of the canyon. However, common usage permanently changed the title to Bridal Veil years later. (Courtesy of Utah State Historical Society.)

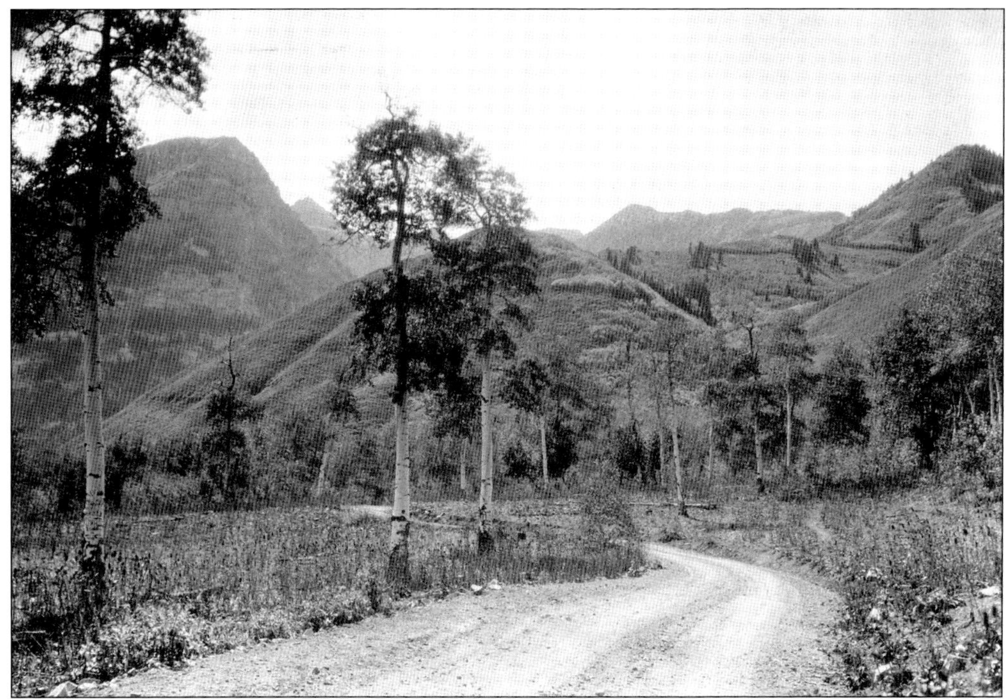

This is a portion of the upper American Fork Canyon during the 1930s. Note the narrow, winding road. Even today, when this area is part of what is known as the Alpine Loop, Utah State Route 92, the highway is not much wider, though it is paved. The road is one of the most scenic canyon roads in Utah and, in the fall, has some of the most vibrant autumn leaves. (Courtesy of Utah State Historical Society.)

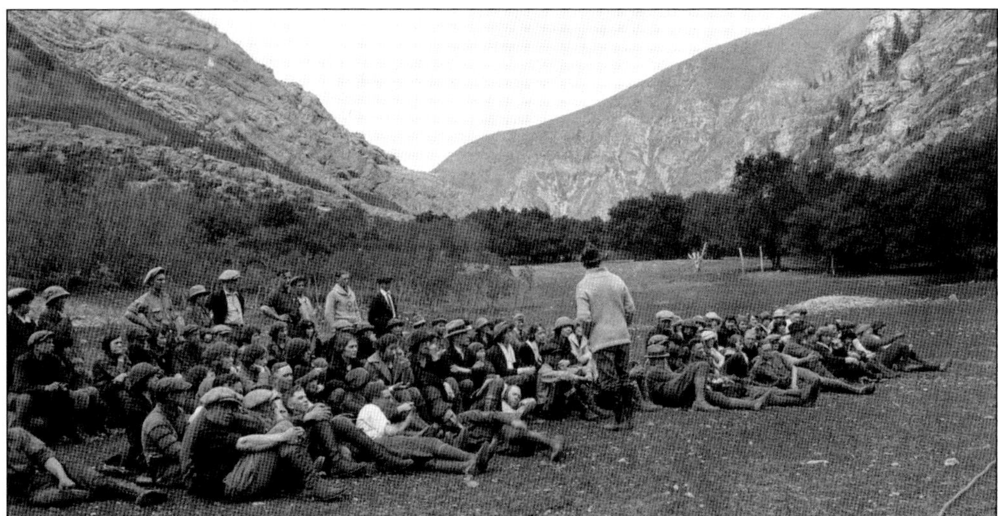

Vivian Park in Provo Canyon has a long, storied history. Here, more than 100 Wasatch Mountain Club members relaxed there on Decoration Day (today's Memorial Day) in 1923. William Ferguson owned the land until 1896, and he likely named it after an "adorable child" he knew, Vivian McBride. The McBrides ran a store and post office in Provo Canyon in the late 19th century. Later, a café, skating rink, and dance hall existed there. The official park came along in 1974. (Courtesy of J. Willard Marriott Digital Library, the University of Utah.)

This is a US government photograph from 1869 showing Provo Falls. It would later be known as Bridal Veil Falls and feature a short-lived aerial tram, billed as the steepest in the world: 1,753 feet long, with a vertical climb of 1,228 feet. The tram opened in 1961 and closed on January 2, 1996, after an avalanche damaged it. Eventually, all traces of the tram and building on top were removed. (Courtesy of Library of Congress.)

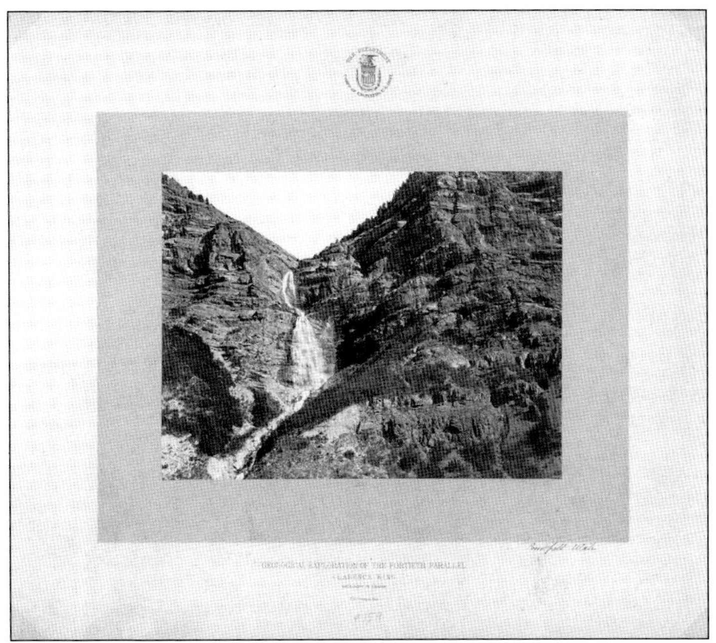

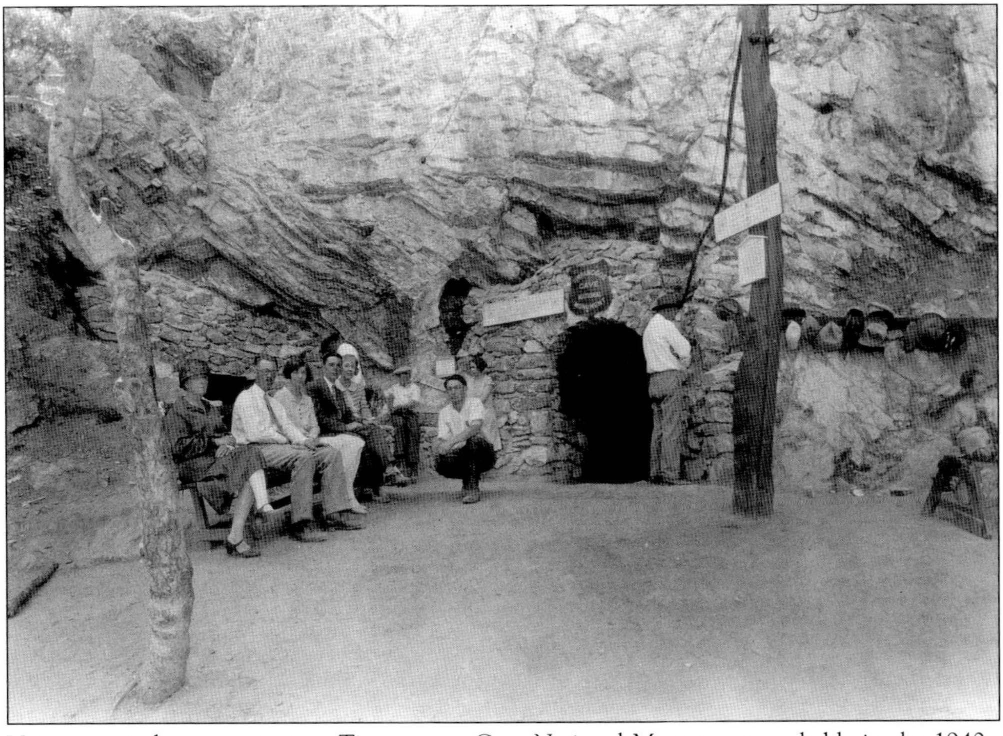

Visitors wait their turn to tour Timpanogos Cave National Monument, probably in the 1940s. Note all the hats hanging on a rack attached to the mountain. The cave was first discovered in October 1887 and was first known as Hansen Cave, after its discoverer, Martin Hansen. It was later renamed Timpanogos Cave when it was designated as a national monument on October 14, 1922. A steep, 1.5-mile hike on a paved trail is required to access it. (Courtesy of Utah State Historical Society.)

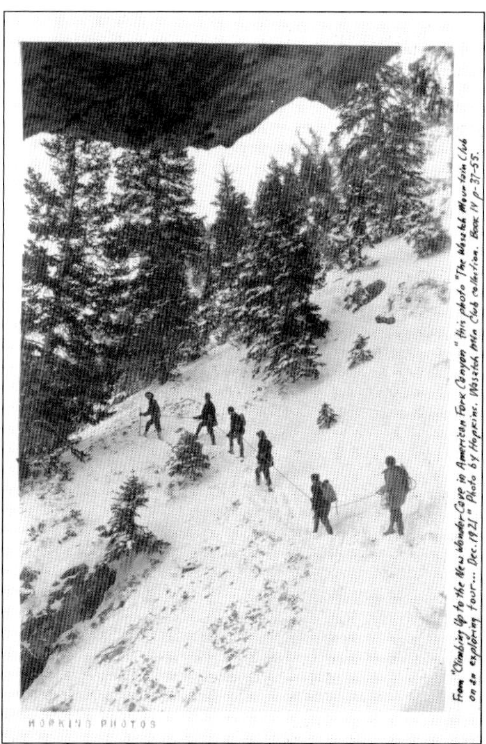

Before it was a national monument, the Wasatch Mountain Club hiked to Timpanogos Cave in the winter of 1921. The club declared it the "New Wonder Cave." Note that the group is safely roped together during this steep winter climb. Timpanogos Cave is the most famous of the caves in the Wasatch Mountains. Another large Wasatch cave is in southern Idaho, named Minnetonka Cave. (Courtesy of J. Willard Marriott Digital Library, the University of Utah.)

If one thinks the Alpine Loop Road in American Fork Canyon is narrow today, look at it here on July 29, 1925, as an even narrower dirt path. Buses, operated by the Brigham Stage company, traverse what was known as the "Z Dugway" back then. American Fork Canyon has some of the most spectacular scenery in the entire Wasatch Mountains. (Courtesy of Utah State Historical Society.)

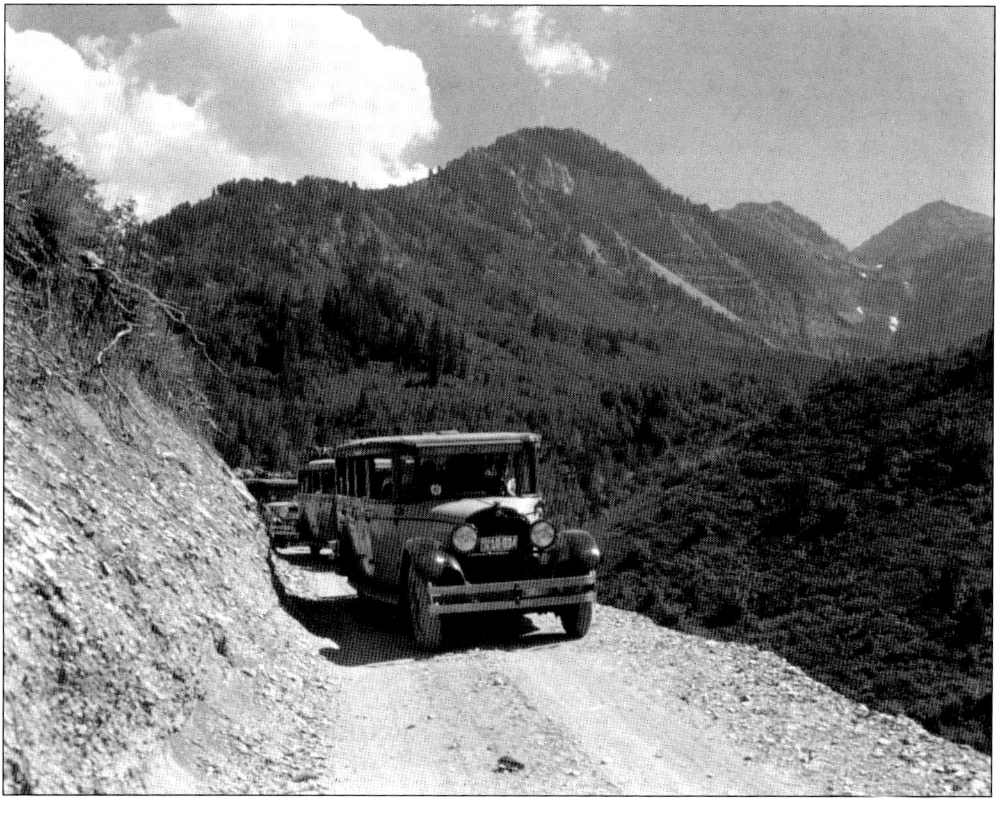

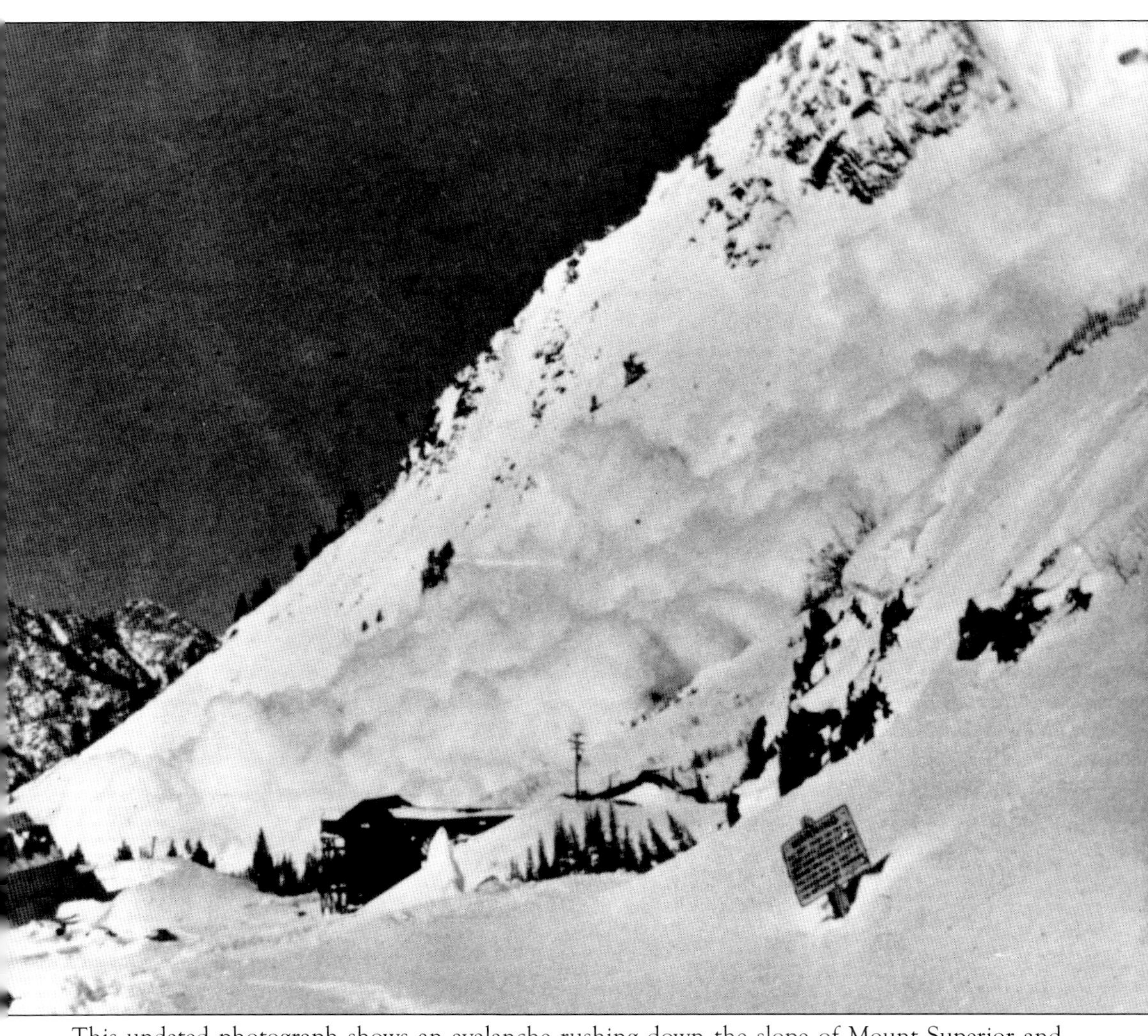

This undated photograph shows an avalanche rushing down the slope of Mount Superior and hitting near the Alta Ski Resort. The resort's Peruvian Lodge is in the left foreground. Avalanches are the biggest danger in the Wasatch Mountains during the winter season. Avalanches can move downhill at up to 80 miles per hour and have killed more than 120 people in Utah since 1958. (Courtesy of Utah State Historical Society.)

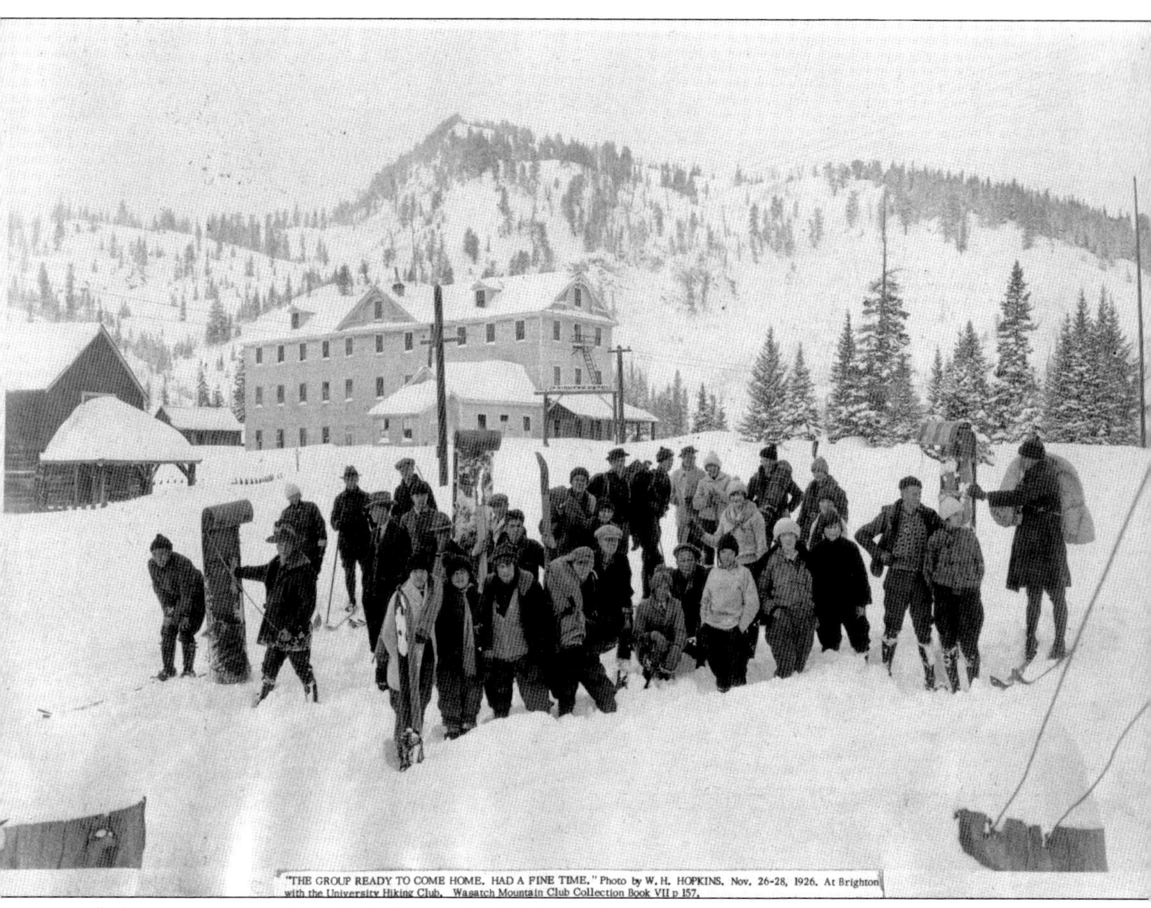

"The University of Utah Hiking Club" (likely alias, the Wasatch Mountain Club) is pictured in a November 28, 1926, photograph by William H. Hopkins. Club members played with skis and toboggans in the deep snow of Brighton. "The group ready to come home, had a fine time" is captioned on the picture. The Brighton Hotel is in the background. (Courtesy of J. Willard Marriott Digital Library, the University of Utah.)

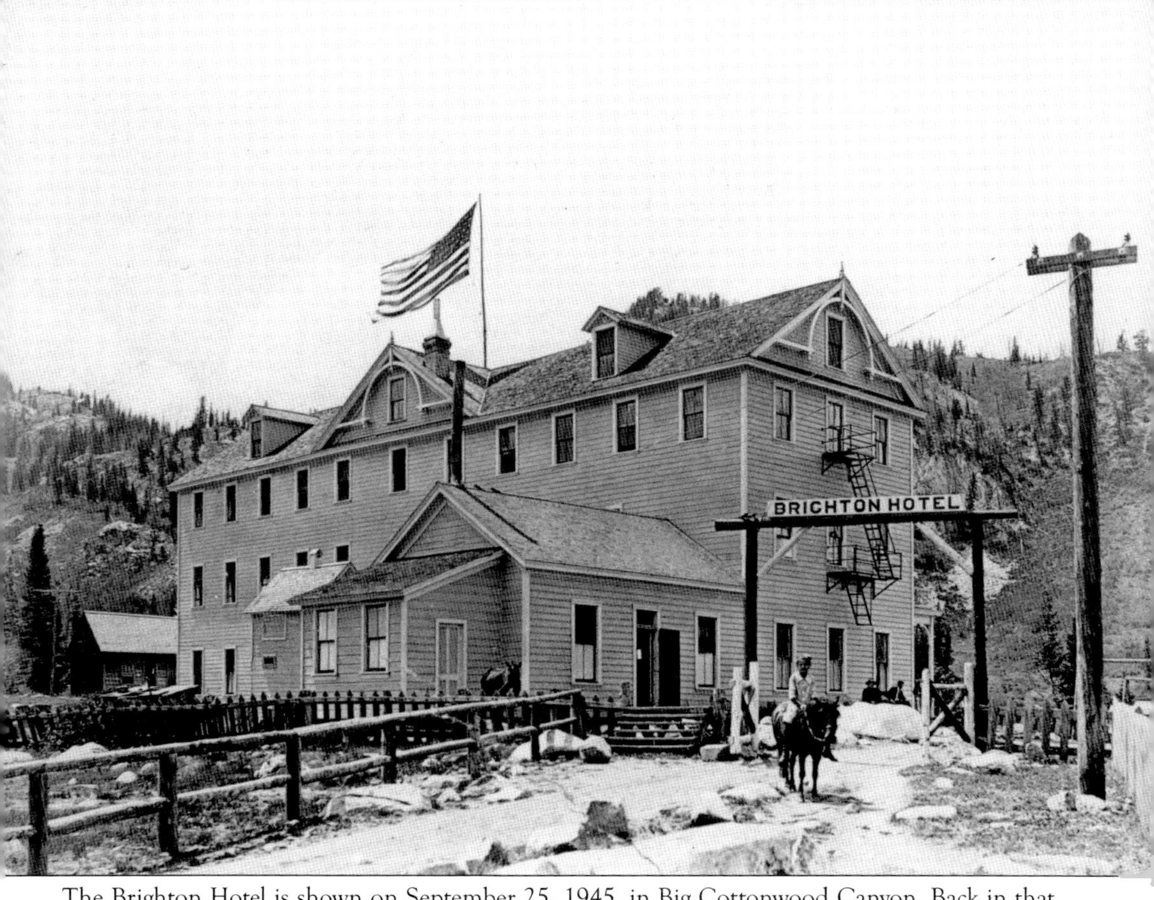

The Brighton Hotel is shown on September 25, 1945, in Big Cottonwood Canyon. Back in that era, the hotel was famous for offering horseback riding as a summer and early fall activity. The first and original hotel was built here in 1874 and was just a two-story structure. This newer version had three stories. (Courtesy of Utah State Historical Society.)

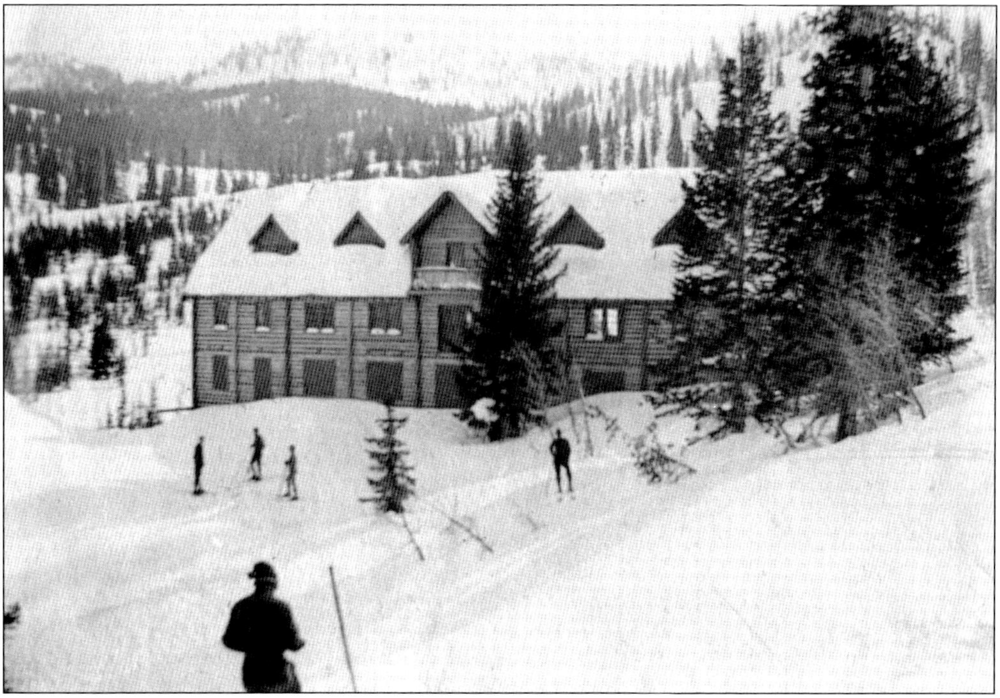

Skiers with the Wasatch Mountain Club are shown outside the Brighton Hotel during a ski activity on Washington's birthday in 1923. Club members skied from Park City to Brighton that day. Going over Guardsman Pass, this route traverses some of the most pristine scenery in the Wasatch Mountains. (Courtesy of J. Willard Marriott Digital Library, the University of Utah.)

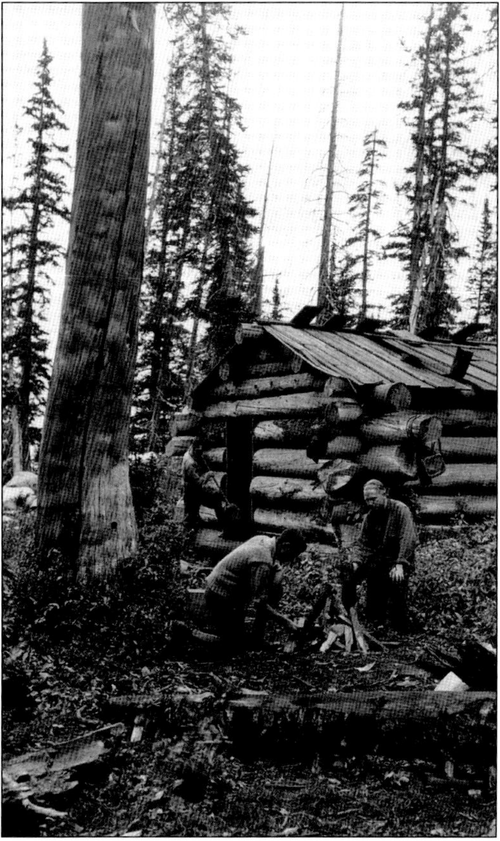

From left to right, Wasatch Mountain Club members Leon Stoney, Jack Kent, and Sylvan Dunn are shown camping at an old log cabin at Lake Martha in the summer of 1920. Kent and Dunn are attempting to start a campfire while Stoney is sweeping out the cabin entrance. Lake Martha is south of Brighton, off Big Cottonwood Canyon, at an elevation of about 9,600 feet. (Courtesy of J. Willard Marriott Digital Library, the University of Utah.)

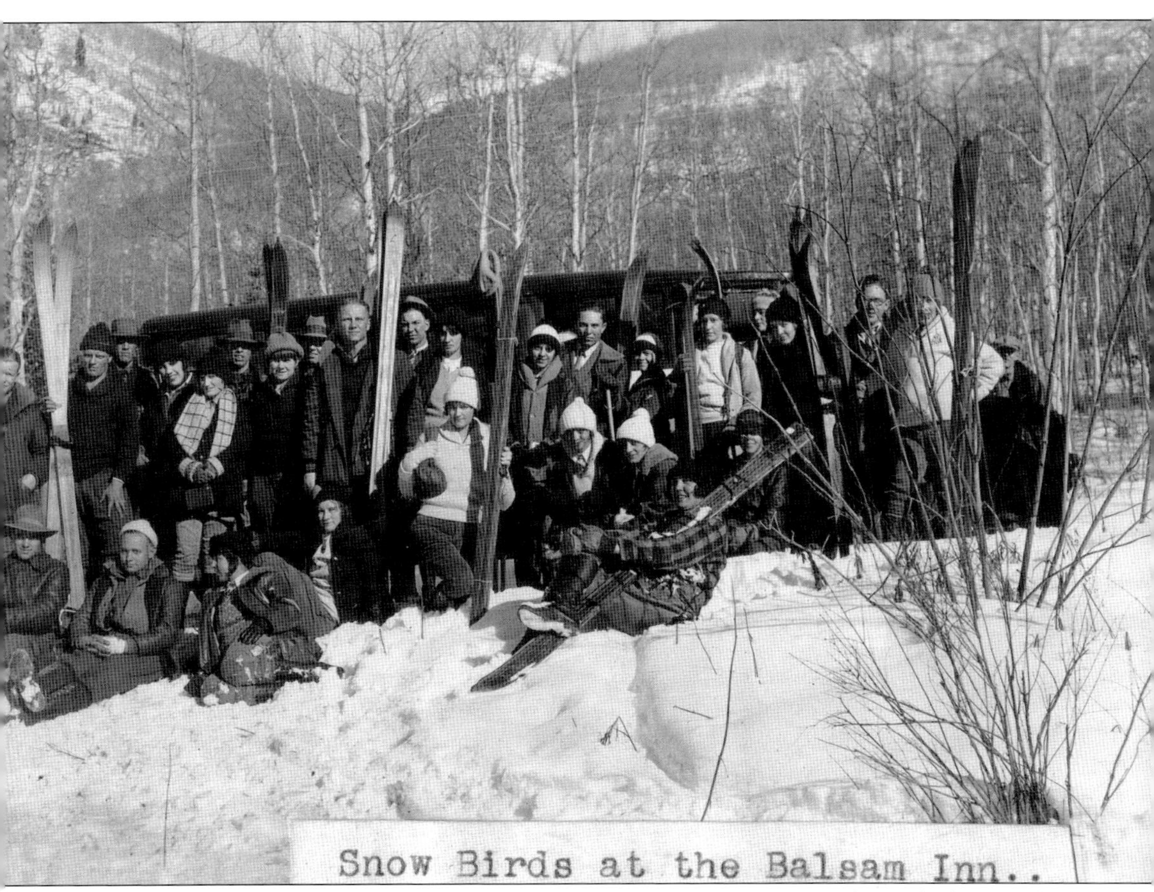

More than two dozen members of the Wasatch Mountain Club pose beside a vehicle outside the Balsam Inn at Brighton over Thanksgiving weekend in 1928. The club members spent three nights there on an outing, skiing and socializing. The picture is marked "snow birds at the Balsam Inn." Obviously, almost a century ago, "snow birds" meant those who loved the winter and snow, whereas now it denotes people who leave cold/snowy areas and go south for the winter. (Courtesy of J. Willard Marriott Digital Library, the University of Utah.)

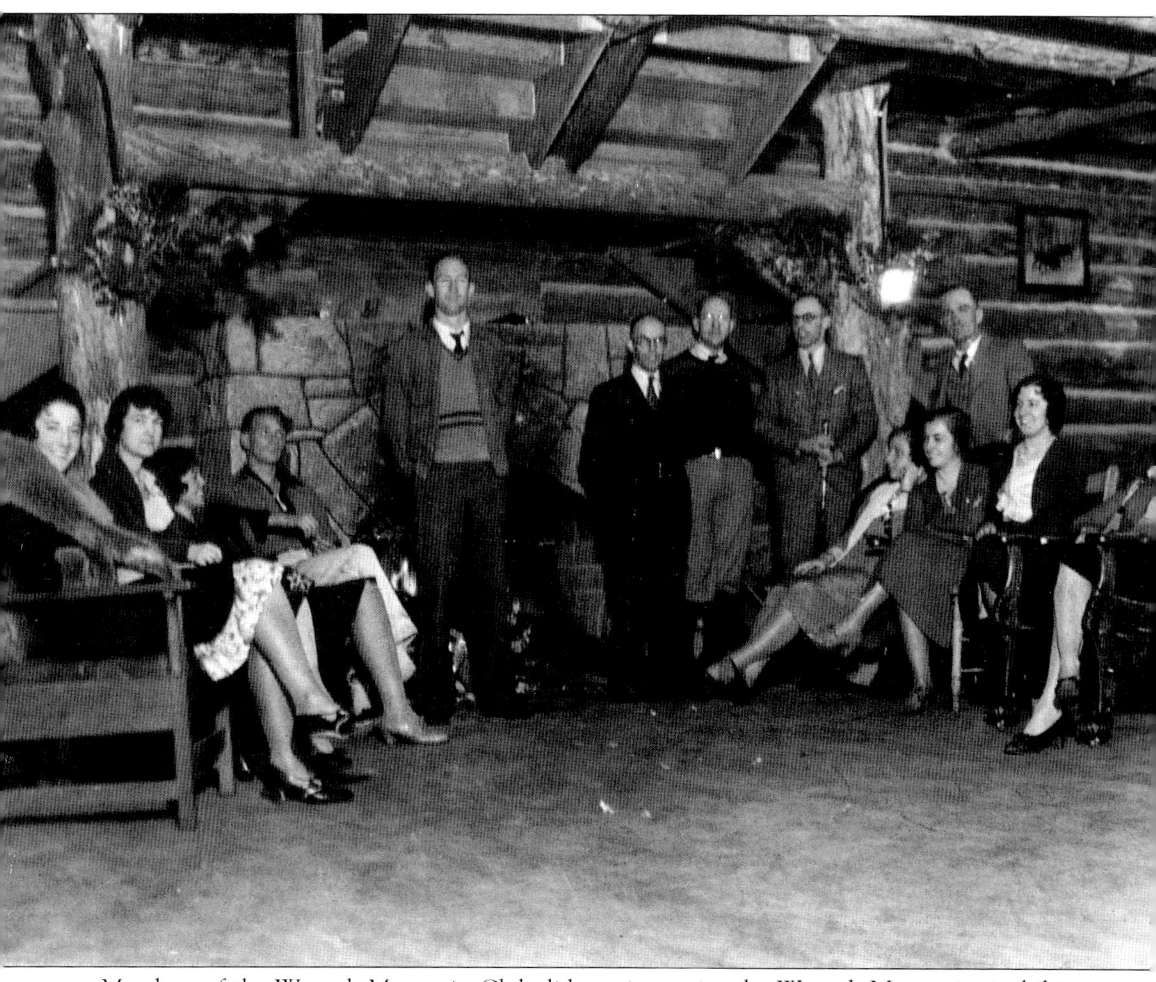

Members of the Wasatch Mountain Club did not just enjoy the Wasatch Mountains in hiking, skiing, climbing, and camping. In the winter, they also liked to socialize high in the mountains, like in this picture from the 1930s at a Brighton lodge proves. Thirteen club members are all dressed up for some evening socializing. (Courtesy of J. Willard Marriott Digital Library, the University of Utah.)

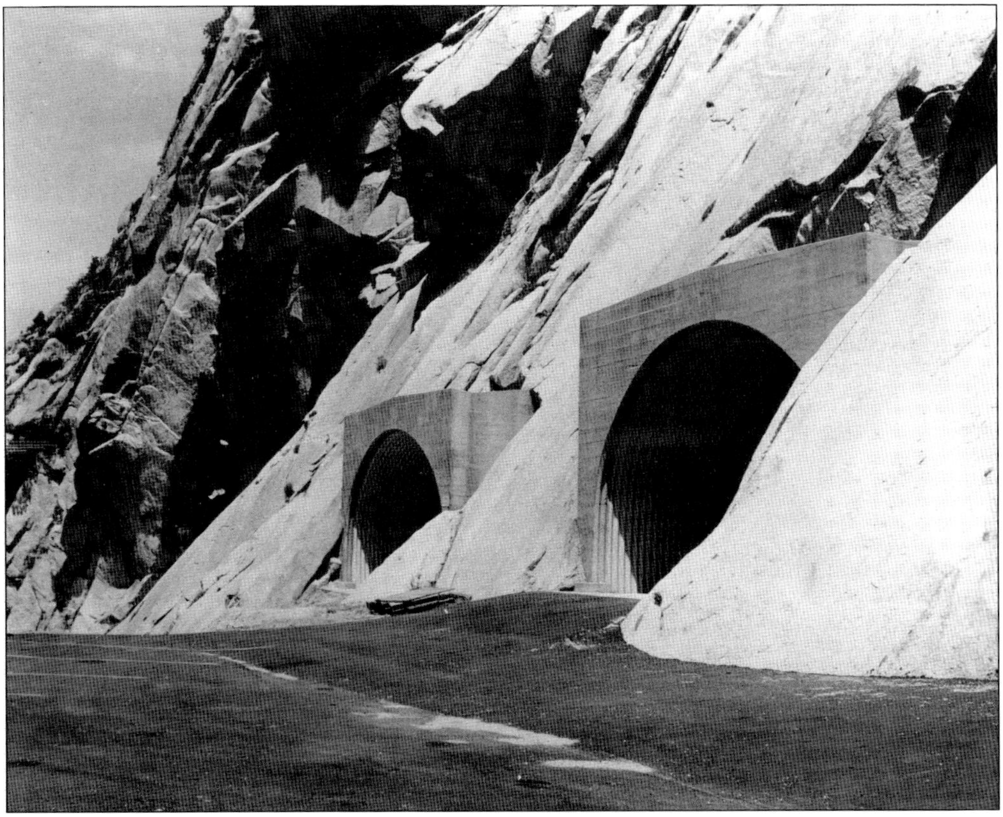

This is the Granite Mountain Records Facility in Little Cottonwood Canyon, likely in the early 1960s, just before completion. Operated by the Church of Jesus Christ of Latter-day Saints, 700-foot tunnels were drilled in the mountainside for a records depository. The vaults were opened for use in 1963. (Courtesy of Utah State Historical Society.)

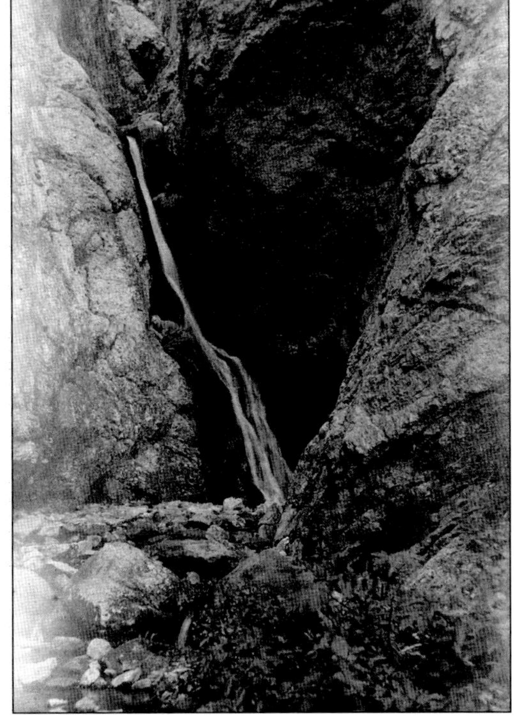

This is Hidden Falls in lower Big Cottonwood Canyon, as it appeared in the late spring of 1923. The falls are so named because they are almost hidden in a rocky recess. Hidden Falls is less than five miles up the canyon and is accessible by a several-minute, easy hike from a parking lot. The elevation is about 6,200 feet. The Wasatch Mountains contain many waterfalls, and they are at their prime in late spring and early summer. (Courtesy of J. Willard Marriott Digital Library, the University of Utah.)

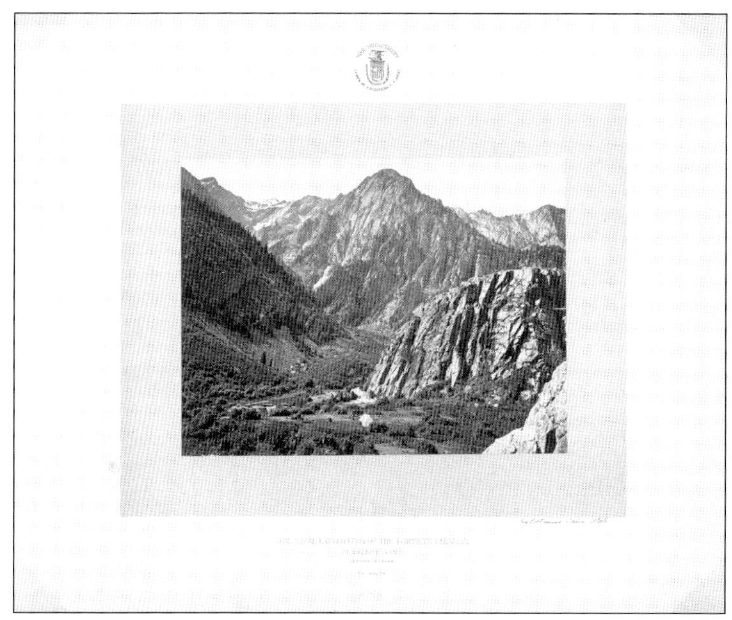

This is Big Cottonwood Canyon, as it appeared in 1869. This picture was taken by Timothy H. O'Sullivan as part of the US Geological Survey, led by Clarence King. Note that there are two large tents at the bottom of the picture, possibly part of the US Government Survey camp. (Courtesy of Library of Congress.)

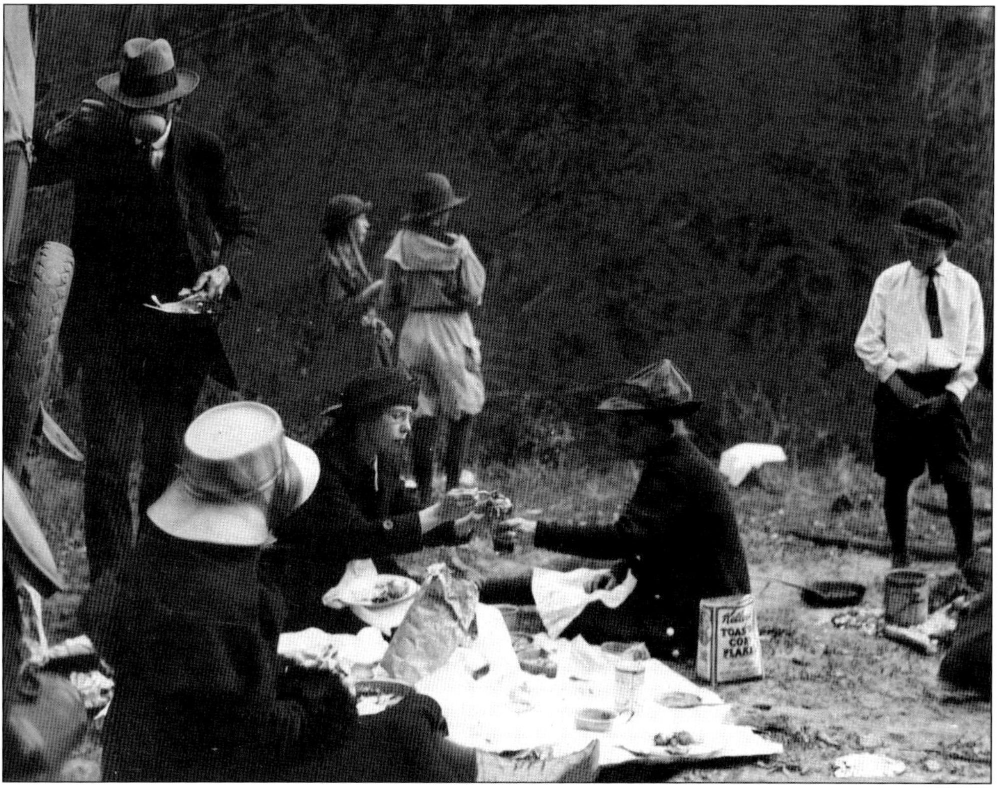

A group of Girl Scouts and their leaders picnic in Salt Lake's Millcreek Canyon in 1922. Millcreek Canyon is especially popular because its lower elevations mean it is snow-free sooner each year and thus has a longer season of use than many other Wasatch Mountain canyons. Today, there are a lot of private cabins in the canyon, too. (Courtesy of J. Willard Marriott Digital Library, the University of Utah.)

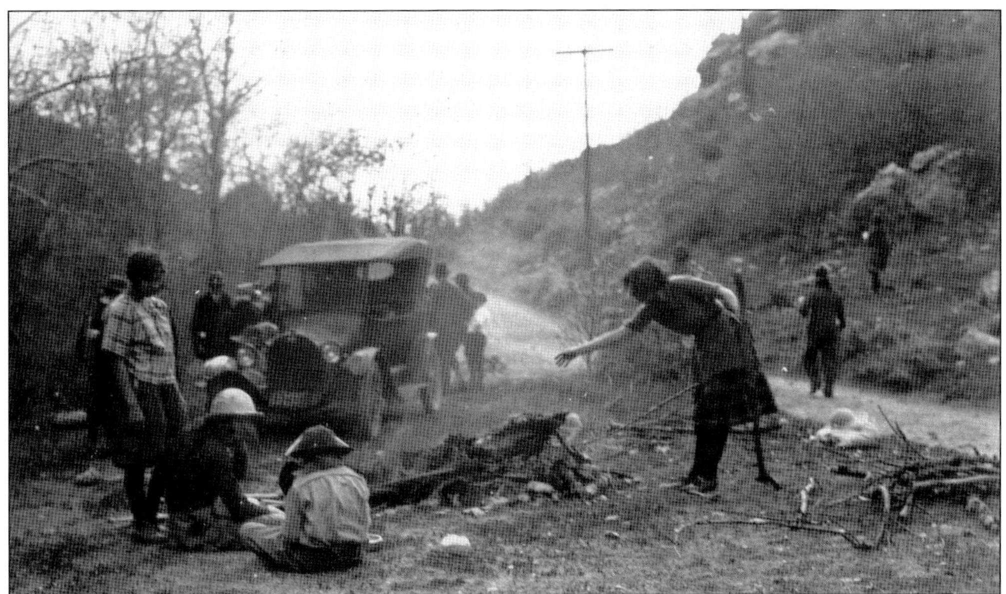

Girl Scouts from Salt Lake City enjoy an outing in upper Millcreek Canyon in the summer of 1922. The girls appear to be building a campfire. Note the rough dirt road leading to the site. Desolation Lake, Dog Lake, Grandeur Peak, and the Pipeline Trail are all accessible highlights in the canyon. (Courtesy of J. Willard Marriott Digital Library, the University of Utah.)

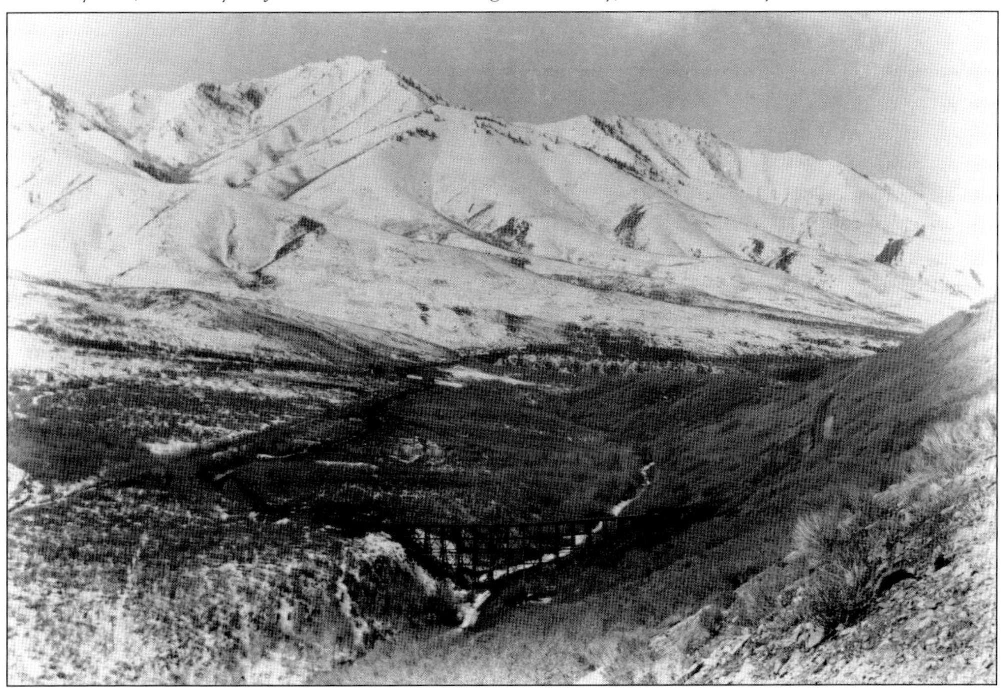

A section of Parley's Canyon is shown during the 1890s in this nostalgic picture. The Denver & Rio Grande Western Railroad bridge and line are clearly shown. (Today, no railroad operates in the canyon.) Note that the highway through the canyon is on the far north side. Parley's Canyon is named for Parley P. Pratt, who built the first road going through the area in 1848. (Courtesy of Utah State Historical Society.)

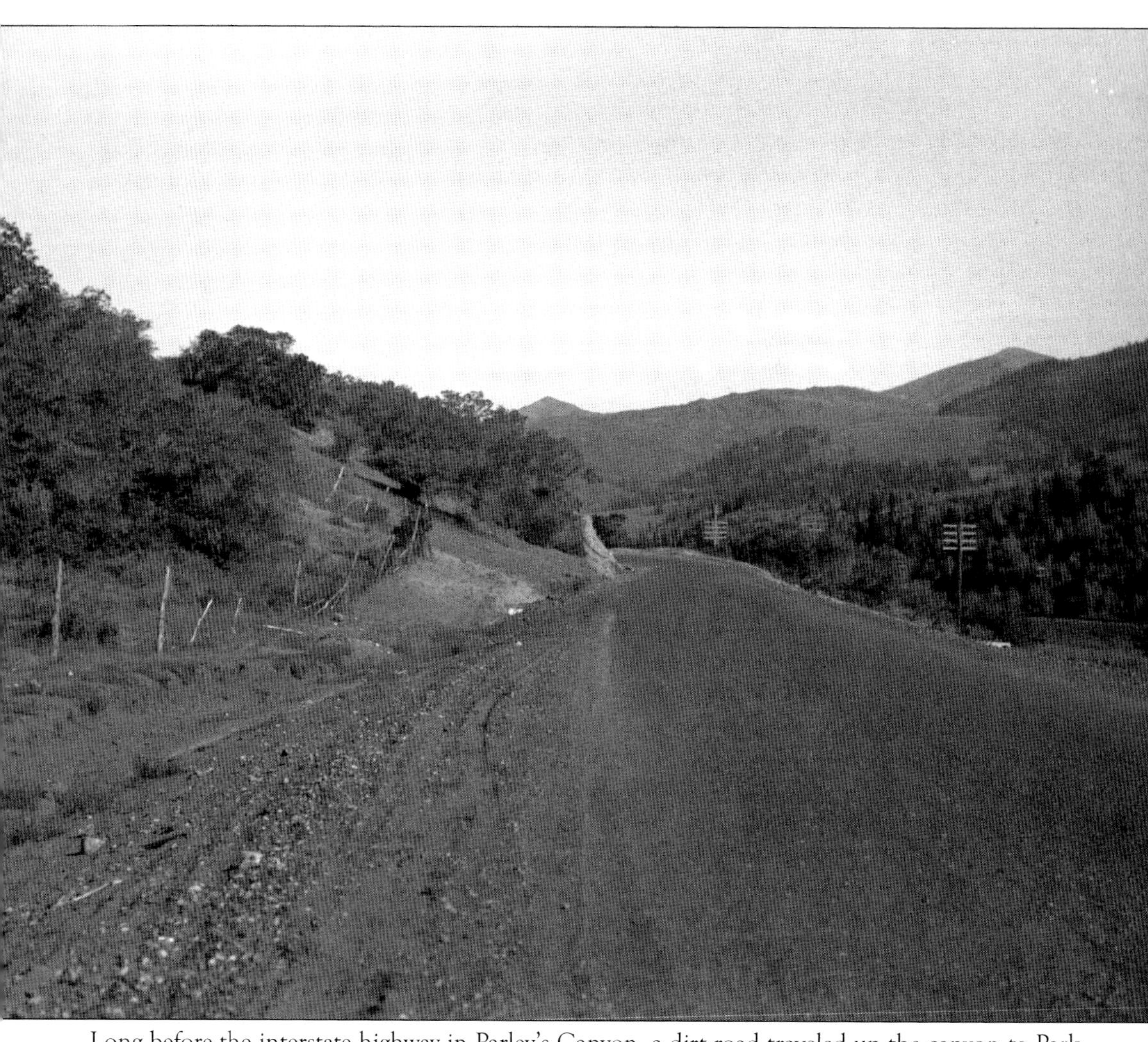

Long before the interstate highway in Parley's Canyon, a dirt road traveled up the canyon to Park City and other eastern Wasatch Mountain destinations. This picture was taken on September 1, 1934, at Higgenbotham. Note the railroad line in the lower right-hand corner of the picture. Train traffic in Parley's Canyon ceased permanently in 1956. (Courtesy of Utah State Historical Society.)

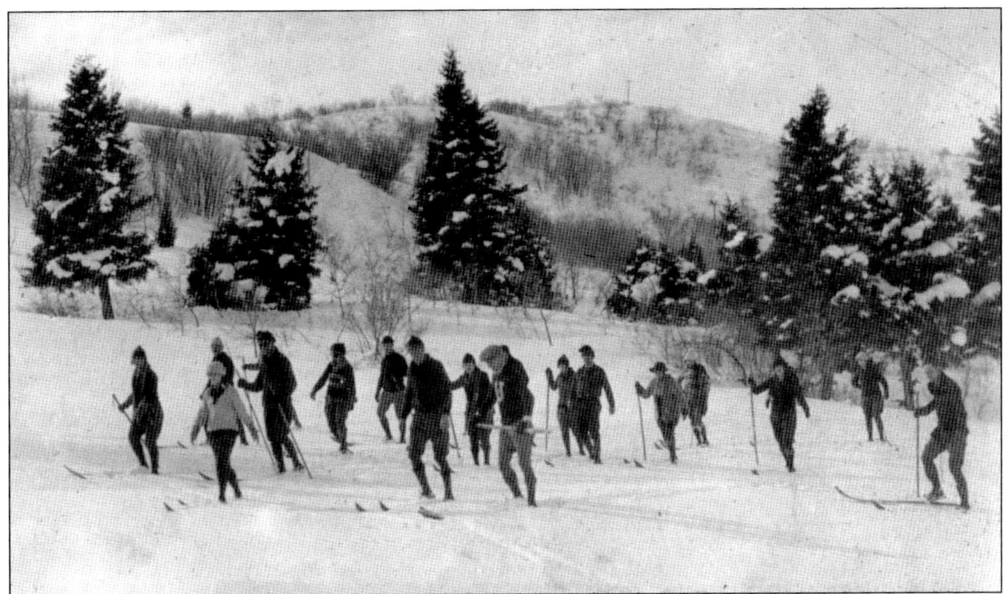

Eighteen members of the Wasatch Mountain Club enjoy a ski outing on a Sunday afternoon in the mid-1920s in upper Parley's Canyon. In that era, Parley's Summit was the traditional skiing place in the area. Park City Ski Resort did not come along until the 1963–1964 winter season. (Courtesy of J. Willard Marriott Digital Library, the University of Utah.)

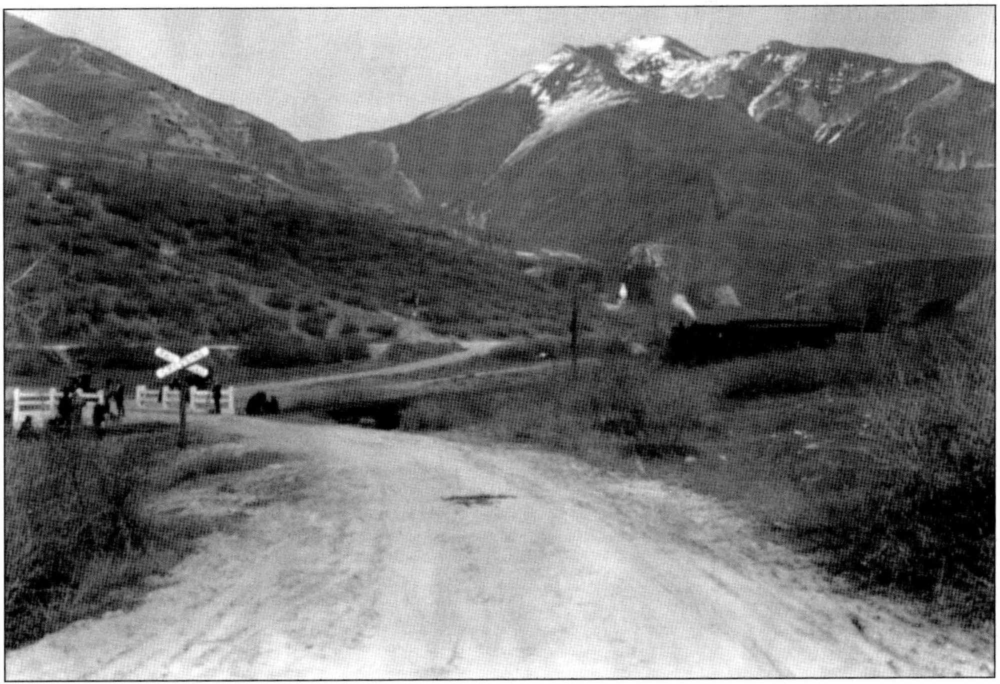

Bridge crossing No. 5 in Parley's Canyon is pictured here on April 21, 1924. A group of men appear to be working on the bridge as a two-car Denver & Rio Grande Western train approaches. Note the small dirt road that goes through the canyon over a century ago. Contrast that with the major freeway, Interstate 80, which traverses the canyon now at up to 65 miles per hour. Also, there is no train traffic in Parley's Canyon today. (Courtesy of Utah State Historical Society.)

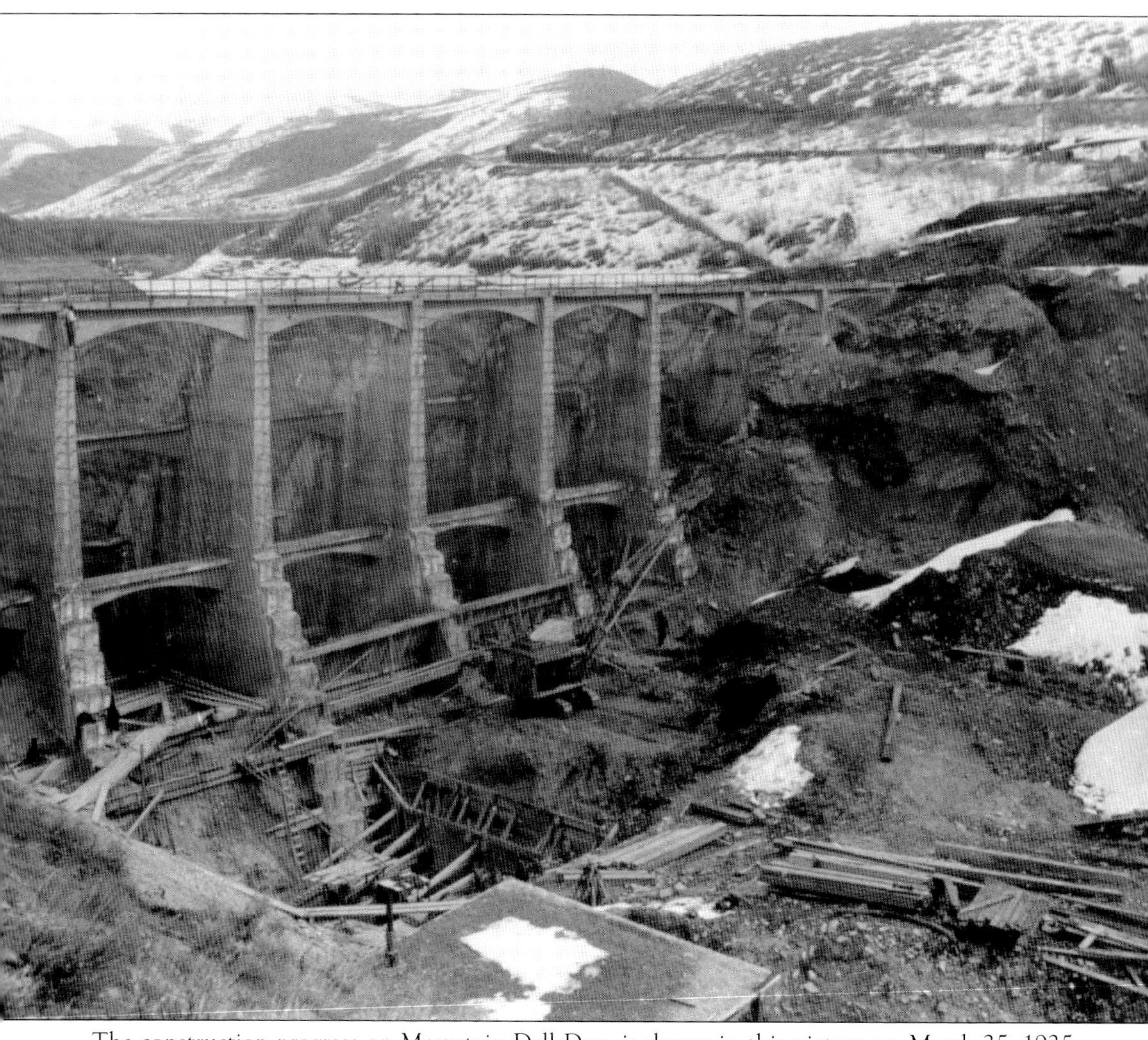

The construction progress on Mountain Dell Dam is shown in this picture on March 25, 1925. This dam is located about 10 miles up Parley's Canyon. It was built in two stages. The first stage was completed in 1917, and the second followed in 1925. The dam is 140 feet high and can hold up to 850 million gallons. (Courtesy of Utah State Historical Society.)

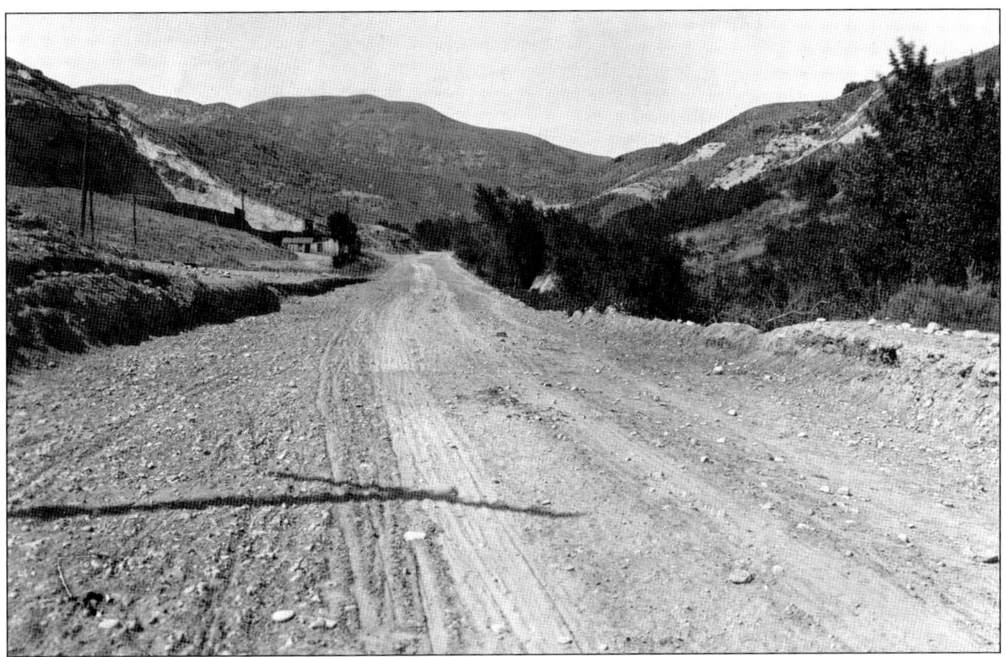

City Creek Canyon is shown on June 6, 1902. Located just north of Salt Lake City, the canyon in this area was once home to a gravel pit and a prisoner's pen. Note the wide gravel road. City Creek was so named by the early Mormon pioneers because of its prime location in their new downtown city. (Courtesy of Utah State Historical Society.)

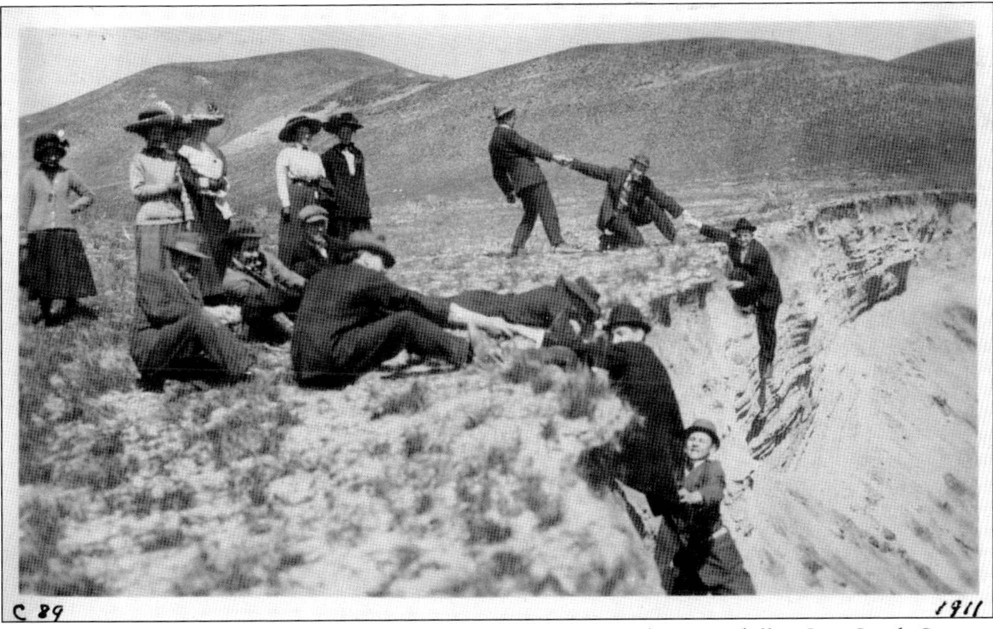

University of Utah geology students are shown clowning around a steep cliff in City Creek Canyon during an excursion there in 1911. Note that everyone is wearing a hat. The women are also just wisely watching the male students' risky behavior. City Creek water was the primary source of Salt Lake City's drinking water until 1882. (Courtesy of J. Willard Marriott Digital Library, the University of Utah.)

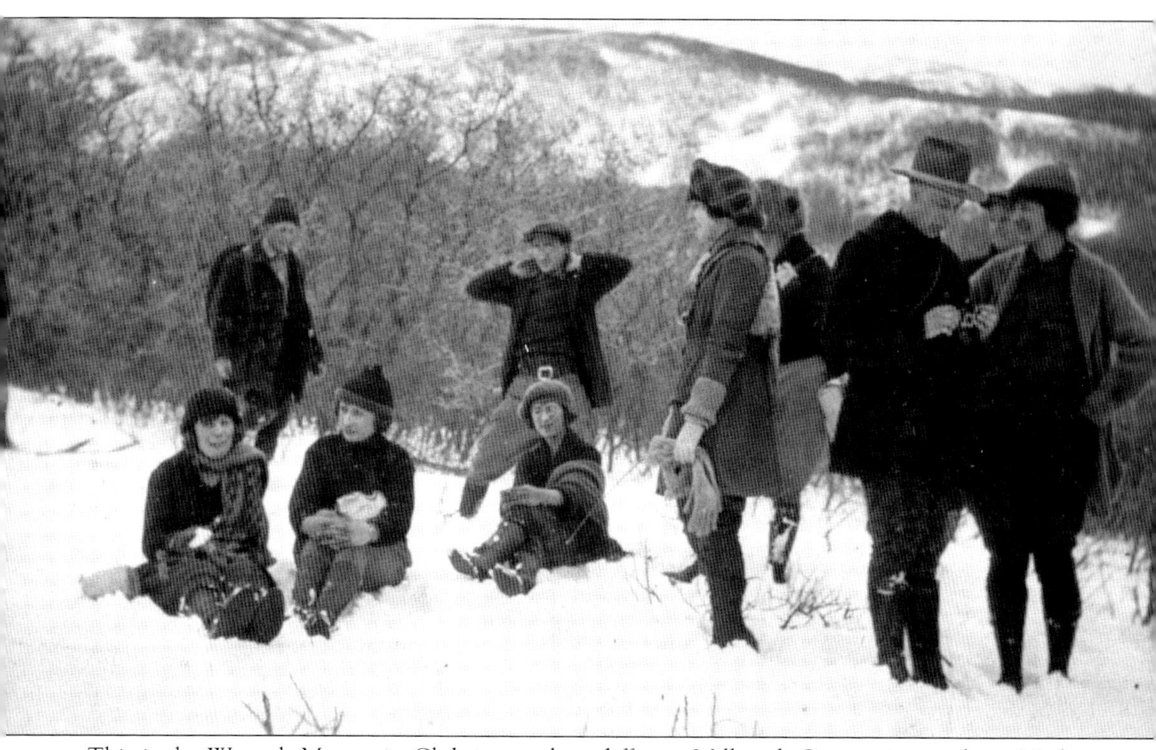

This is the Wasatch Mountain Club in another, different Millcreek Canyon in northern Utah. This one is located east of Bountiful in Davis County. The date is February 1922. North Mill Creek Canyon was one of Bountiful's four temporary names before the Bountiful title was given to the city. Today, Mueller Park is a very popular recreation area that is located near the mouth of Millcreek Canyon. (Courtesy of J. Willard Marriott Digital Library, the University of Utah.)

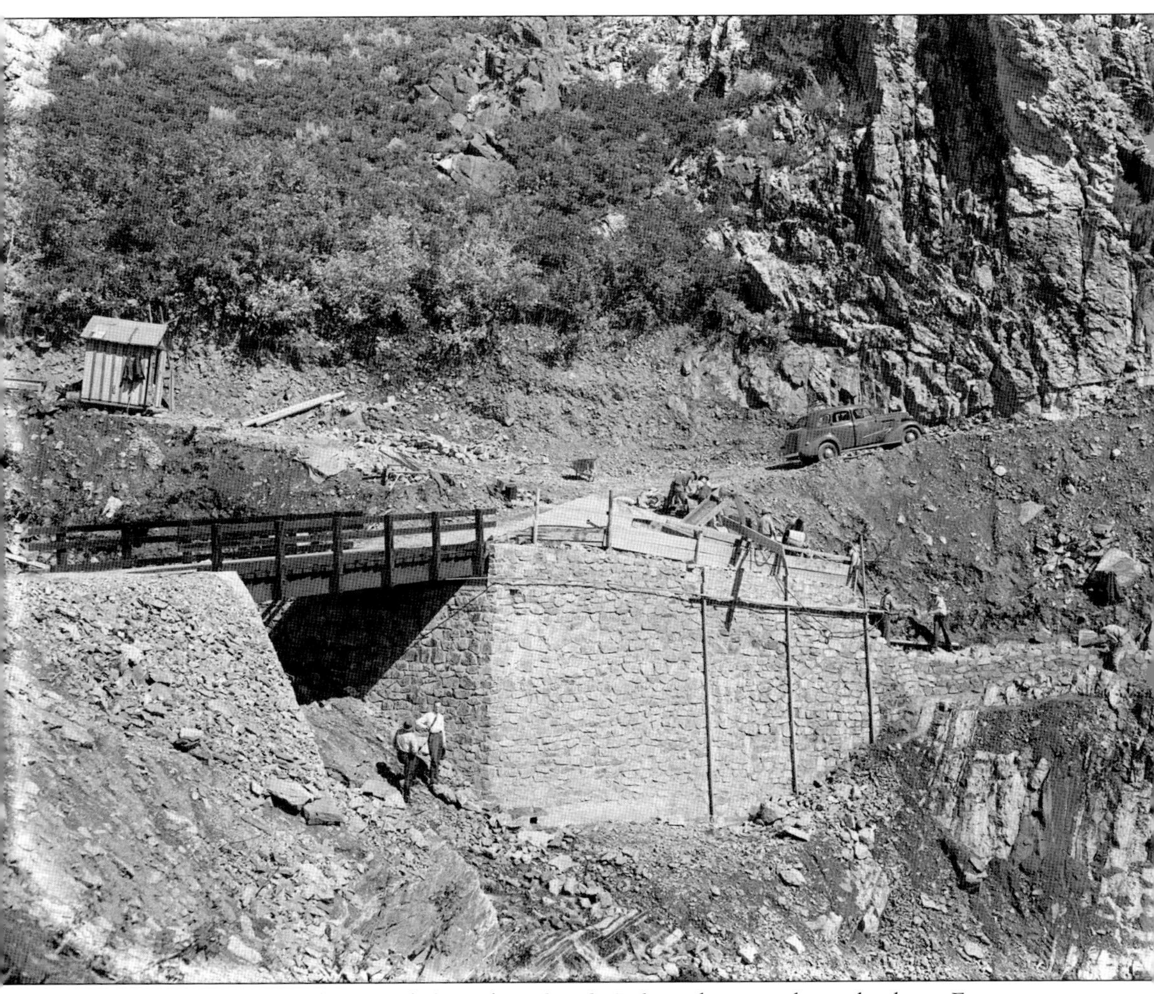

This August 31, 1937, photograph from the *Salt Lake Tribune* shows work on a bridge in Farmington Canyon. The bridge appears completed, and workers are fine-tuning the accompanying retaining walls. Farmington Canyon is now part of a scenic backway, a dirt road that leads to the Francis Peak radar station on the north or loops southward down into Bountiful, with its other segment. (Courtesy of Utah State Historical Society.)

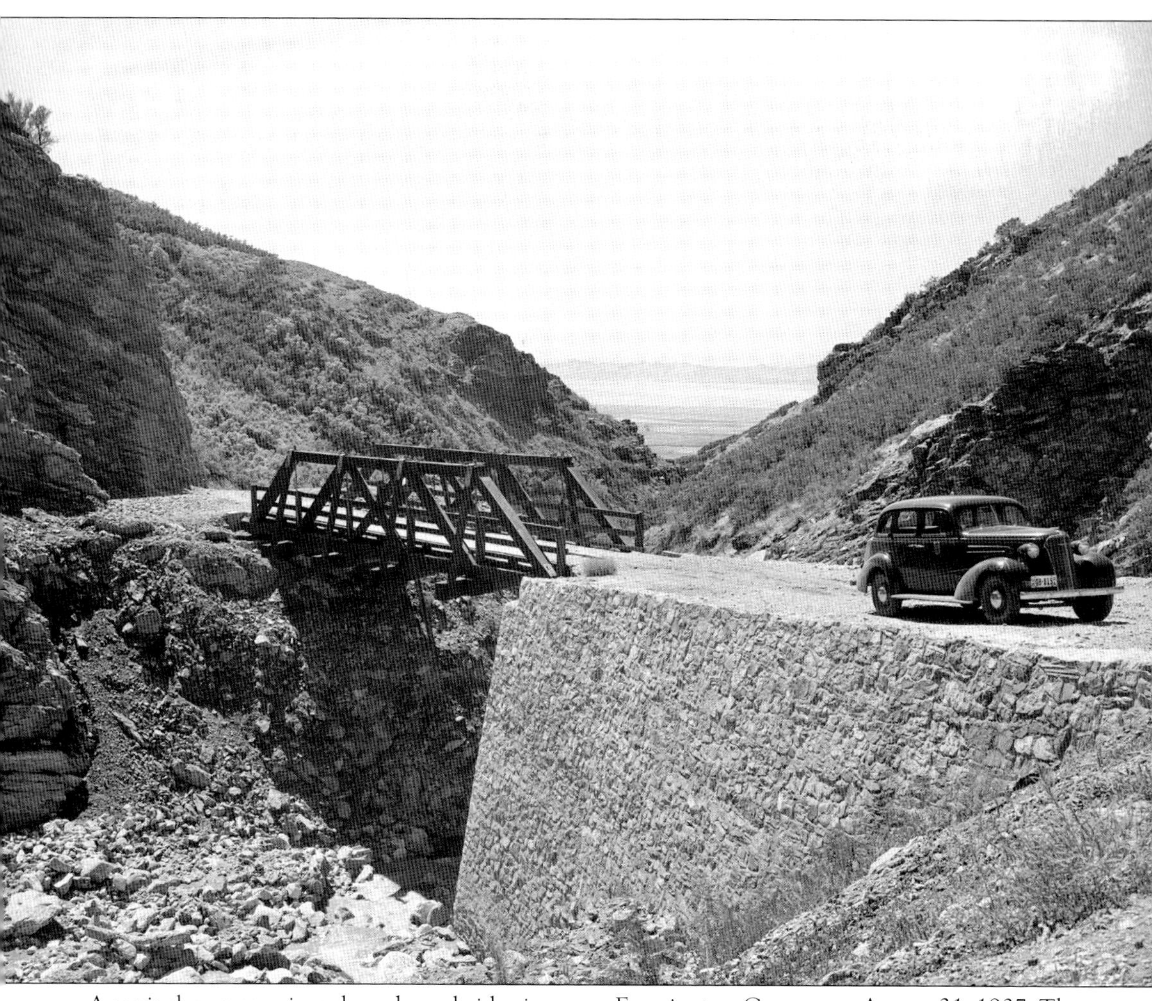

A car is shown crossing a brand-new bridge in upper Farmington Canyon on August 31, 1937. The Civilian Conservation Corps built most of the road in the early 1930s. The road was primarily constructed to aid in erosion control, as the early 1920s produced significant flooding through and near the canyon. (Courtesy of Utah State Historical Society.)

Bair-Gutsman mountain race runners dot the top of Bair Canyon as they approach the jeep road on the mountain saddle during the August 1981 rendition of the race. The race was started by Jan Cheney of Kaysville. Seen in the valley below is Fruit Heights City, Interstate 15, and the outskirts of the Great Salt Lake. (Photograph by author.)

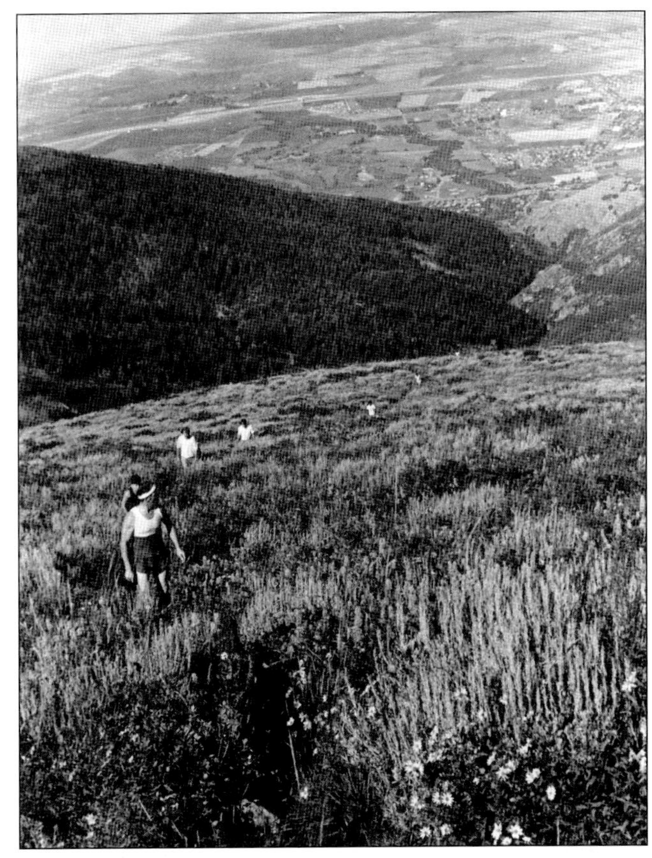

Dozens of runners line the jeep road, located north of Francis Peak, during the August 1981 running of the annual Bair-Gutsman mountain race. This picture was taken just south of the junction of Bair Canyon, where the race course was the steepest of all. Today, this and a number of similar mountain races, some even totaling 100 miles in length, are held annually in the Wasatch Mountains. (Photograph by author.)

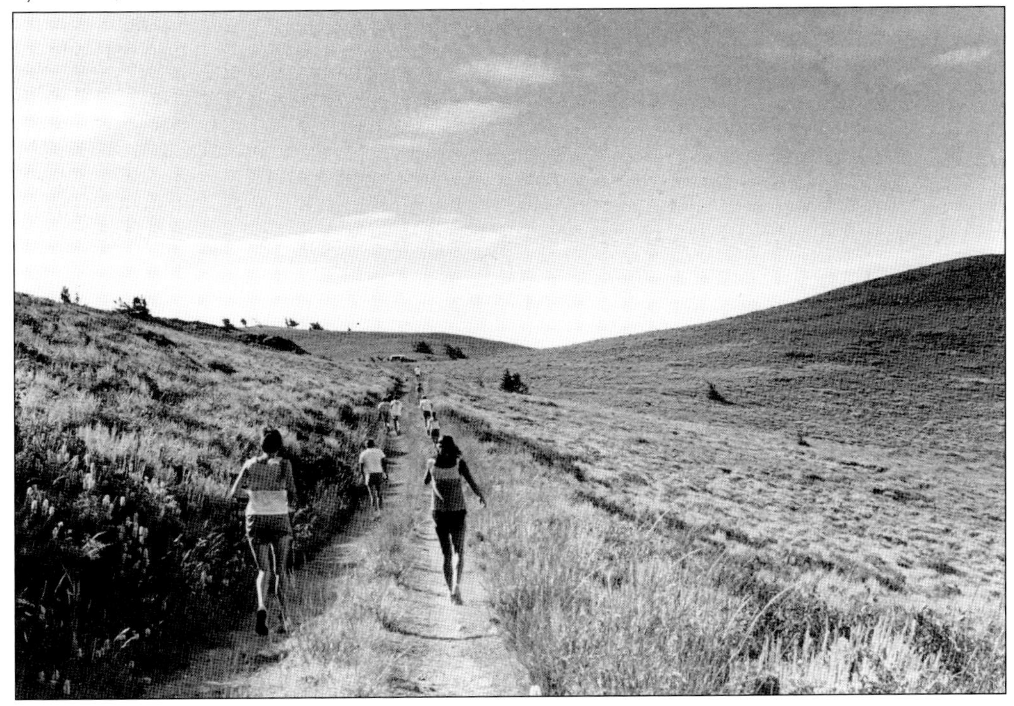

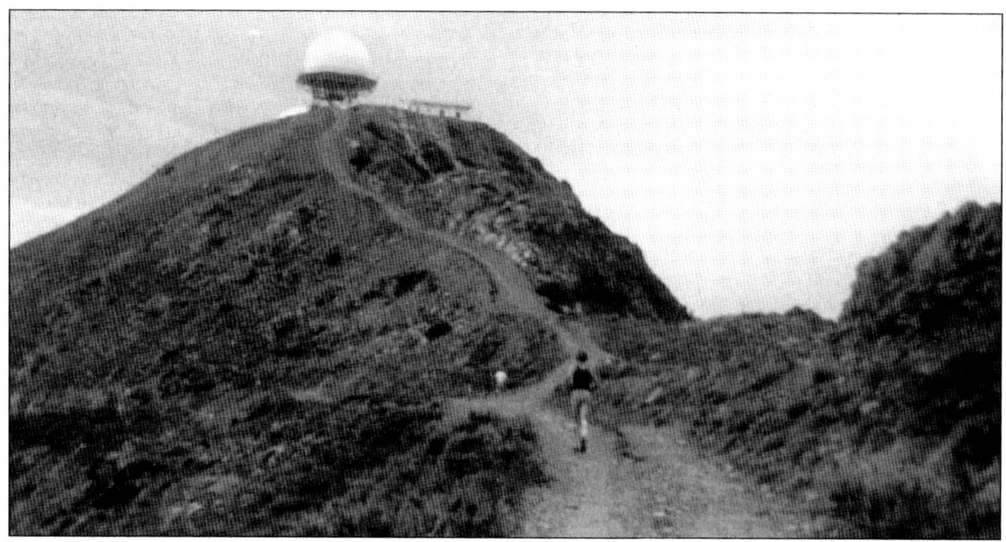

This is an August 1981 photograph of the dirt road below Francis Peak and its radar domes during one of the early years of the 12-mile Bair-Gutsman mountain footrace. The race originally began at the Rockloft in Fruit Heights, climbed Bair Canyon, proceeded past the radar domes, and ended at a road junction at the top of Farmington Canyon. Today, the race's starting point is farther north. (Photograph by author.)

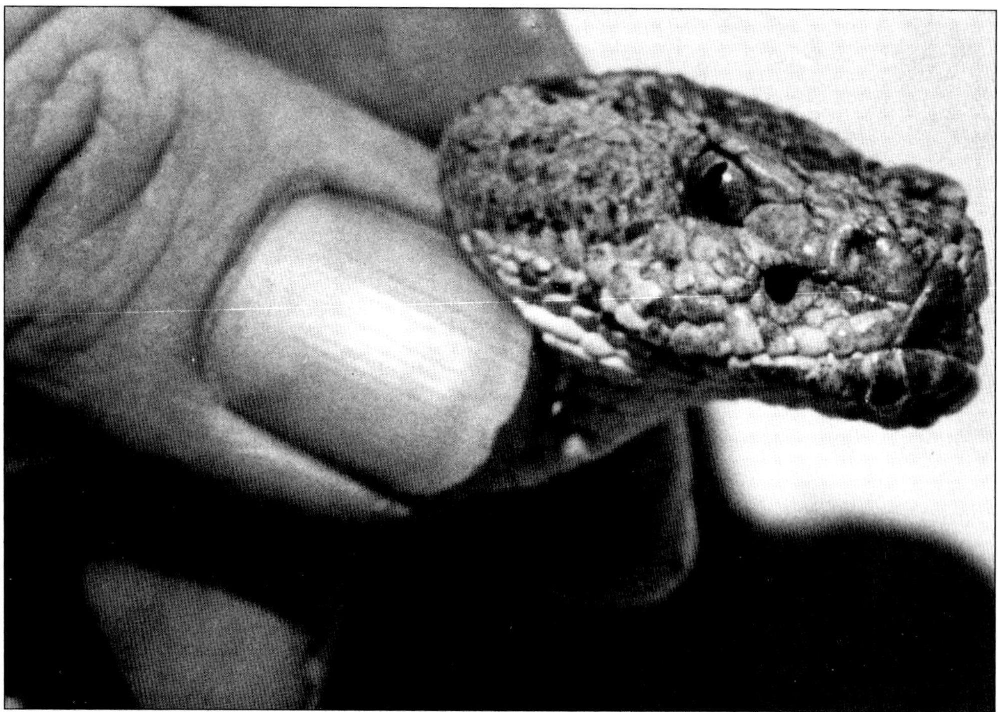

A young Great Basin rattlesnake, one of several such species in Utah, is held by a Hogle Zoo worker in 1979. These venomous snakes are found all over the Wasatch Mountains and even at some of its upper elevations. For example, when workers constructed the Francis Peak radar domes in the late 1950s, they disturbed the dens of these rattlers at 9,500 feet above sea level, even though wildlife experts claimed the reptiles could not live that high. (Courtesy of *Deseret News* Archives.)

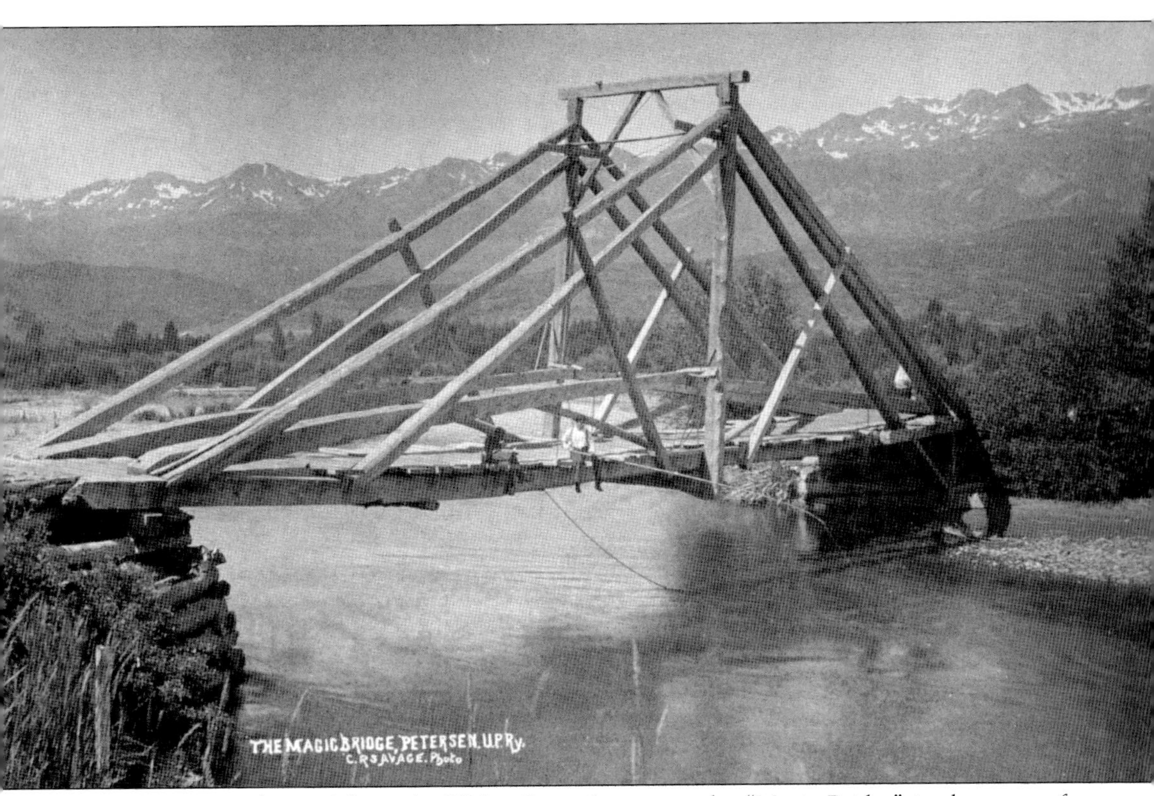

Several men are shown fishing the Weber River from atop the "Magic Bridge" in the town of Peterson in 1888. C.R. Savage took the photograph. The wooden bridge appears somewhat risky by today's standards. Note the eastern side of the main Wasatch Mountain range shown in the background, straddling Morgan and Davis Counties. (Courtesy of Utah State Historical Society.)

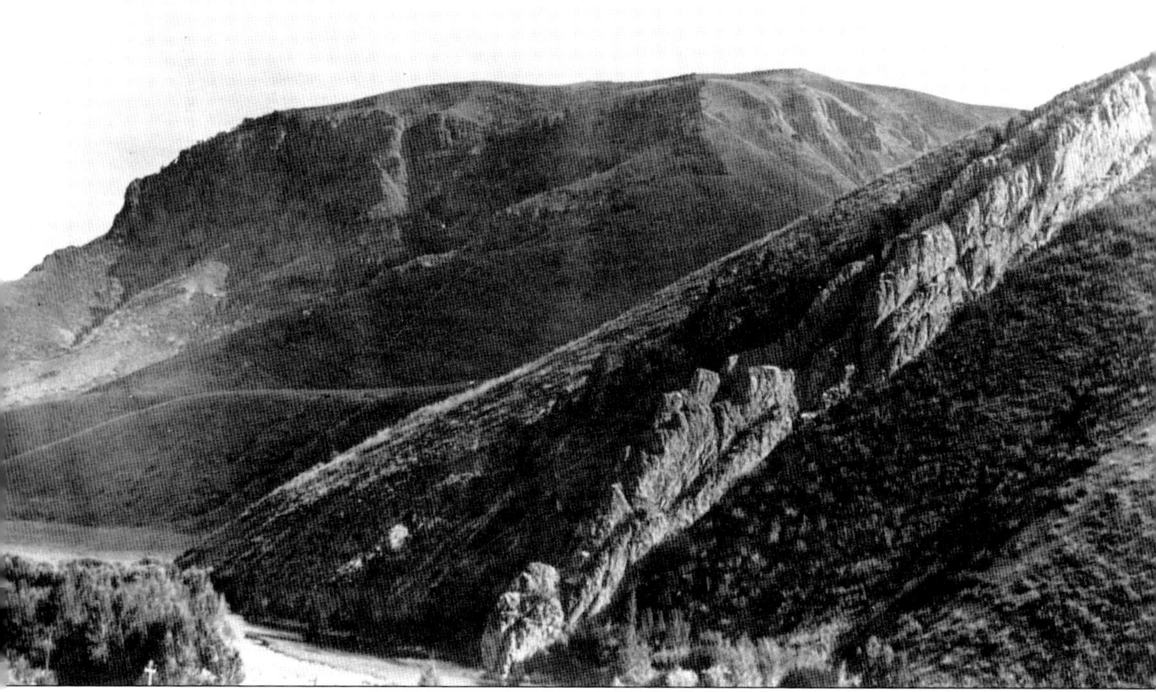

This is a look at Devil's Slide in Weber Canyon during the 1880s from a west-side angle. Devil's Slide has long been a curiosity in Weber Canyon ever since the first pioneers laid eyes on it. It is a good example of the oddities in rock that the Wasatch Mountains contain. (Courtesy of Utah State Historical Society.)

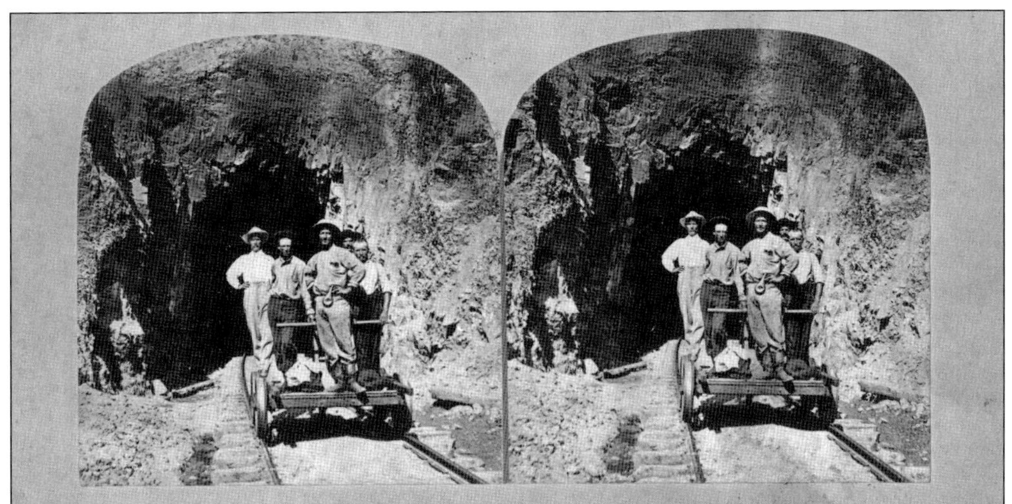

Five workers pose on a handcart at one of the entrances of railroad tunnel No. 4 in Weber Canyon, probably during the late 1860s, in this stereographic picture. Portions of the upper canyon east of Morgan were so narrow that railroad tunnels had to be drilled through the mountainside. (Courtesy of J. Willard Marriott Digital Library, the University of Utah.)

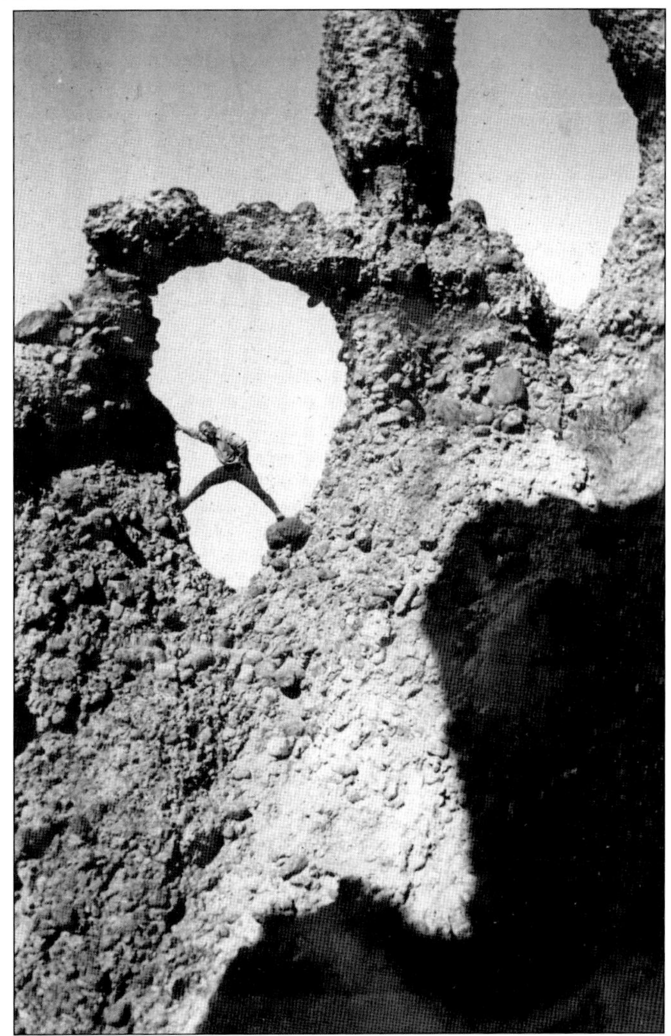

An unidentified member of the Wasatch Mountain Club stretches inside an arch at "Chinatown," a rare collection of red rock above Weber Canyon, during a visit in the 1930s. This place fascinated early-20th-century Utahns, but now private land issues have made this slice of Cedar Breaks National Monument in northern Utah all but off-limits. (Courtesy of J. Willard Marriott Digital Library, the University of Utah.)

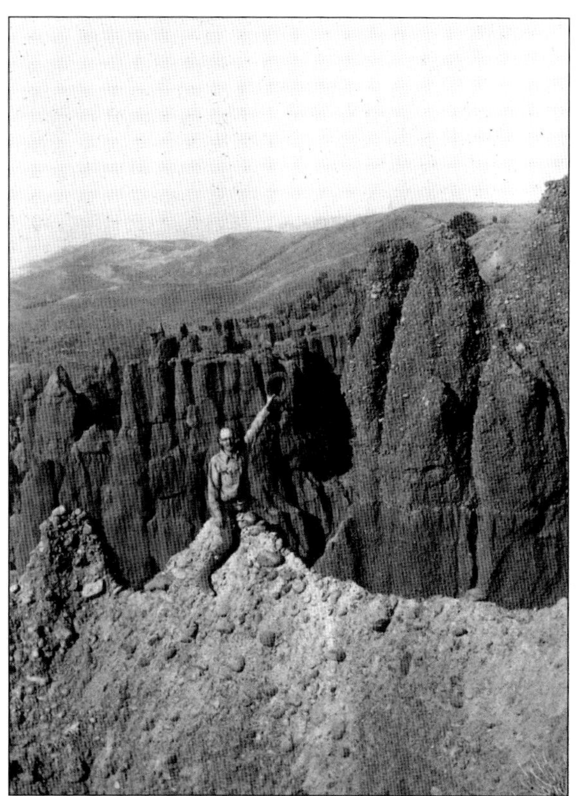

A daring man sits on a hump of rock in Morgan County's Chinatown as if it were a horse. Note the pagoda-like rock shapes that the man is pointing to in the background. Chinatown is located on a plateau on the north slope of Weber Canyon. It is not visible from the canyon below. The best access is from Lost Creek over a dozen miles of dirt roads and through many private gates. (Courtesy of J. Willard Marriott Digital Library, the University of Utah.)

A group of fancy-dressed guests mingle outside the front of the Hermitage Inn in Ogden Canyon in the summer of 1901—possibly the first season it was open. Located halfway through the canyon, this resort was a frequent stopping point as well as a good place to host elaborate parties. The inn burned down in 1939. Resorts like this were plentiful in Ogden Canyon and many other canyons of the Wasatch. (Courtesy of Utah State Historical Society.)

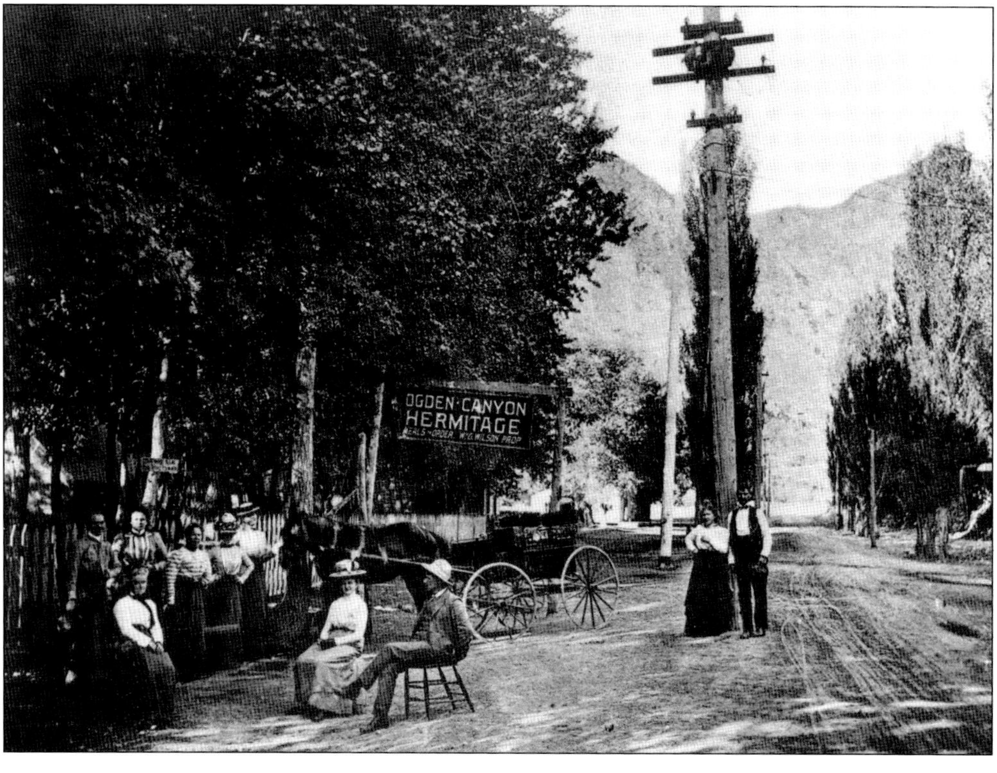

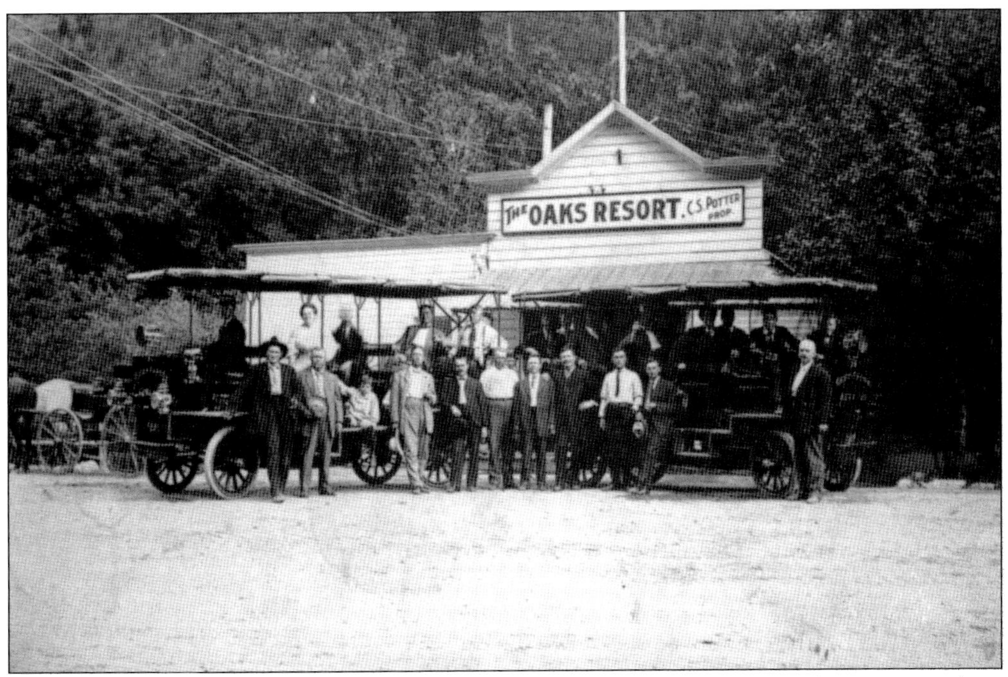

This is the Oaks Resort in Ogden Canyon, possibly in the 1910s. Opened by the Potter Brothers of Ogden, the Oaks had an emphasis on ginger ale, lemonade, and soda water and less focus on alcohol. Its original location was about a mile away from its modern placement, as the Oaks moved to higher ground to experience less flooding from the adjacent Ogden River. The Oaks has had several closings and revivals over the decades. It closed in 2023 and may reopen in 2025 or thereafter. (Courtesy of Utah State Historical Society.)

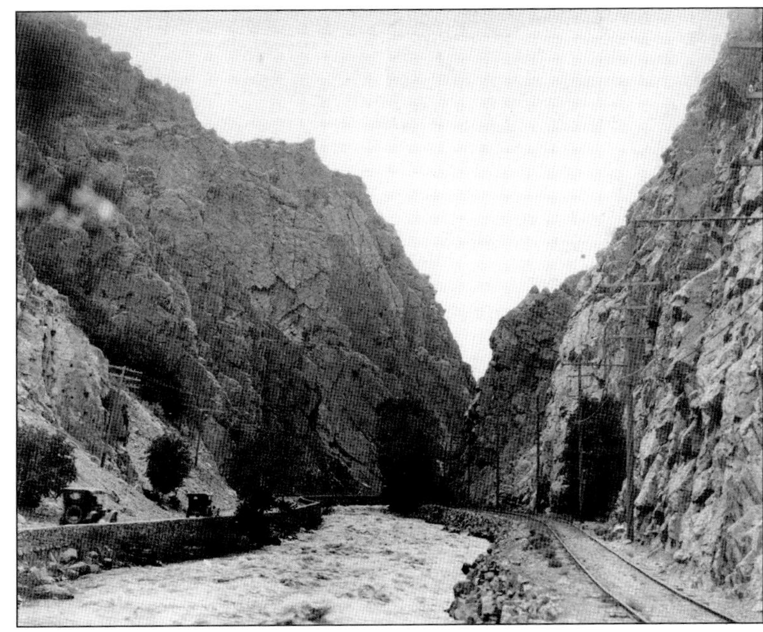

This is the west end of Ogden Canyon, probably in the late 1920s. Back then, the highway was on one side of the river, and the trolley tracks were on the other side. The trolley operated from Ogden City, through the canyon, to Ogden Valley from 1909 to 1932. Utah State Route 39 has suffered from occasional landslides over the decades. (Courtesy of Utah State Historical Society.)

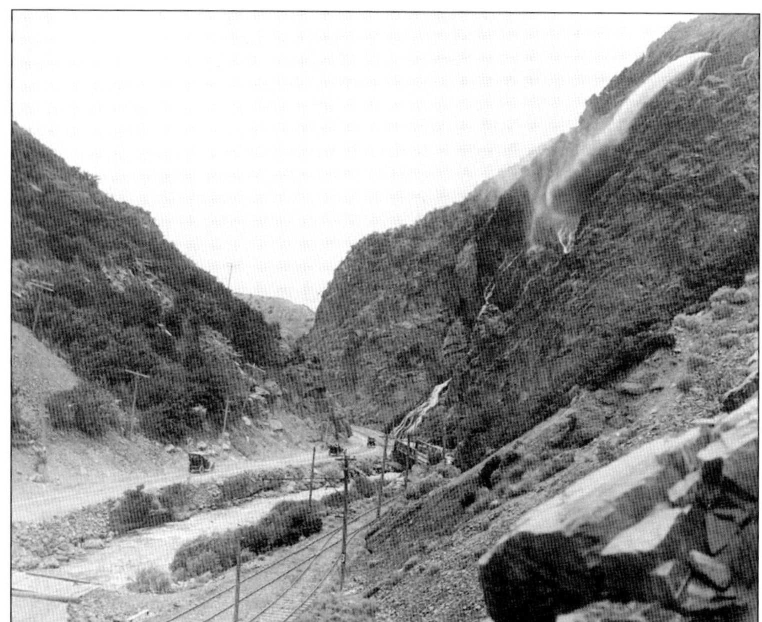

Ogden Canyon is shown as it appeared around 1920. This picture was taken just east of the mouth of the canyon. Note the artificial waterfall created by excess discharge in the water pipeline system through the canyon. Also, note the narrow section of the canyon, where the highway and trolley run side by side around a corner. (Courtesy of Utah State Historical Society.)

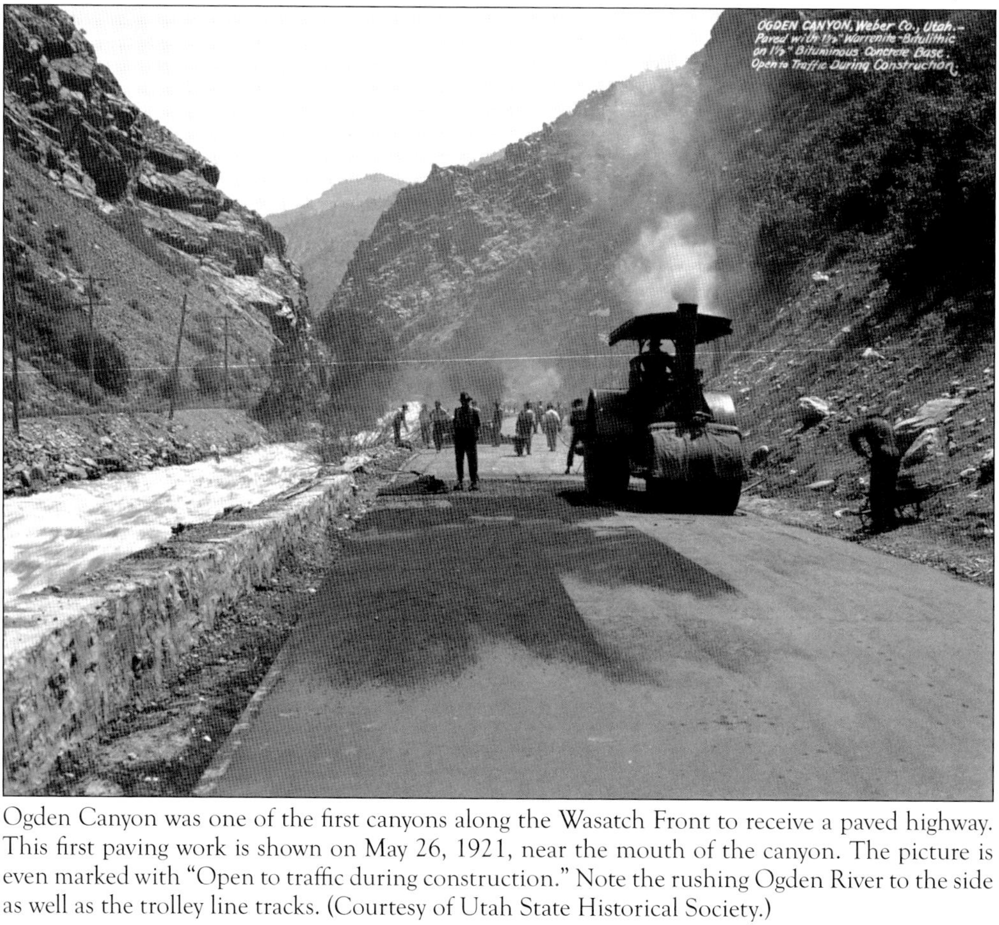

Ogden Canyon was one of the first canyons along the Wasatch Front to receive a paved highway. This first paving work is shown on May 26, 1921, near the mouth of the canyon. The picture is even marked with "Open to traffic during construction." Note the rushing Ogden River to the side as well as the trolley line tracks. (Courtesy of Utah State Historical Society.)

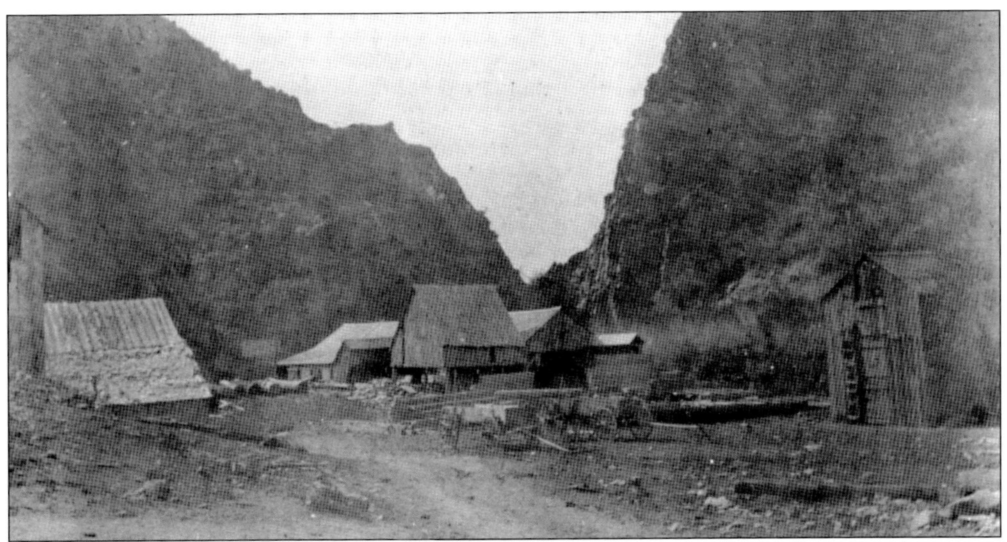

This late-19th-century picture shows a large sawmill operation in Ogden Canyon. There are few details on this mill, but the canyon offered plenty of timber resources, and the free-flowing Ogden River added a power source, too. As Ogden Canyon became more and more of a tourist and recreational area by the early 1900s, such mills were phased out there. (Courtesy of Utah State Historical Society.)

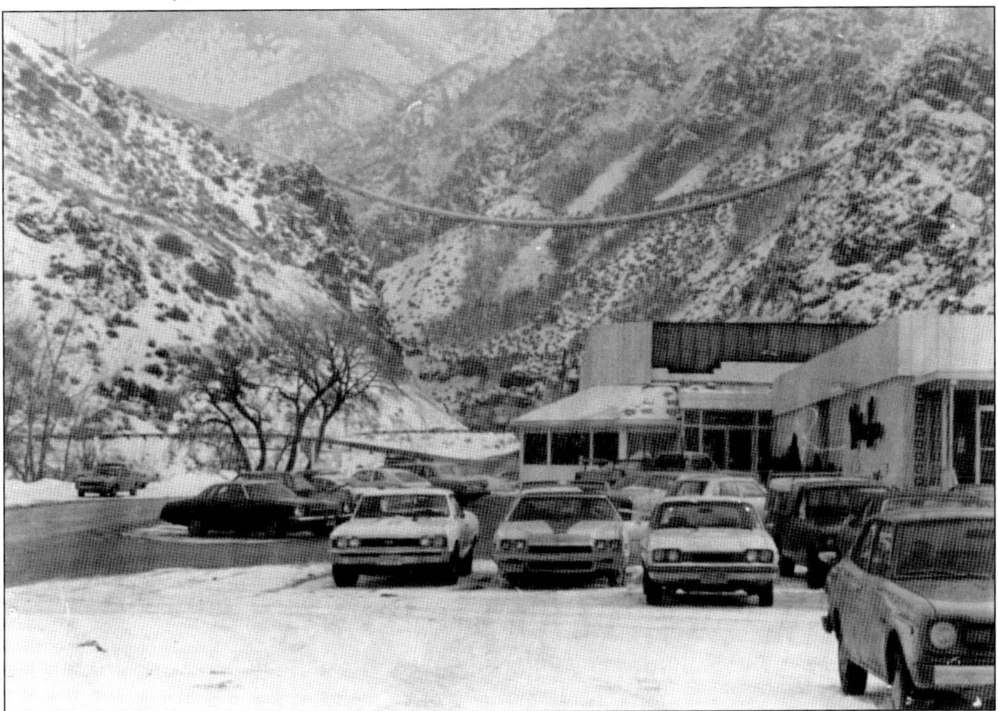

This is an early 1976 picture of the mouth of Ogden Canyon, showing Rainbow Gardens. This commercial enterprise had a gift shop and bowling alley then. (A restaurant, the Greenery, opened in April 1976 to expand the operation, but the bowling alley is now gone.) Note the Weber Basin Conservancy District's water pipeline crossing over the mouth of the canyon. (Courtesy of Utah State Historical Society.)

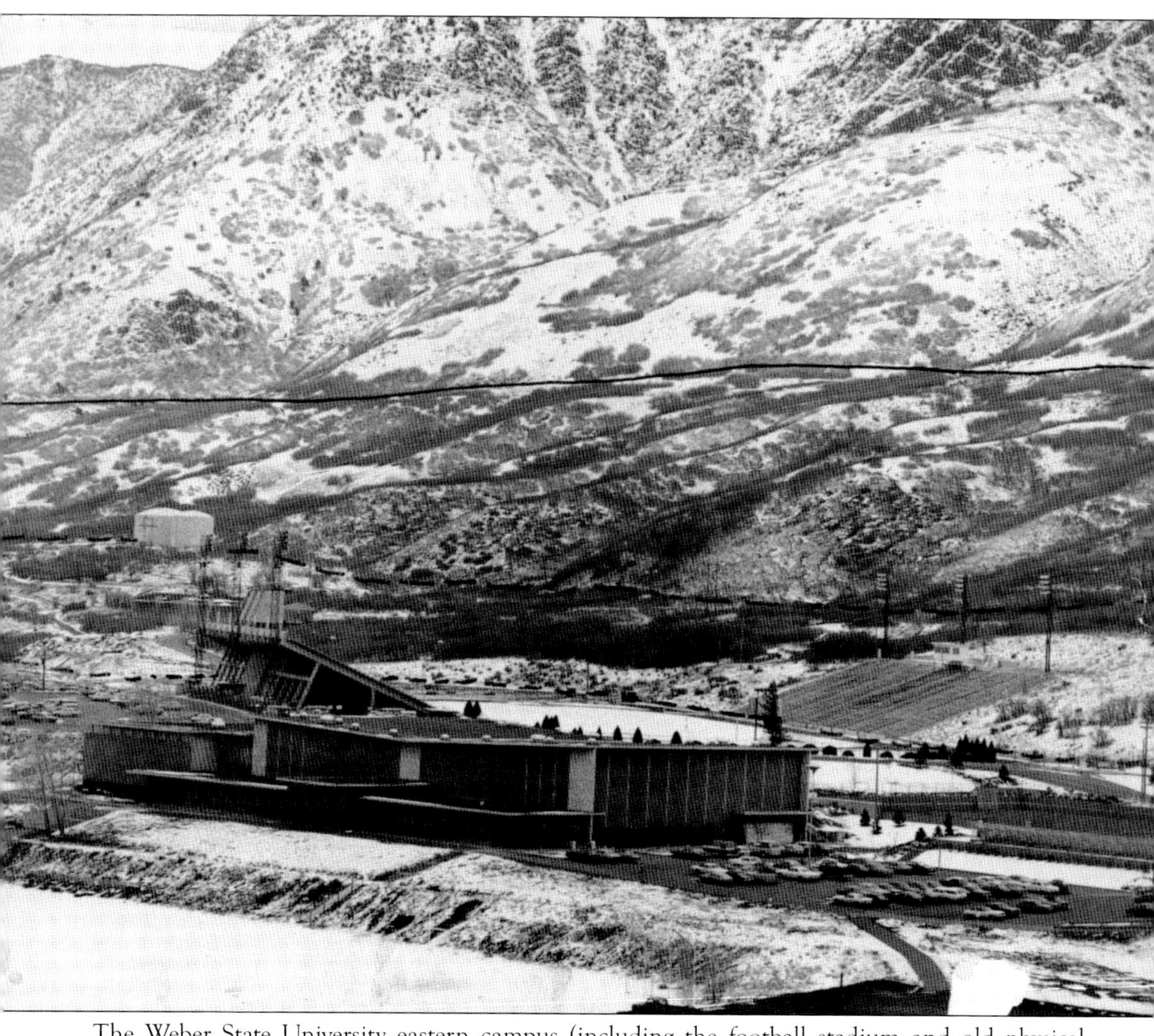

The Weber State University eastern campus (including the football stadium and old physical education building) is shown in this mid-1970s photograph. The solid line marks the ancient Lake Bonneville shoreline level, while the dotted line marks the main Wasatch earthquake fault as it crosses the campus. With the entire length of the Wasatch Mountains comes this geological fault, a feature that has a high risk for future strong earthquakes. (Courtesy of Weber State University *Signpost* newspaper archives.)

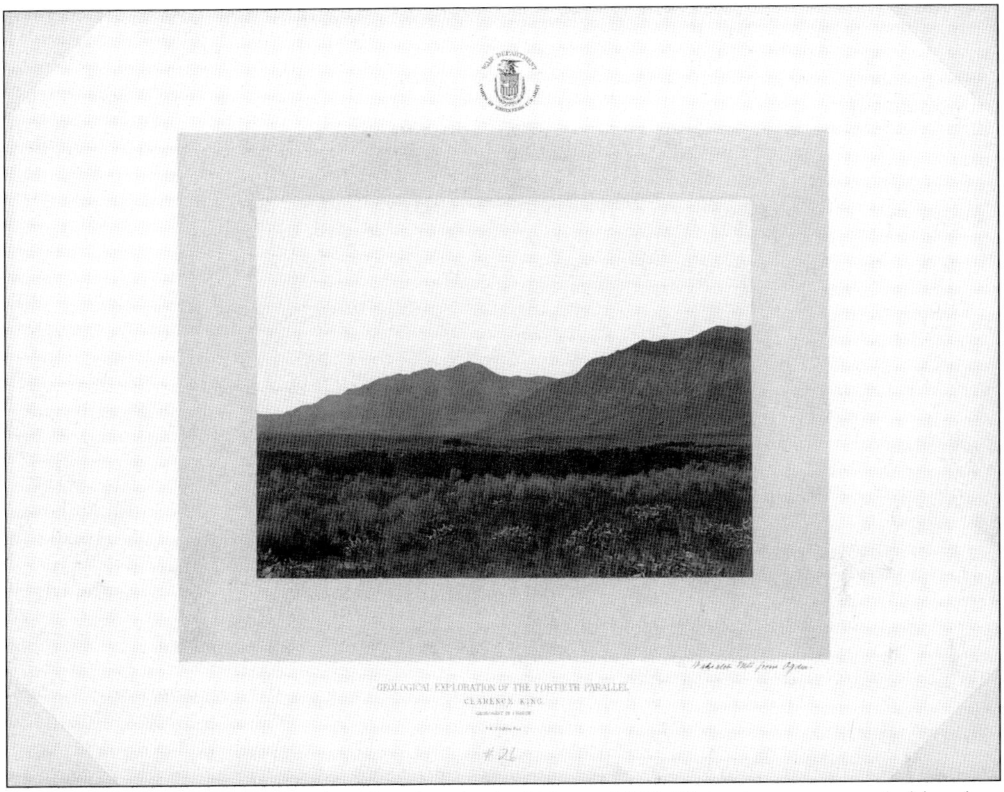

This is what the eastern side of Ogden City looked like in 1869. This picture was probably taken at about today's Twenty-Ninth Street and Harrison Boulevard, looking northeast toward Ogden Canyon and Ben Lomond Peak. Note that there are zero homes and that there is a mixture of dense oak brush and sagebrush all over the area. (Courtesy of Library of Congress.)

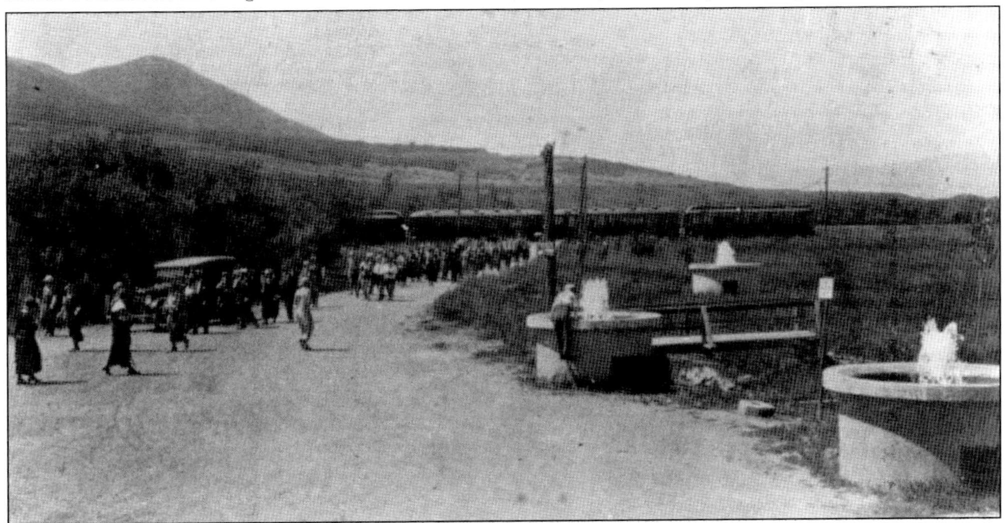

Ogden Valley boasted a famed "Artesian Well Park" in the early 20th century before Pineview Reservoir covered it over. In its heyday, there were 48 such wells providing drinking water. Locals and foreign tourists alike flocked to see the flowing wells, and for a few decades, a train line even offered transportation there, traveling up Ogden Canyon. (Courtesy of Utah State Hisiety.)

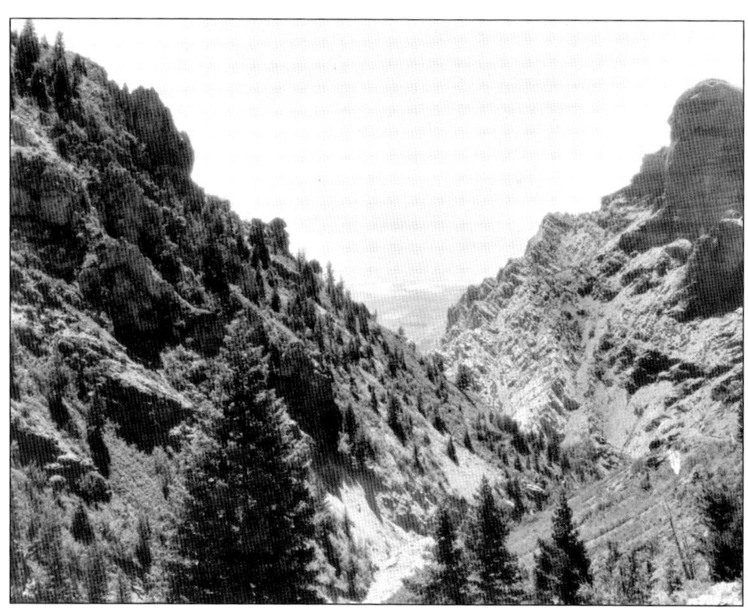

This is a view looking down Willard Canyon in 1937 to the west. This is one of the most rugged and narrow canyons in all of the Wasatch Range. It also produces a bounty of seasonal, sliver-like waterfalls each spring, though actually seeing them requires an extraordinarily difficult climb or the use of an aerial drone. (Courtesy of Utah State Historical Society.)

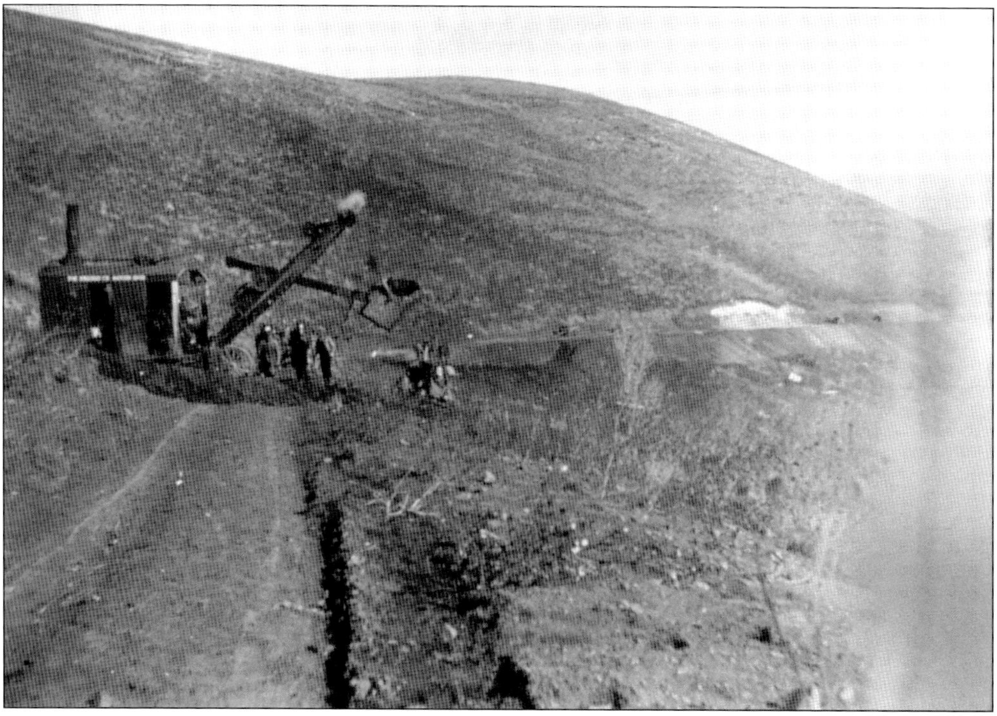

A steam shovel cuts a new, more direct road between Brigham City and the Cache Valley in the fall of 1926. This $5,000 project was designed to eliminate some of the sharp curves in the previous road in Sardine Canyon, between Mantua and Wellsville. Today, busy US Highway 89 traverses through this same area. This road cuts through the main Wasatch Mountains and has the Wellsville Mountain segment on its west side. (Courtesy of Utah State Historical Society.)

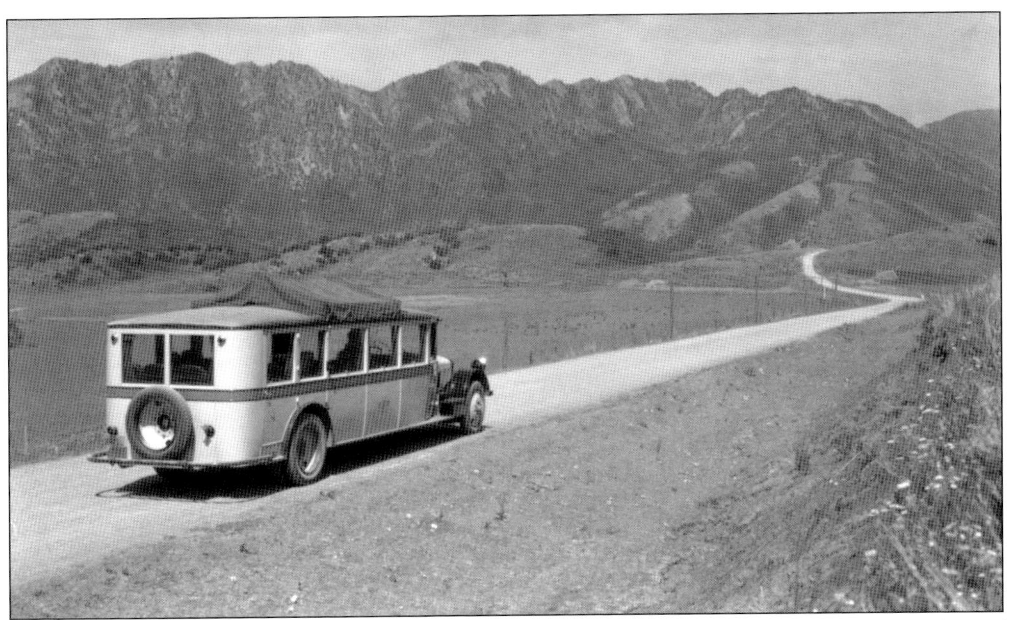

A bus belonging to the Utah-Idaho Central Railroad Company traverses the upper reaches of Sardine Canyon on June 9, 1926. The very steep Wellsville Mountains, a spur of the Wasatch Mountains, looms to the left. The highway then appears to be a very smooth gravel surface. (Courtesy of Utah State Historical Society.)

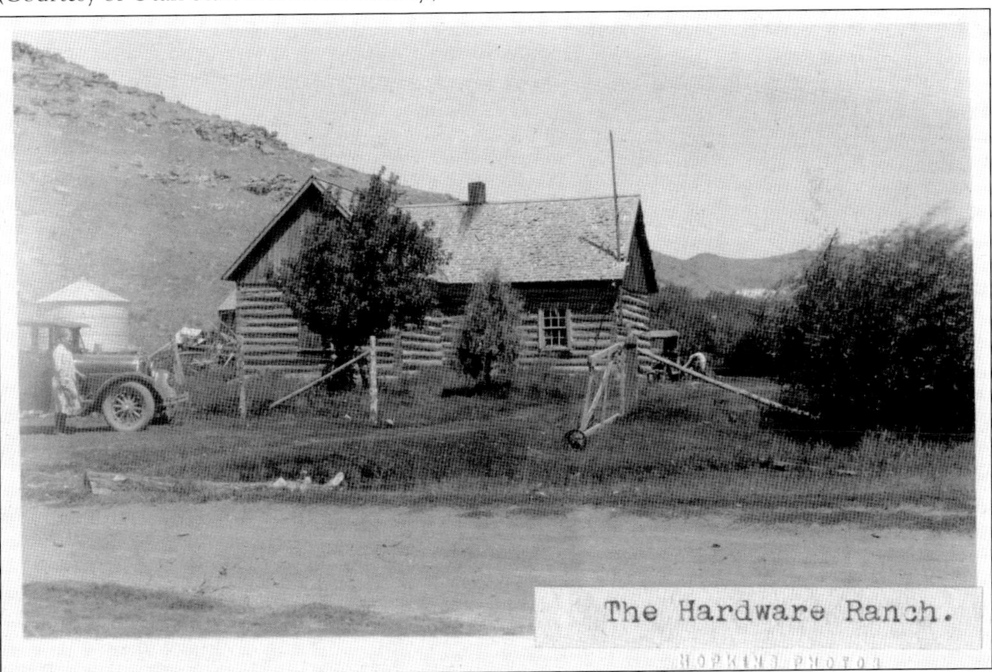

This is the original log house where the managers of the Hardware Ranch Game Management area resided. The date is 1929. Located in upper Blacksmith Fork Canyon in Cache County, the ranch switched operations in 1945 to support a large herd of elk, some 600 strong, in the area. The habitat in the area is not suitable naturally to support such a large group of animals. (Courtesy of J. Willard Marriott Digital Library, the University of Utah.)

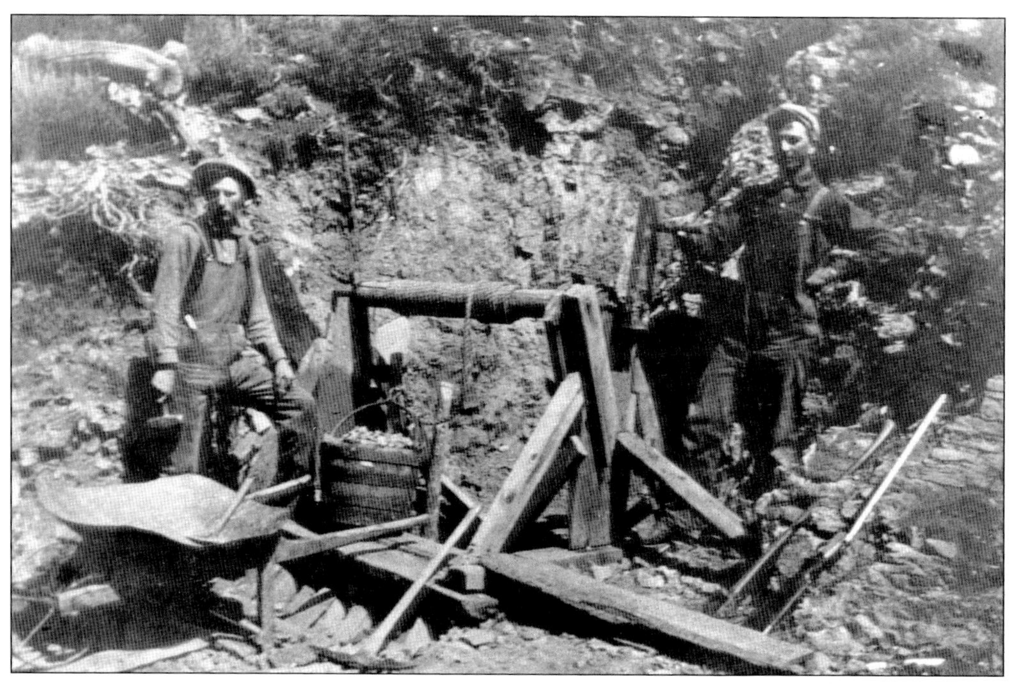

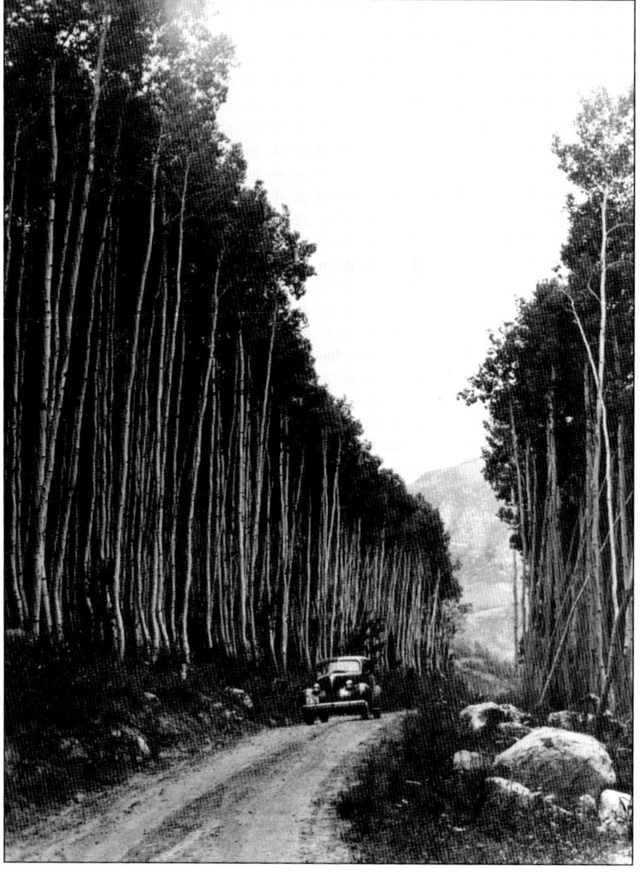

Mining minerals was explored significantly in the 19th century and early 20th century in the Wasatch Mountains. This is the Amazon Mine in Logan Canyon in 1895. N.M. Hansen Jr. and John E. Johnson are shown working at the mine. This was a lead, copper, and silver mine located in upper Logan Canyon near the middle Sinks area at an elevation of 7,500 feet above sea level. (Courtesy of Utah State Historical Society.)

An automobile passes through a thick grove of Aspen trees on the way to Tony Grove, probably in the 1930s. Located as an offshoot of Logan Canyon, Tony Grove features a lake and camping, fishing, and hiking. In this era, getting there was over a narrow dirt road. Today, it is a paved two-lane road to Tony Grove, one of the most serene of locations in the Wasatch Mountains. (Courtesy of Utah State Historical Society.)

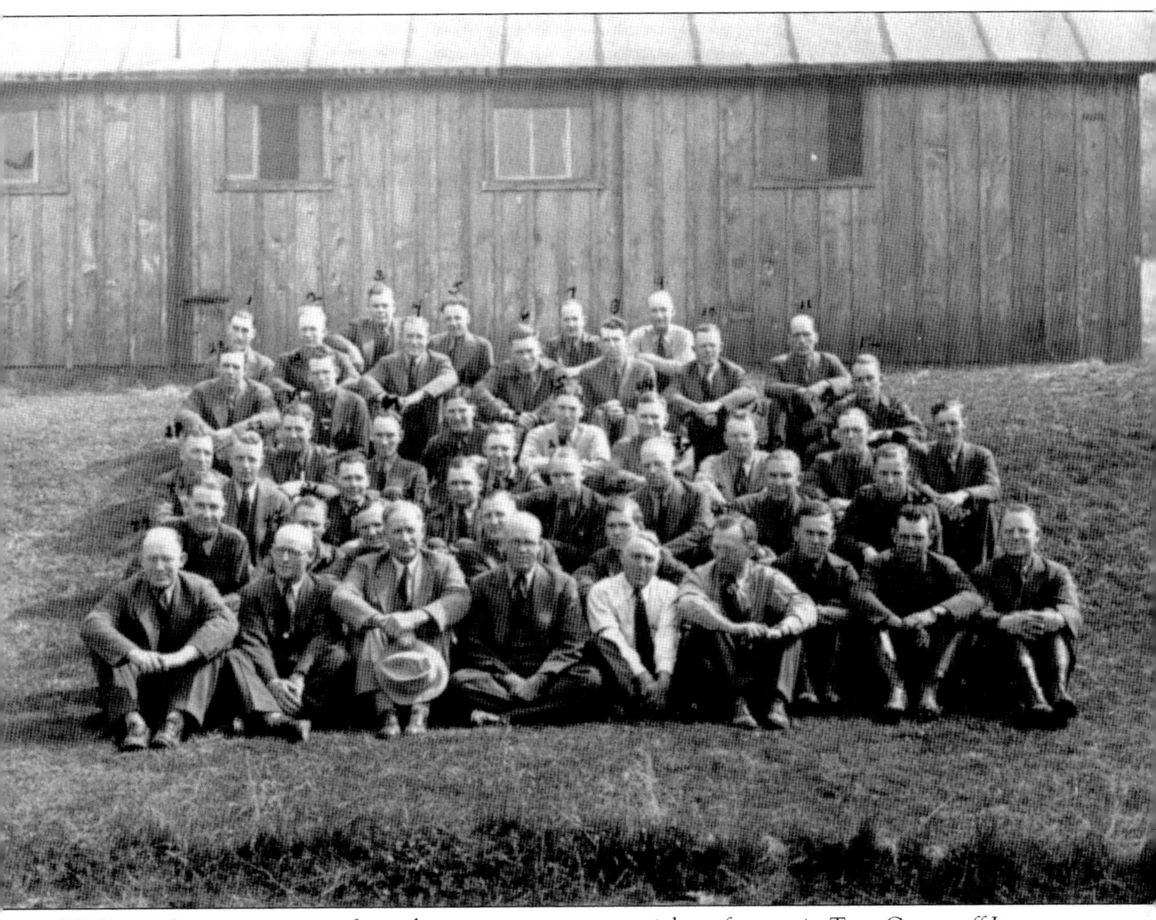

US Forest Service managers from three states met at a special conference in Tony Grove, off Logan Canyon, during the summer of 1936. A duty of the US Forest Service is to efficiently manage the resources and recreation of the Wasatch Mountains, and rangers have been doing this job well for more than a century. (Courtesy of Utah State Historical Society.)

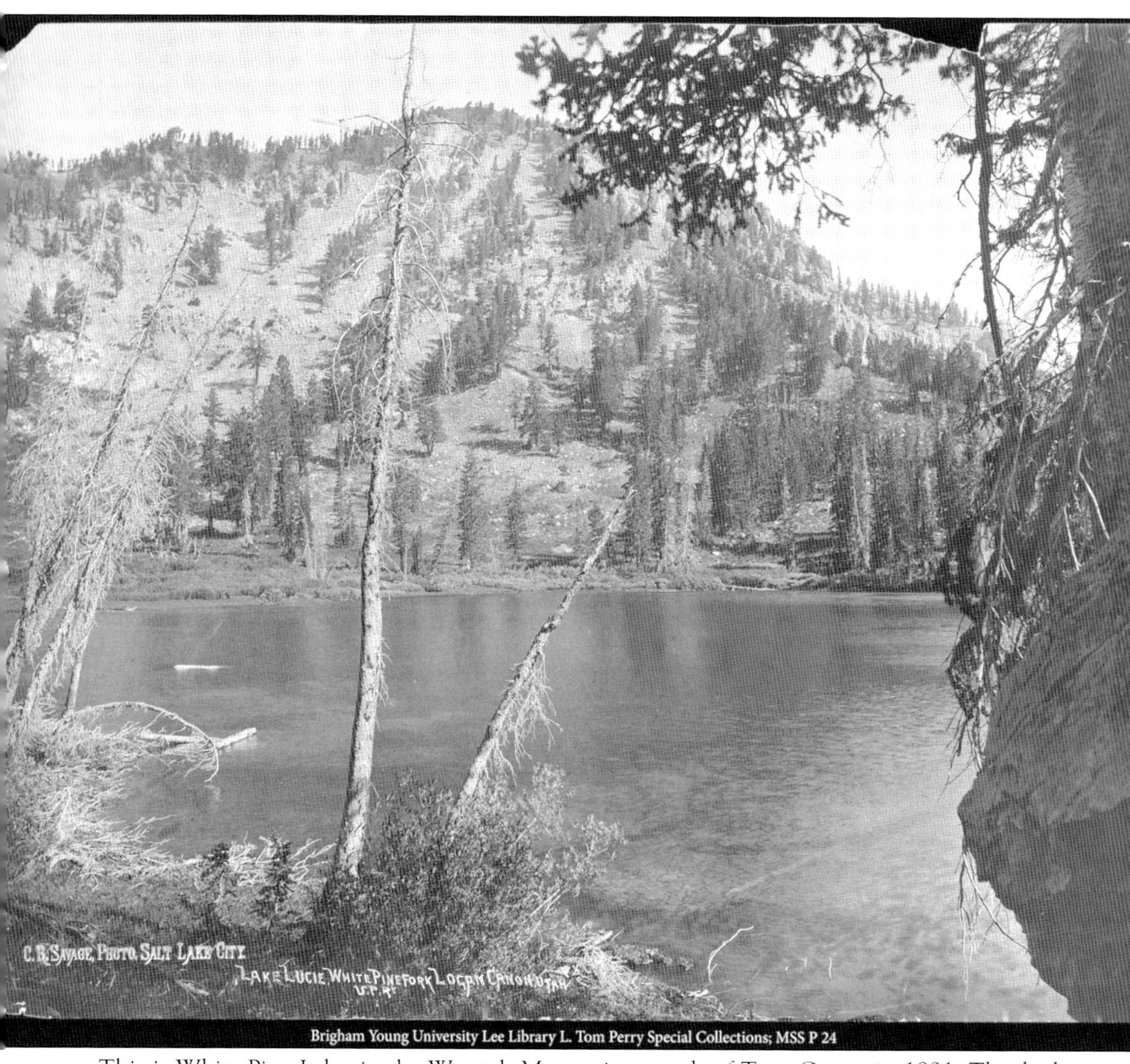

Brigham Young University Lee Library L. Tom Perry Special Collections; MSS P 24

This is White Pine Lake, in the Wasatch Mountains, north of Tony Grove, in 1891. This high-elevation lake is bordered by the Biblically named Mount Magog (shown in the picture behind the lake) on its south side and Mount Gog on its north side. Charles Savage took this photograph. (Courtesy of Utah State Historical Society.)

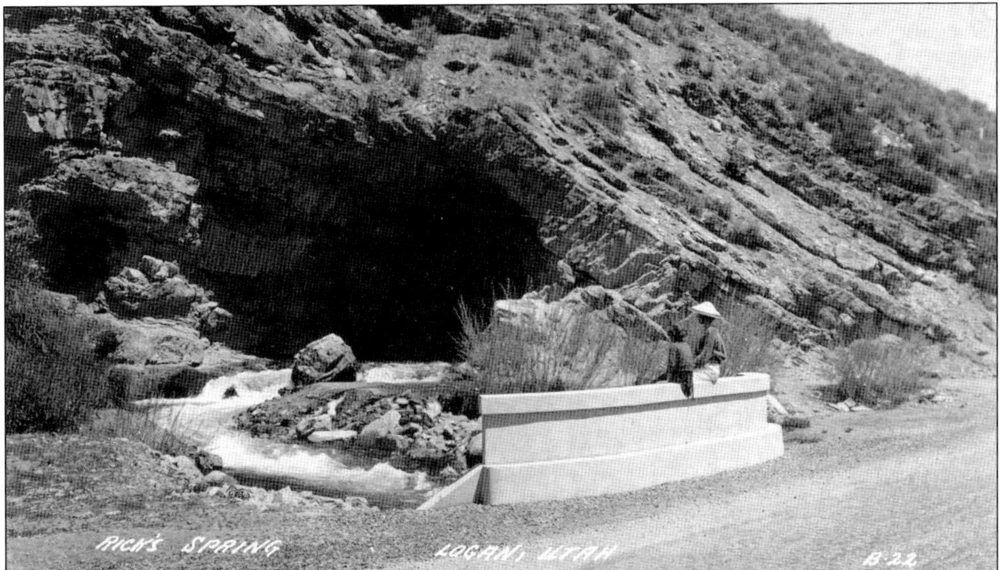

Ricks Springs is shown in Logan Canyon, probably during the 1940s. Two unidentified people admire the rushing water while sitting on a cement barrier. Travelers often drank the water here; however, in the early 1970s, it was discovered that the water is primarily not from a spring but is a diversion of the Logan River itself, supplemented by a small amount of spring water. (Courtesy of Utah State Historical Society.)

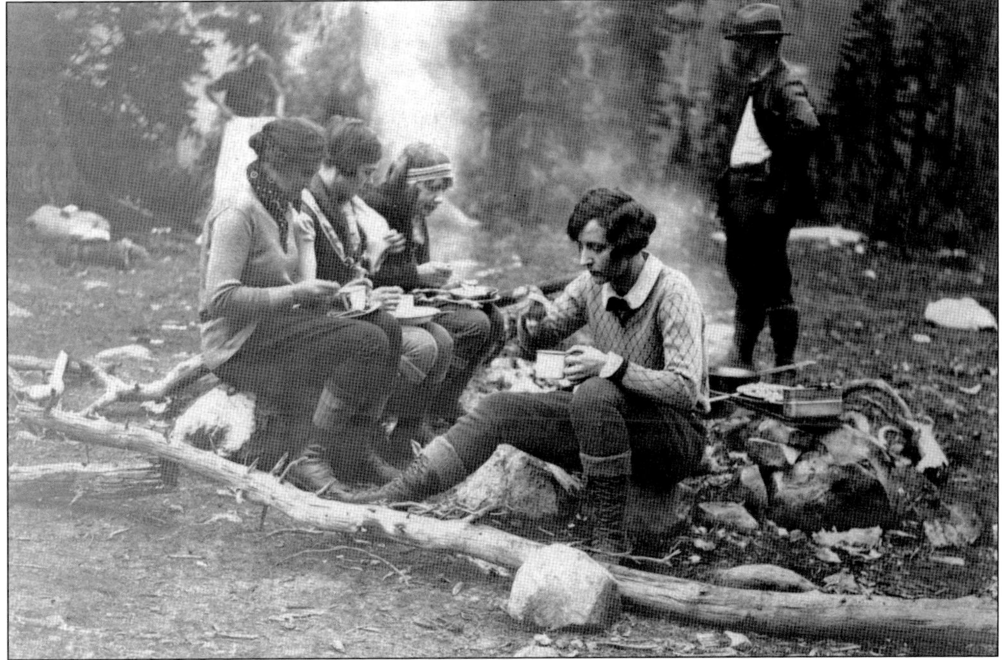

Four female members of the Wasatch Mountain Club are shown having a hot breakfast in the Wasatch Mountains, possibly in Logan Canyon, during the late 1920s or the early 1930s. The club sponsored hikes and camping all over the Wasatch Mountains and wisely chronicled its outdoor adventures in photographs. (Courtesy of J. Willard Marriott Digital Library, the University of Utah.)

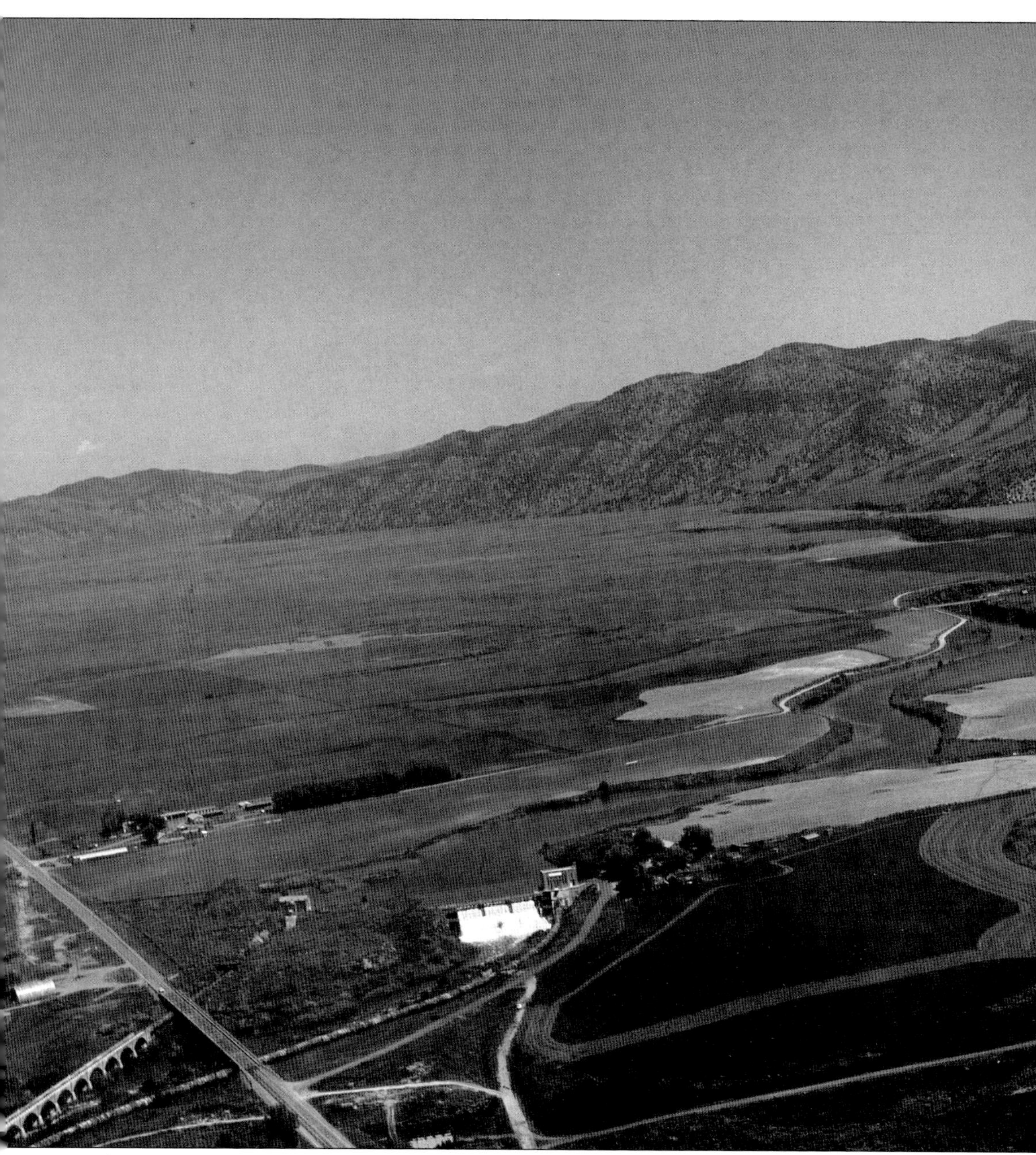

This is an aerial photograph of just north of Grace, Idaho, from the 1970s or 1980s. In the background is the extreme northern end of the Wasatch Mountain Range, at Soda Point/Sheep Rock, where the Bear River loops around the range (also sometimes referred to as the Bear River Mountains) and heads south toward the Great Salt Lake. Also pictured is the Alexander Dam on the Bear River and several farms, including the Rigby Ranch (which the author's maternal grandparents used to operate) on the north. (Courtesy of J. Willard Marriott Digital Library, the University of Utah.)

Six

Modern-Era Mountains

It is impossible for this book to highlight but a fraction of the history, legends, and impressive bucket list that the Wasatch Mountains offer.

Two golden assets in the Wasatch Mountains are the Mount Nebo Scenic Byway and the Skyline Drive Scenic Backway. The Mount Nebo Byway is a paved, 38-mile-long route that climbs to just over an elevation of 9,000 feet behind Mount Nebo, the tallest Wasatch mountain. The road goes from Juab County to Utah County, and its southern end is also the south end of the Wasatch. The Skyline Drive is a rugged dirt road, 24 miles long. It stretches from Farmington Canyon to Bountiful.

Notwithstanding, portions of the Wasatch Mountains are becoming overcrowded and stricken with possible environmental problems. In essence, Utahns love these mountains, which are extremely close to population centers, way too much. For example, controversy over a possible gondola in Little Cottonwood Canyon to more efficiently (and with less pollution) access the canyon has been a key issue in Salt Lake County for years.

Also, the US Forest Service, in Salt Lake's Mill Creek Canyon, installed user fees, starting in 2020. They also put restrictions on bicycle use and dogs in the canyon and on trails.

Provo Canyon recently went through some upgrades and widening projects. Some of this was necessary because of the "Wasatch Back," the growing communities on the east side or in the middle of the Wasatch Mountains.

A drought in the early 21st century has also produced its share of wildfires in the Wasatch Mountains. Hunting and wildlife issues are always paramount concerns, too. Some eight major reservoirs store water for a thirsty Wasatch Front.

The Salt Lake 2002 Winter Olympic Games happened primarily because of the Wasatch Mountains, and the games will return to Salt Lake—and the Wasatch Mountains—in 2034.

(Note that the Wasatch Mountain range stops on the north end, just past Grace, Idaho. Ironically, the author's maternal grandparents owned a large ranch in north Grace and had the last house northward on the Wasatch Range's westward side since the mid-1930s. Relatives of the author still live on that farm, in the northwesternmost home on the Wasatch.)

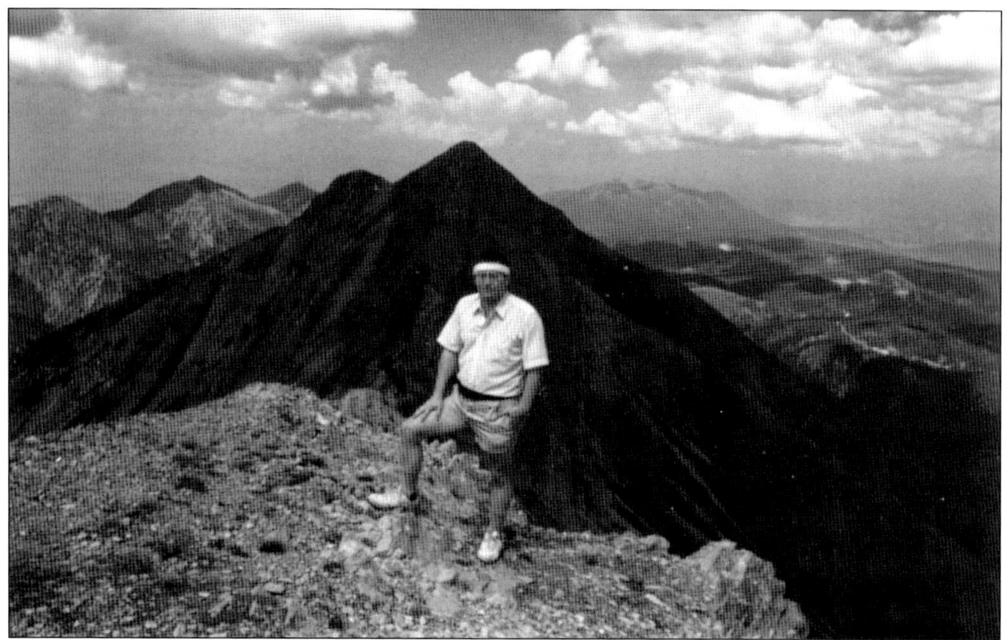

Ray Boren stands atop Mount Nebo's South Peak during an August 1994 hike there with two companions. Note Mount Nebo's Middle and North Peaks in the background. The trail from Salt Creek Canyon accesses the South Peak via a steep five-mile trek. Proceeding to the other two Nebo peaks from there requires a long scramble over a knife edge. (Courtesy of Ravell Call.)

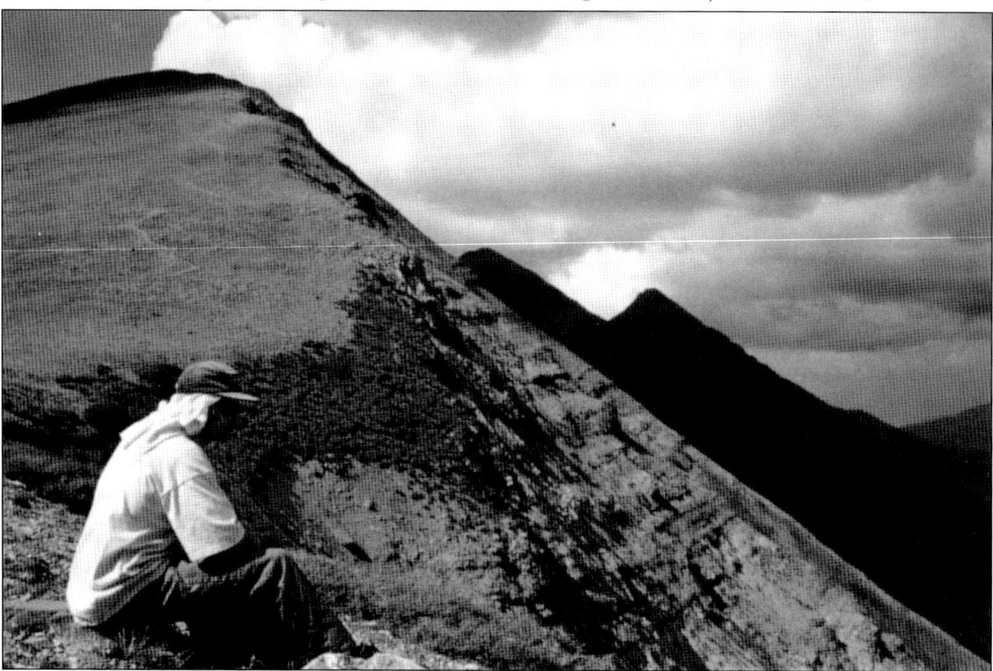

Ravell Call pauses for a rest just below the South Peak of Mount Nebo during a 1994 hike there. All three Nebo peaks are clearly visible in the picture. The Mormon pioneers gave the mountain this Old Testament name after the high peak in Moab, east of the Jordan River, where Moses apparently died or was translated. (Photograph by Ray Boren.)

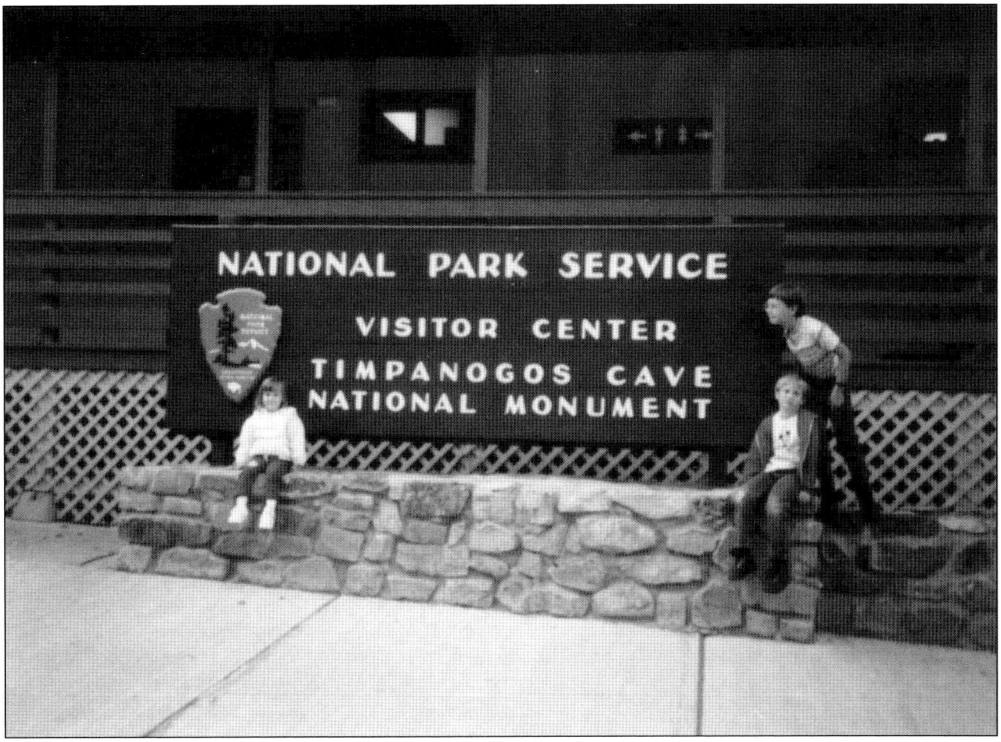

Timpanogos Cave National Monument is located 10 miles east of Interstate 15 exit No. 284 (Alpine-Highland) along Utah Highway 92. The cave is generally open from mid-May through mid-October, weather permitting. Because tickets for cave tours are often sold out on the day of, it is recommended that advance tickets are purchased online. (Photograph by author.)

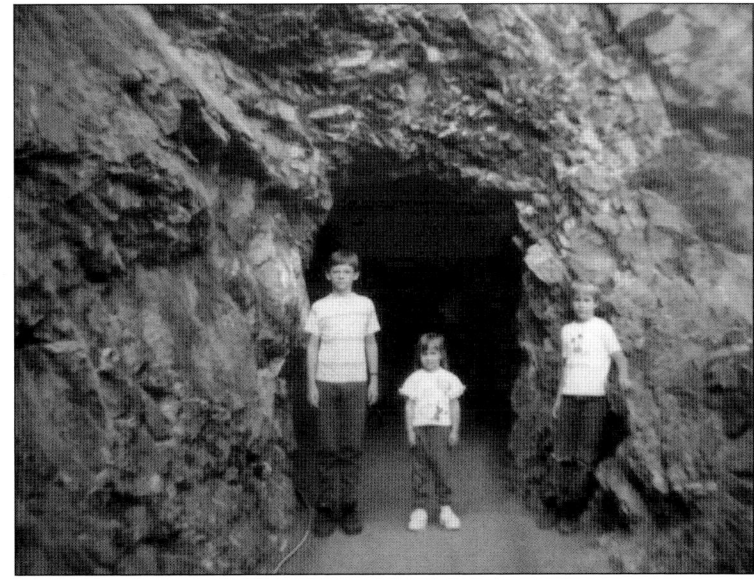

From left to right, Roger, Elizabeth, and Steven Arave pose at the entrance to Timpanogos Cave after a 1997 hike there. To reach the cave entrance, visitors must hike up a 1.5-mile paved trail that climbs a total of 1,092 feet in elevation. Hikers also must have a reservation to visit the cave first. (Photograph by author.)

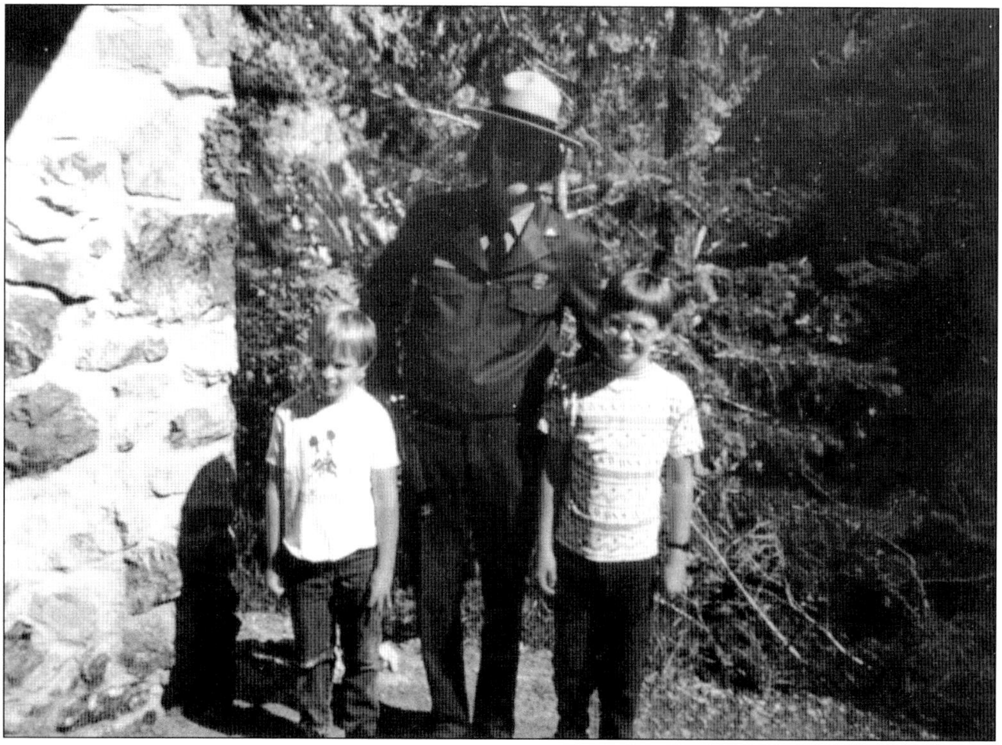

A Timpanogos Cave National Monument ranger poses with Steven (left) and Roger (right) Arave after a tour of the cave. Rangers are essential to a visit here because all tours of the cave are guided by them. Only 16 people are allowed per tour. Timpanogos Cave is named after the mountain above it. (Photograph by author.)

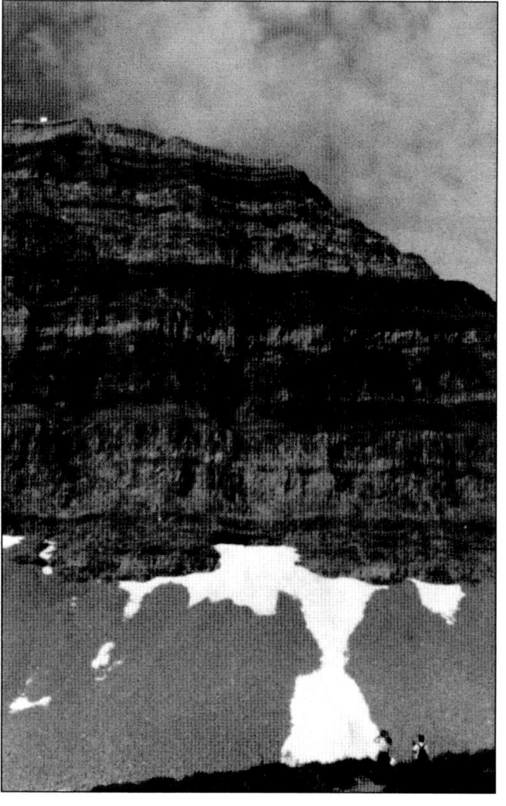

This is the backside (east side) of Timpanogos Peak, as shown in a 1991 photograph. This picture was taken near Emerald Lake. Often, those hikers who lack the stamina to reach the actual Timp summit stop here and at least feel rewarded with this stunning alpine view in the area. (Photograph by author.)

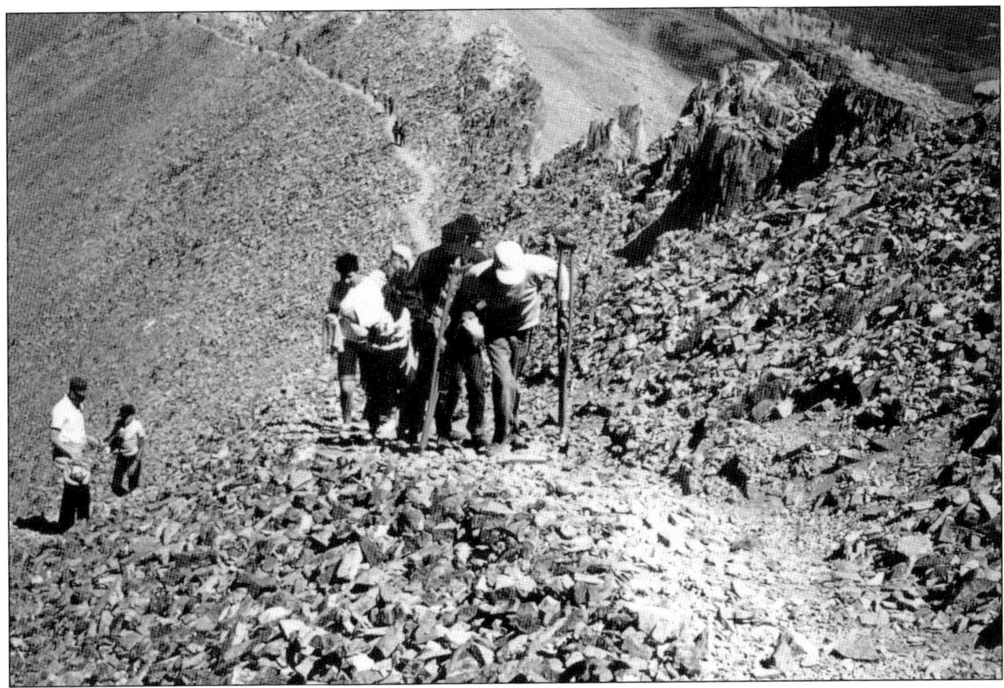

The extended Stewart family is shown during a summer hike to Mount Timpanogos in 1980. Note that one family member of the large group was making the long and steep hike on crutches. The group is approaching the mount saddle, just below the summit of Timp. The Stewart family was the first to homestead in the Aspen Grove area, below the majestic mountain, in the 19th century. Some geological features in the area are also named for the Stewart family. (Courtesy of J. Willard Marriott Digital Library, the University of Utah.)

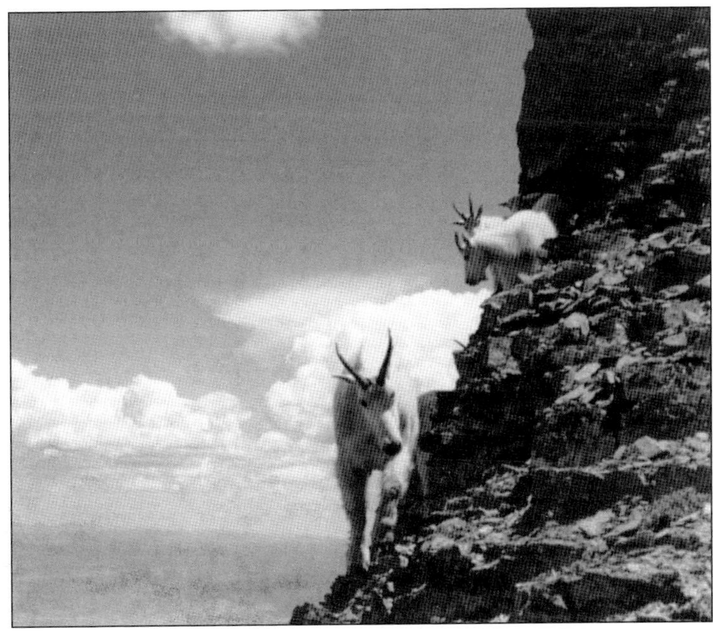

A pair of curious mountain goats peer around a corner, just below the Mount Timpanogos summit, during a 1991 hike there. Mount Timpanogos is the crown jewel of hiking, especially for Utah and Wasatch Counties, at an elevation of 11,752 feet above sea level. The Timp summit is a 14-mile, round-trip hike from Timpooneke or 13.5 miles from Aspen Grove. About 4,300 feet in elevation gain is required from Aspen Grove. (Photograph by Ray Boren.)

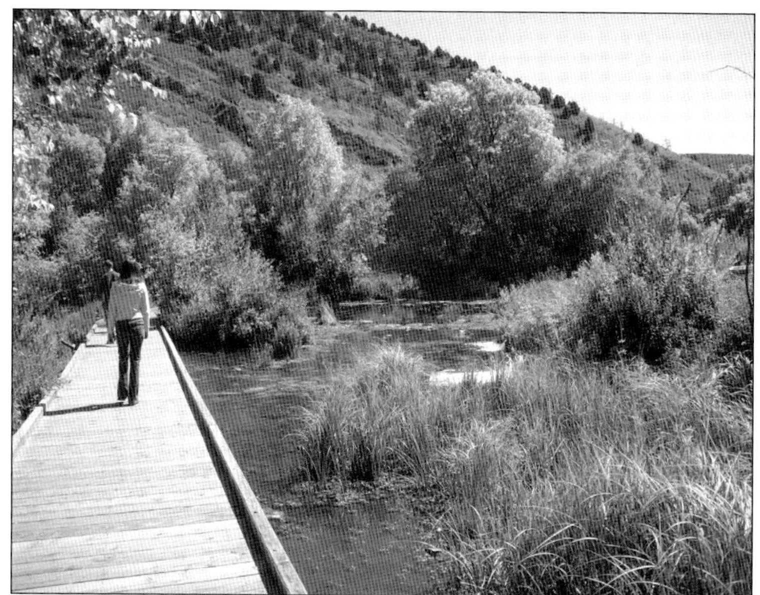

This is one of the many boardwalks around Cascade Springs in the Wasatch Mountains. The artesian wells here produce some seven million gallons of water a day. In the summer season here, there are also many wildflowers dotting the landscape. Cascade Springs is accessible off the Alpine Loop Highway or from State Highway 220 in Midway. (Photograph by author.)

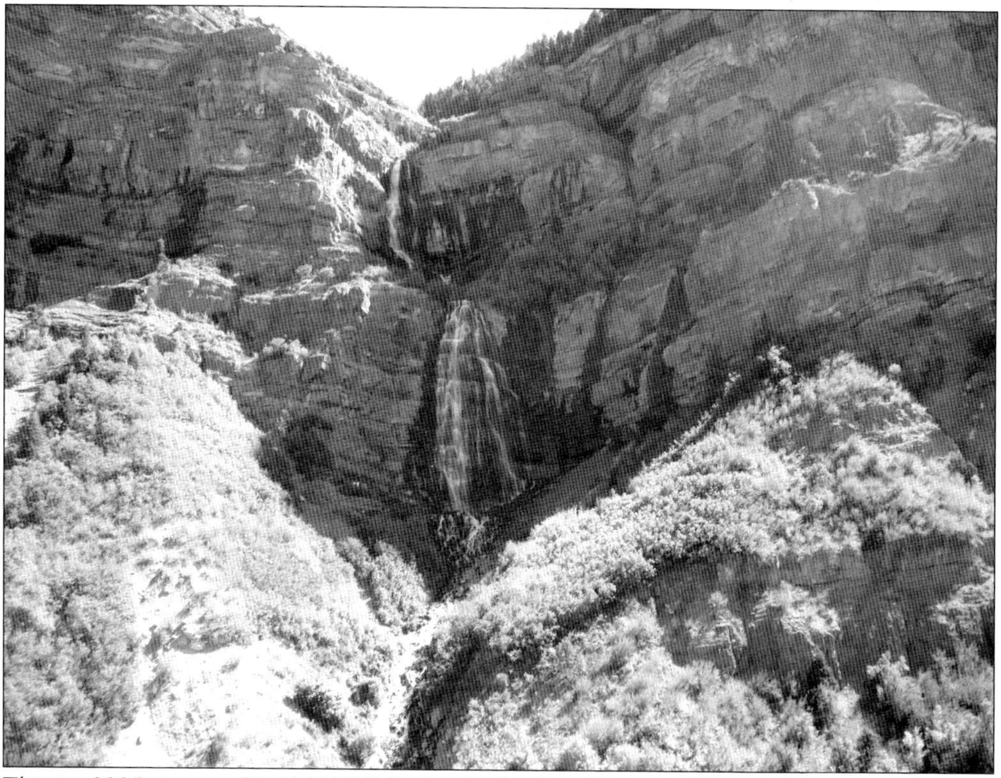

This is a 2005 picture of Bridal Veil Falls. It is by far the tallest waterfall in the Wasatch Mountains at 607 feet. The falls' original name was Beautiful Cascade in 1859, but that was later changed to the current moniker. Bridal Veil is readily accessible off US Highway 189 in Provo Canyon. An aerial tramway used to travel above the falls, but it closed permanently in 1996 and has since been removed. Caution is advised when hiking around the falls, as many accidents and even some fatalities have occurred there. (Photograph by author.)

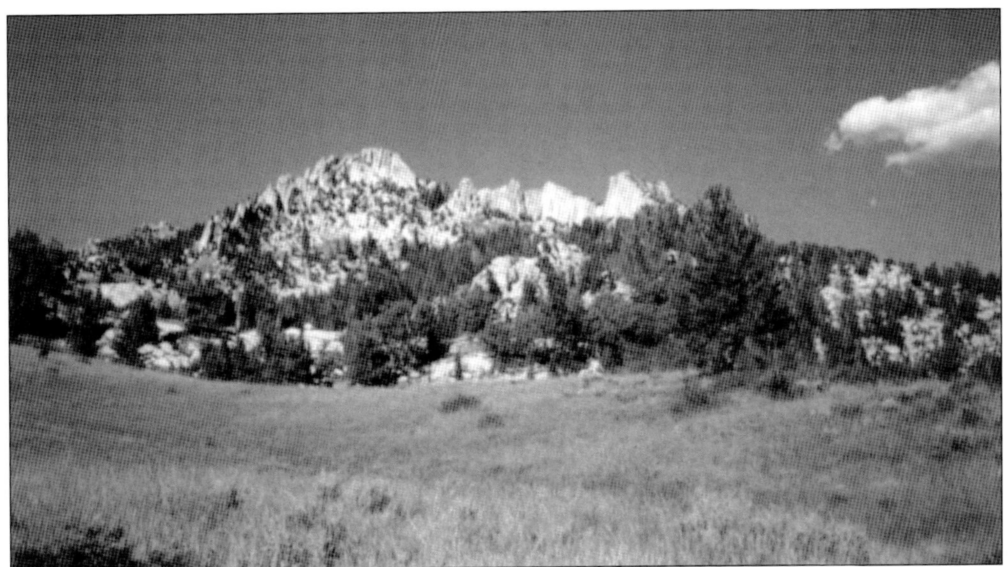

This is a 2002 picture of the large cirque below Lone Peak. This relatively flat/grassy bowl is a popular resting, picnicking, and camping spot for hikers to Lone Peak, shown in the distance. The peak's name comes from its solitary stature on the mountainside between Twin Peaks and Mount Timpanogos. (Photograph by author.)

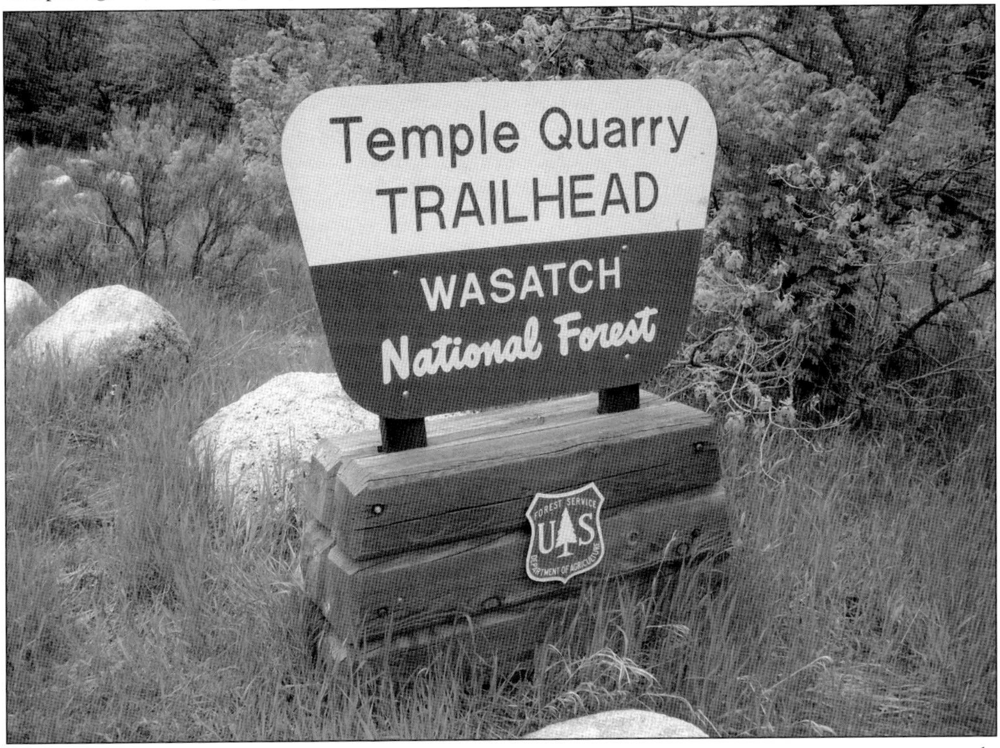

This sign near the mouth of Little Cottonwood Canyon designates the Mormon pioneer temple rock quarry trailhead. The one-half-mile trail has interpretive signs that outline what life was like in the late 1800s. Note that there was originally a stream here, but water was diverted up the canyon decades ago to provide hydroelectric power for the Salt Lake Valley. (Photograph by author.)

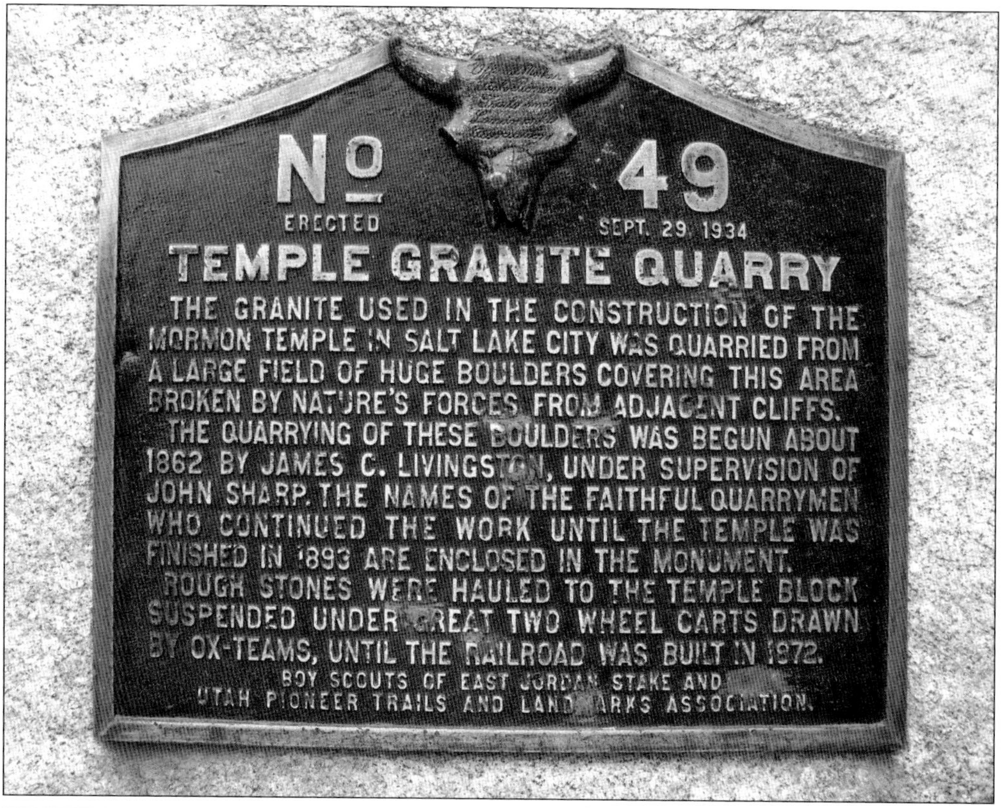

Nº 49

ERECTED SEPT. 29, 1934

TEMPLE GRANITE QUARRY

THE GRANITE USED IN THE CONSTRUCTION OF THE MORMON TEMPLE IN SALT LAKE CITY WAS QUARRIED FROM A LARGE FIELD OF HUGE BOULDERS COVERING THIS AREA BROKEN BY NATURE'S FORCES FROM ADJACENT CLIFFS.

THE QUARRYING OF THESE BOULDERS WAS BEGUN ABOUT 1862 BY JAMES C. LIVINGSTON, UNDER SUPERVISION OF JOHN SHARP. THE NAMES OF THE FAITHFUL QUARRYMEN WHO CONTINUED THE WORK UNTIL THE TEMPLE WAS FINISHED IN 1893 ARE ENCLOSED IN THE MONUMENT.

ROUGH STONES WERE HAULED TO THE TEMPLE BLOCK SUSPENDED UNDER GREAT TWO WHEEL CARTS DRAWN BY OX-TEAMS, UNTIL THE RAILROAD WAS BUILT IN 1872.

BOY SCOUTS OF EAST JORDAN STAKE AND UTAH PIONEER TRAILS AND LANDMARKS ASSOCIATION.

This is the rock and bronze monument near the mouth of Little Cottonwood Canyon that was erected in 1934. All of the granite blocks used in the construction of the Salt Lake Temple, the Church of Jesus Christ of Latter-day Saints, were hewn from here and transported a dozen miles to downtown Salt Lake City. (Photograph by author.)

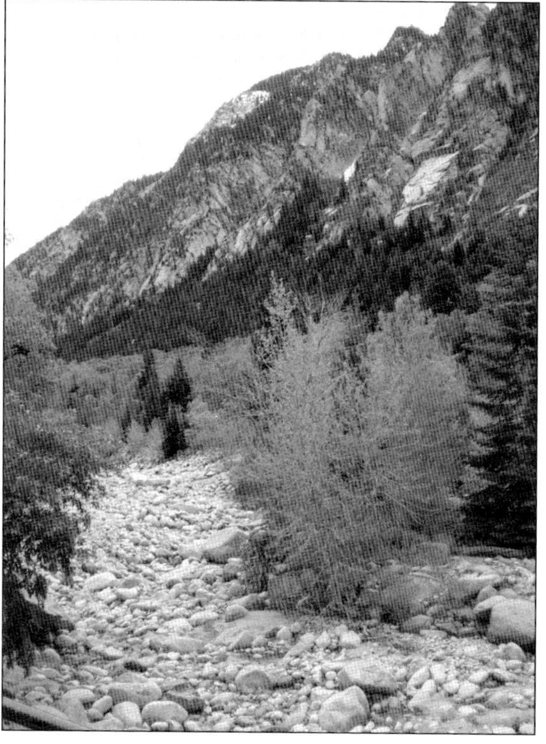

The mouth of Little Cottonwood Canyon is shown in a 2011 photograph. This is near the Temple Quarry Trail. Mining granite blocks from near here means a direct slice of the Wasatch Mountains exists in downtown Salt Lake City since the exterior of the Salt Lake Temple is composed of them. (Photograph by author.)

A pair of women stand on a small mound below one of the Twin Peaks, looming above Snowbird Ski Resort, in the early summer of 2001. The Twin Peaks soar to 11,433 feet, more than 400 feet above the top of the Snowbird Tram at Hidden Peak. (Photograph by LeAnn Arave.)

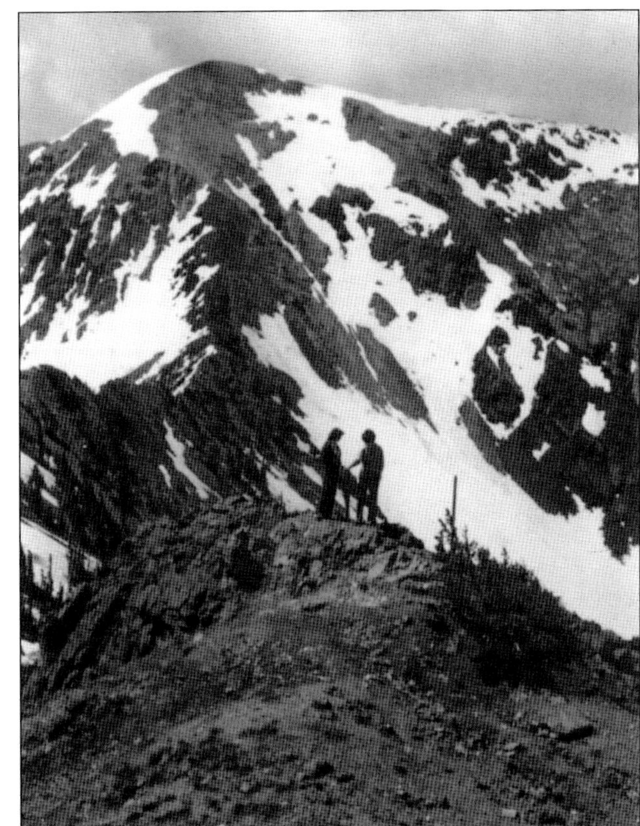

A young boy slides down a snowy hill in Park City on Thanksgiving weekend in 1989. Park City transitioned from its beginning as a mining town in the 1860s to a ghost town in the 1950s as the mining resources bottomed out and finally to a skiing and outdoor mecca in the 1960s. (Photograph by LeAnn Arave.)

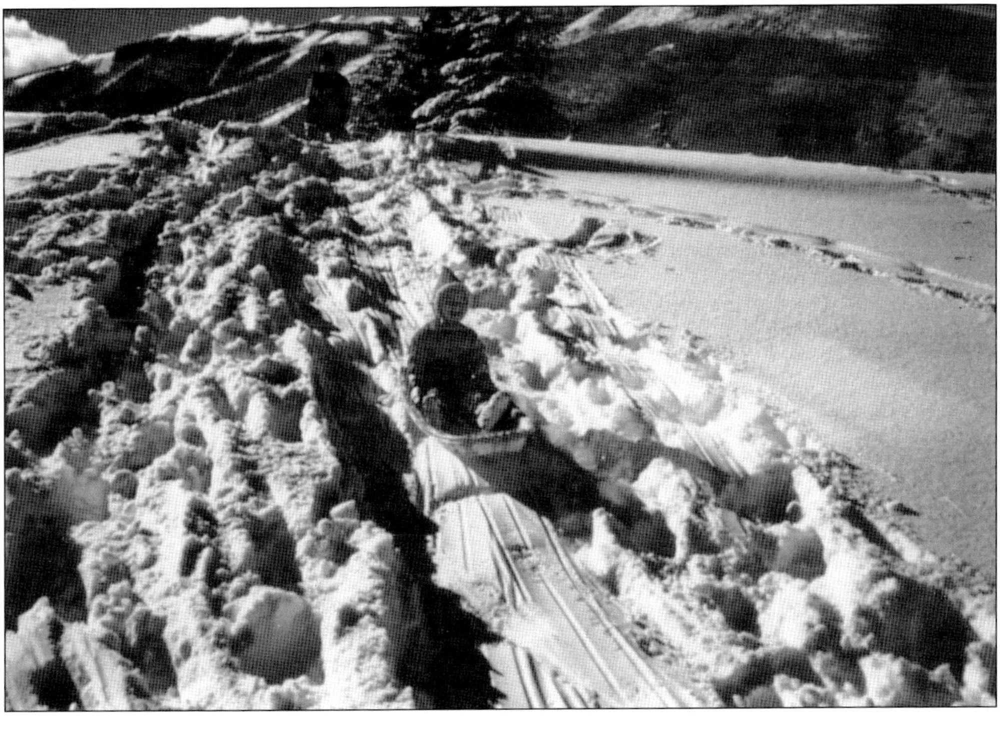

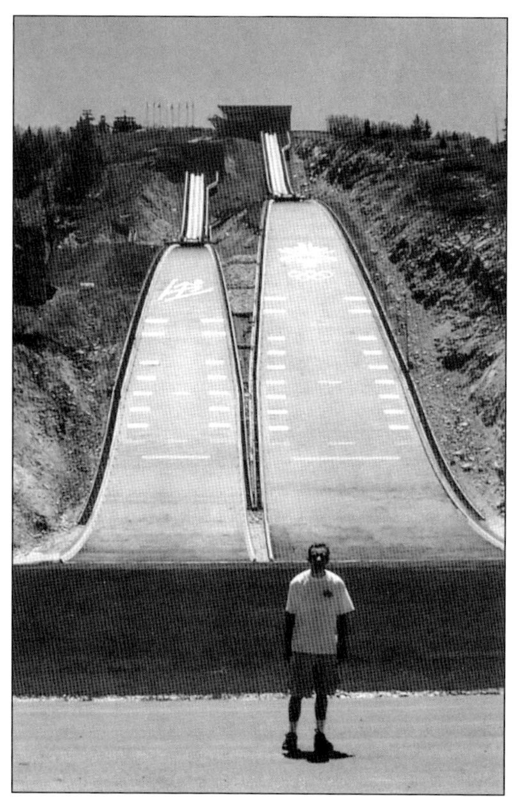

Roger Arave poses at the bottom of one of the Olympic ski runs from the 2002 Salt Lake Winter Games. Located in the Utah Olympic Park at Park City, these facilities are still used for training and competitions. At no other time than February 2002 has the Wasatch Mountains gained more worldwide publicity than with the 2002 Olympic Games. Salt Lake will also host the 2034 Winter Olympics. (Photograph by LeAnn Arave.)

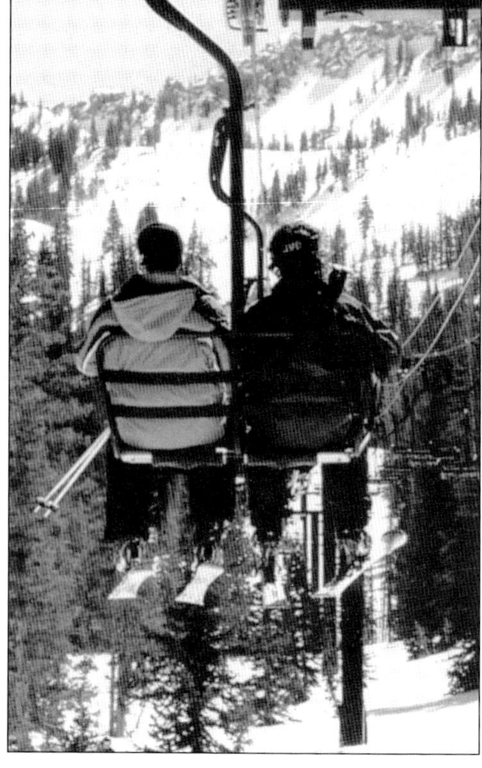

Two unidentified skiers head up the main ski lift at Alta Resort, Little Cottonwood Canyon, for another downhill run in February 2009. Alta is one of the oldest ski resorts in the nation, opening in 1939. Alta was originally a mining town but eventually shifted into a resort town focused on skiing and other winter sports. (Photograph by Steven Arave.)

The south summit of Mount Olympus is shown in this 1991 photograph. At 9,026 feet, this mountain is one of the most picturesque in all of the Wasatch Range. It is not by far the tallest but stands out for its pleasing and yet rugged shape. Located east of Holladay and southeast of Salt Lake City, no one knows who named the peak, but its Greek mountain connection is obvious. (Photograph by author.)

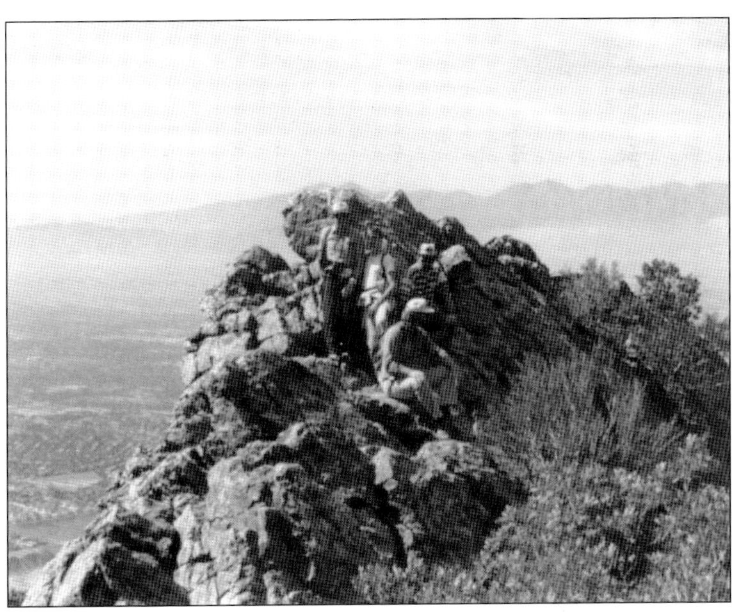

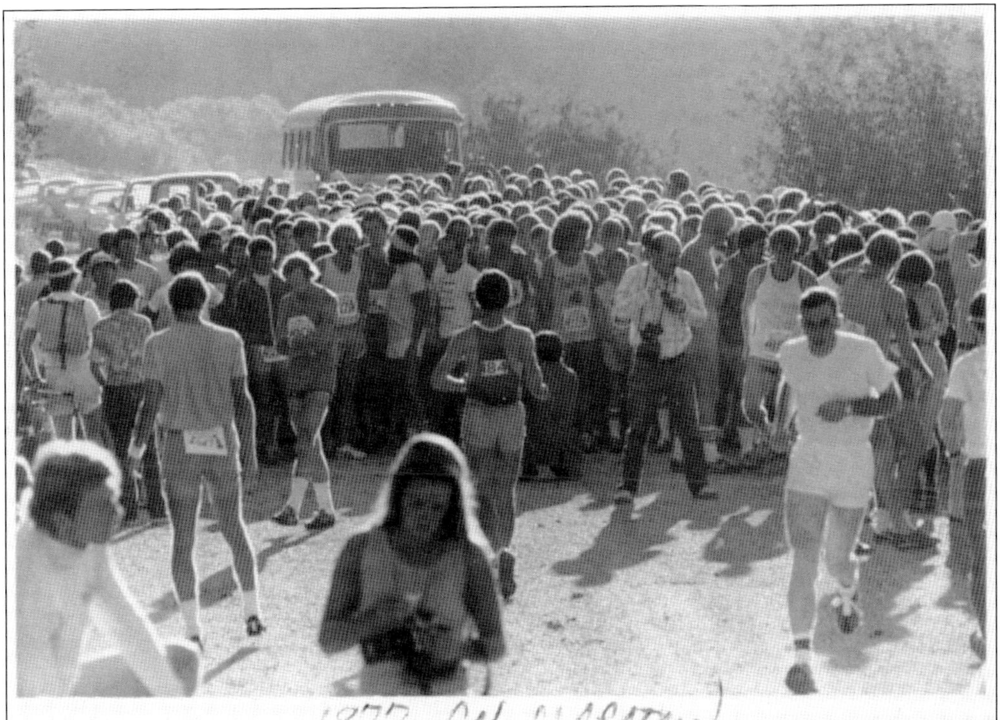

Hundreds of runners line up for the eighth annual *Deseret News* Marathon at the top of Emigration Canyon, near Big Mountain, on July 24, 1977. Demitro Cabanillas won the 26.2-mile race in 2:21:20. The race followed the same mountainous route through the Wasatch Range that the first Mormon pioneers took in July 1847. (Courtesy of *Deseret News* Archives.)

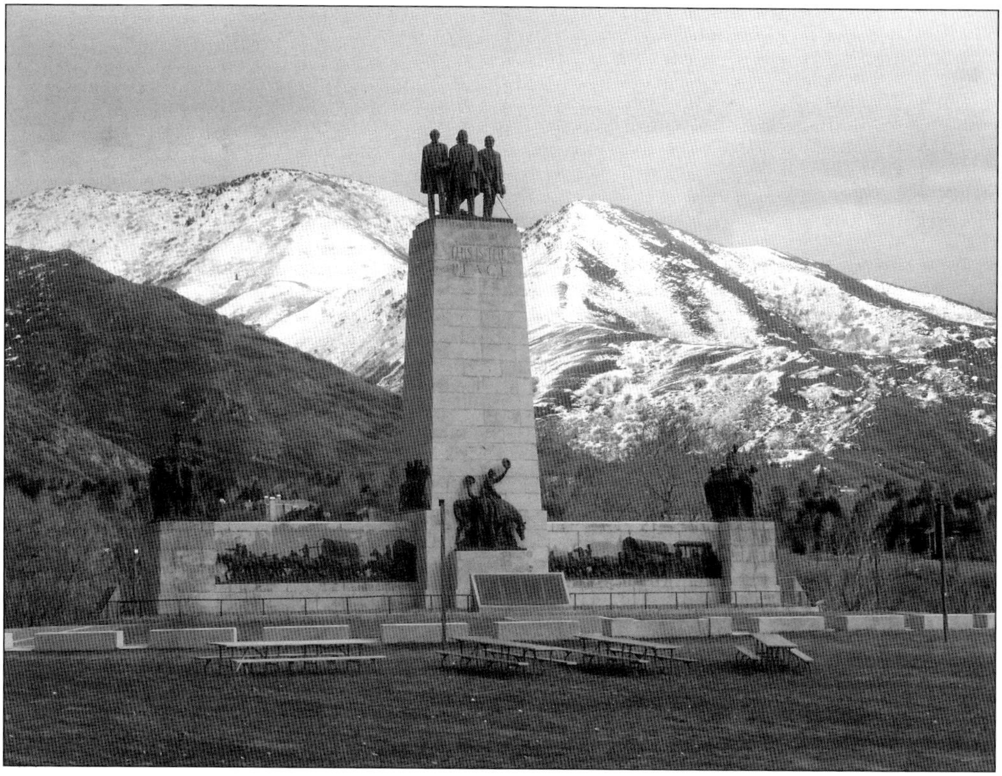

This Is The Place Monument, at the mouth of Emigration Canyon in Salt Lake City, which commemorates the arrival of the Mormon pioneers into the valley on July 24, 1847. This monument was constructed in 1947 and is just north of Hogle Zoo. The monument is now part of This Is The Place Heritage Park, which highlights early pioneer life in the Salt Lake Valley. (Photograph by author.)

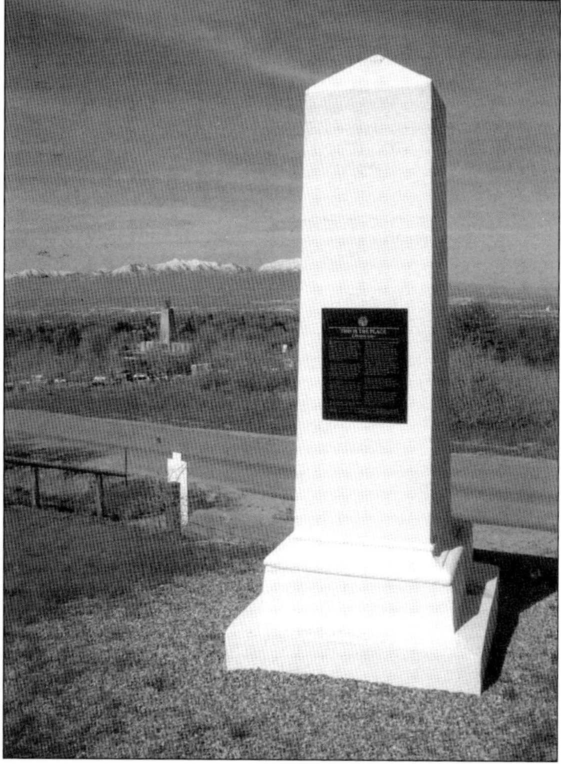

Although somewhat obscured, this is the original This Is The Place Monument, located northeast, on a hill above the larger, modern monument. This 10-foot-high marker, placed in 1921, is believed to more accurately represent the actual location where Brigham Young declared the Salt Lake Valley to be "the right place" on July 24, 1847. (Photograph by author.)

These slabs of rock comprise what has become to be known as "The Living Room" in the foothills above the University of Utah campus. These makeshift slabs of rock create "chairs" that hikers can sit in. There is no denying that the views of Salt Lake City as well as sunsets are fabulous here (though the seats are hard). To hike here requires a 2.3-mile round trip and 871 feet in elevation gain. (Photograph by Liz Arave Hafen.)

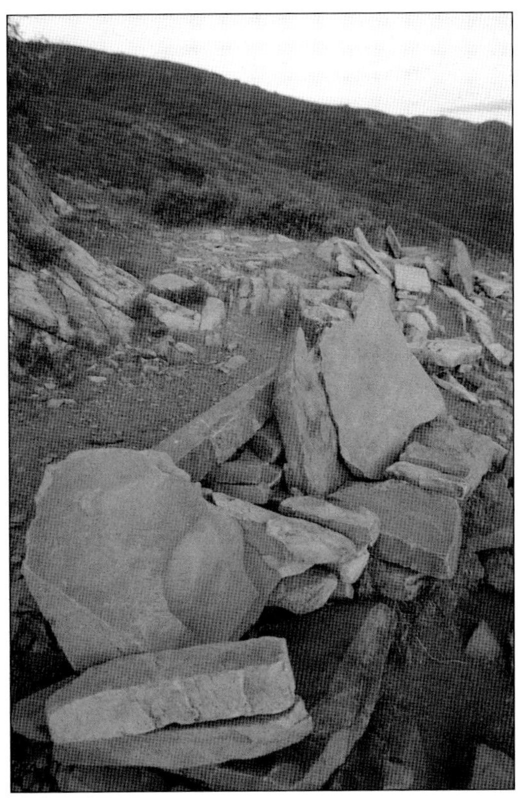

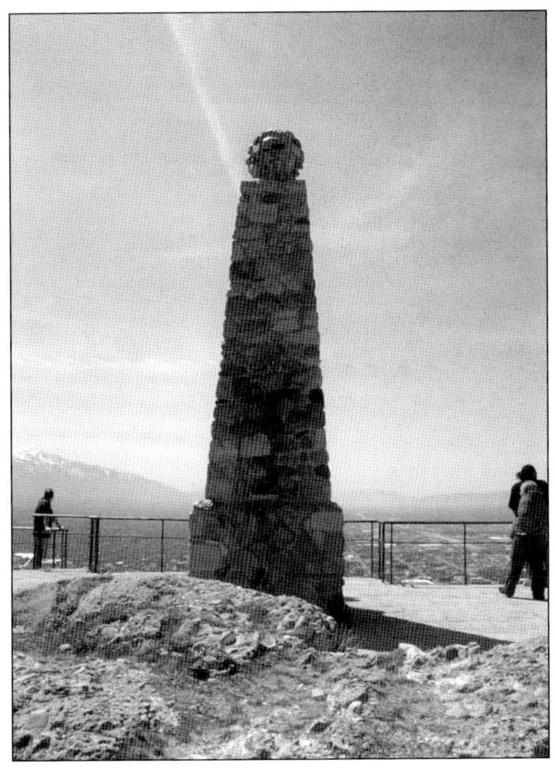

This is the monument atop Ensign Peak in the Wasatch Mountains. This marker was placed there in July 1934. Ensign Peak is only 5,414 feet above sea level, but it was the first summit that the Mormon pioneers climbed just two days after arriving in the Salt Lake Valley. (Photograph by author.)

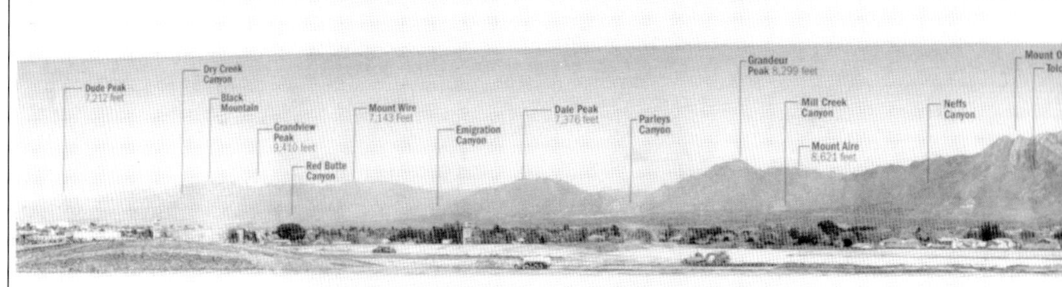

Majestic landmarks of the Wasatch Fro

This is a panoramic view of the entire west side of the Wasatch Mountains in Salt Lake County. Multiple pictures were taken in the summer of 2001 near Airport No. 2 (about the center of Salt Lake County) and then spliced together. Highlighted in the picture are the main mountain peaks

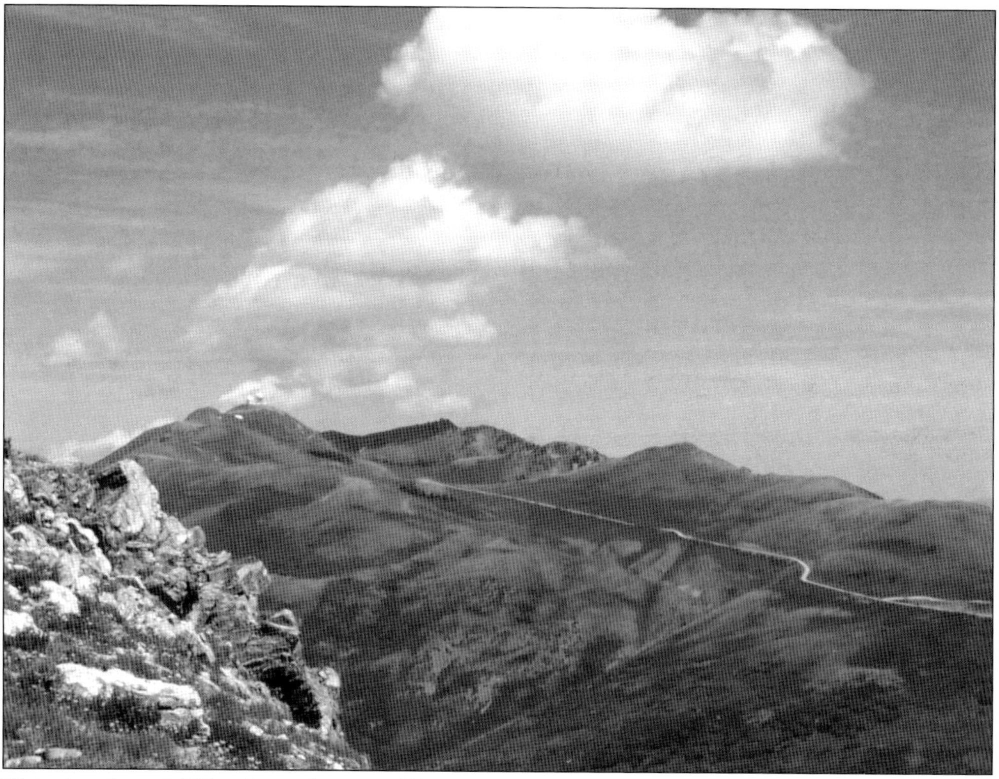

This view from 2007 is from the top of Farmington Canyon, showing Francis Peak with its twin radar domes as well as a lot of backcountry. A wide dirt road leads from here to Francis Peak, or if a right turn is made, another road goes south along the top of the Wasatch Mountains and winds down into Bountiful City. (Photograph by Roger Arave.)

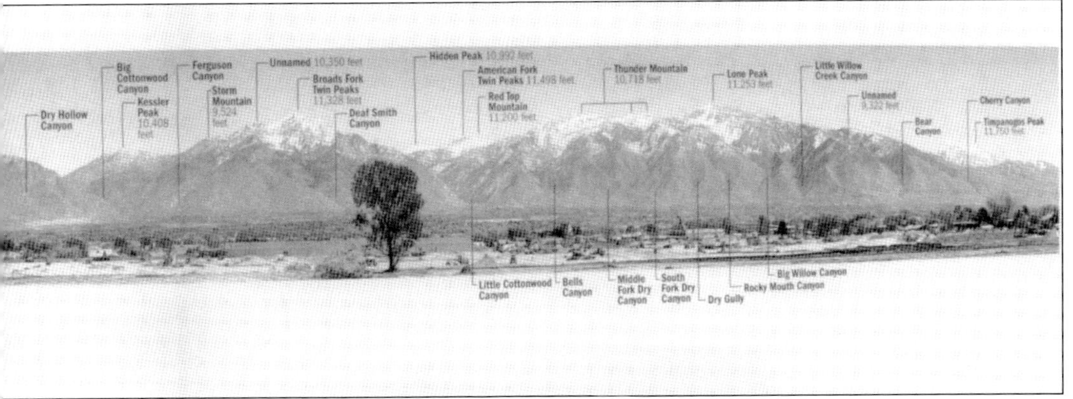

and canyons' names there as researched from various maps. (Photograph by Scott Winterton; courtesy of *Deseret News* Archives.)

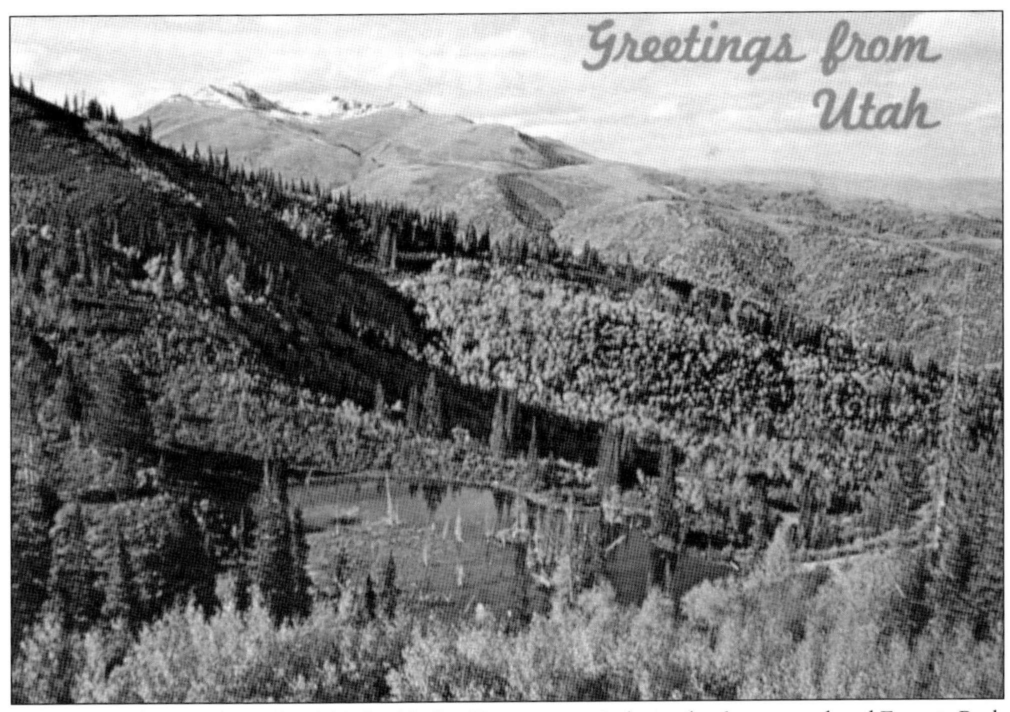

This postcard from the early 1980s highlights Farmington Lake in the foreground and Francis Peak in the background. The picture was taken during the early fall season when the autumn leaves were most colorful. These fall leaves are a coveted seasonal eye candy of the Wasatch Mountains. (Courtesy of author.)

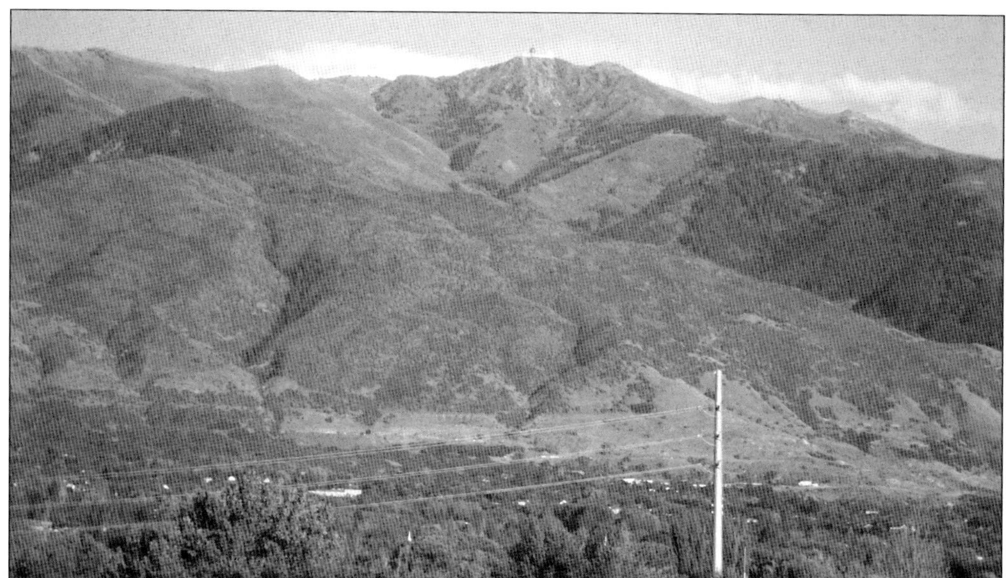

The twin radar domes atop Francis Peak in Davis County are true skymarks and are among the most unusual of features in the entire Wasatch Mountains. As viewed from Layton's South Main Street in 2013, they sit roughly a vertical mile above the valley floor and aid in long-range commercial and military radar operations. (Photograph by author.)

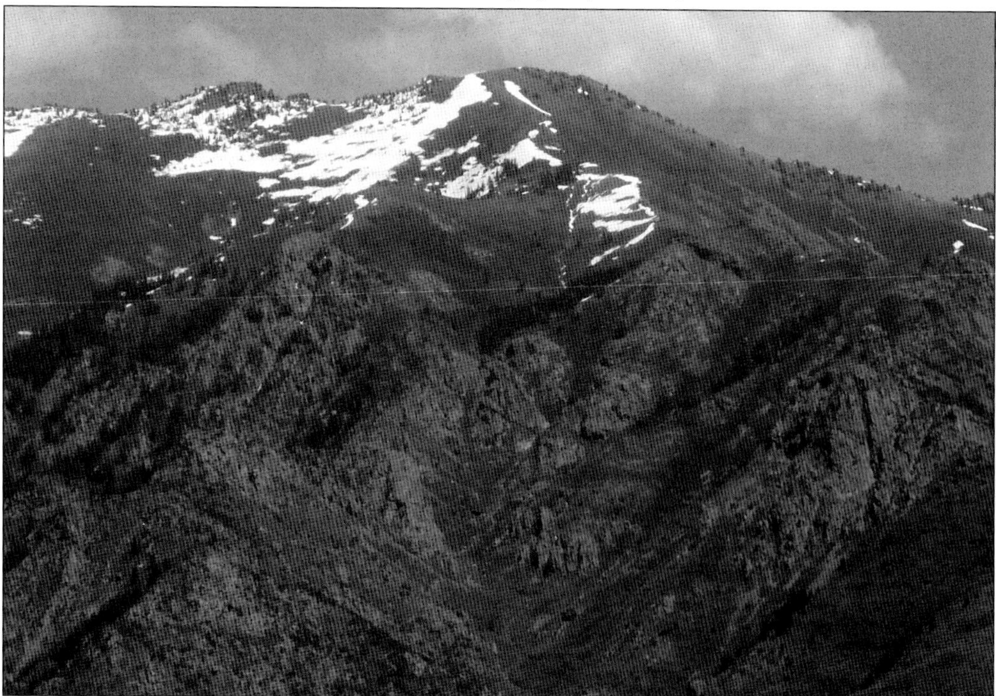

This is Thurston Peak, the tallest mountain in both Davis and Morgan Counties, at 9,706 feet, as it appears from Layton City. The book's author wrote a newspaper story in 1991 highlighting this previously unnamed peak, and soon after, a Morgan County historian launched a campaign to name the peak in 1993 after the Thurston family, who had roots in both Davis and Morgan Counties. (Photograph by author.)

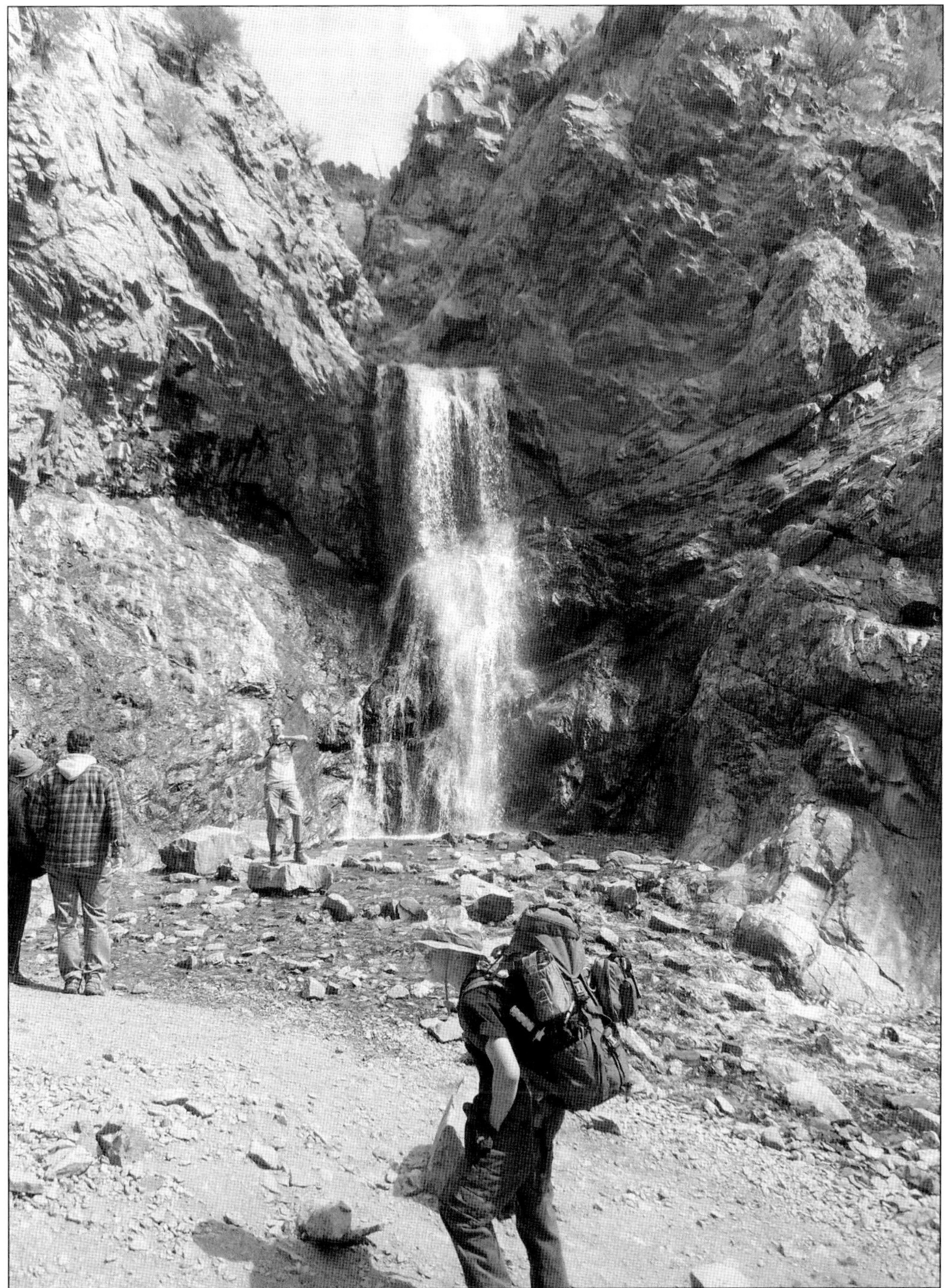

Adams Canyon, east of Layton, boasts the best waterfall in all of Davis County. The 40-foot falls is best in the spring but runs year-round. It is accessible by a three-mile hike, with the trailhead situated at the top of Oak Hills Drive and US Highway 89 in Layton. It is one of many waterfalls that dot the Wasatch Mountains. (Photograph by author.)

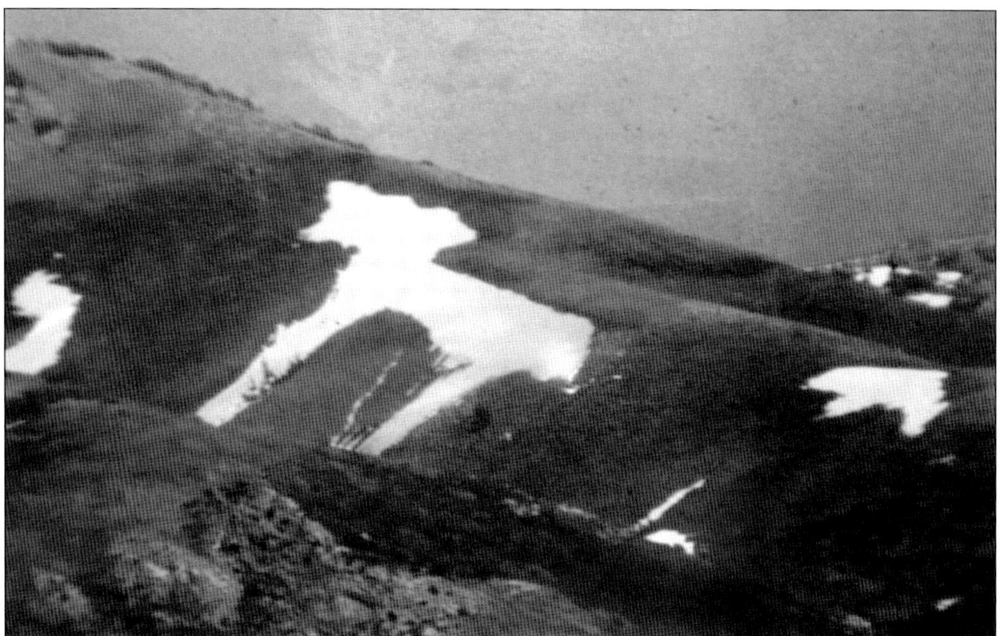

This is the "Snow Horse," east of Layton City. Made out of snow that fills some deep gullies on the Wasatch mountainside, it appears almost every spring around late May to early June. It has been a seasonal landmark since pioneer times, and this photograph hangs in Layton City Hall. There is at least one other such "snow mark" in the Wasatch Mountains—in some winters a smiling face shape can be seen on Ben Lomond Peak. (Photograph by Harris Adams.)

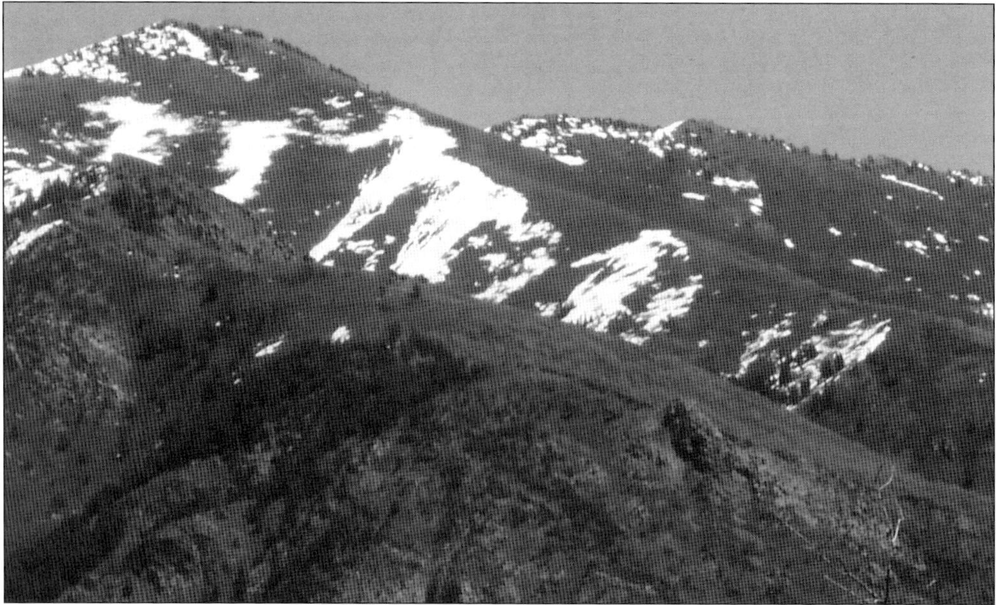

This is a 2016 photograph of the Snow Horse shape east of Layton. The figure becomes slimmer as the snow melts. Also to the left, a "U" letter shape can often be seen, a delight to fans of the University of Utah. The early pioneers in the area used the appearance and staying power of the Snow Horse to gauge how much summer water their farms could rely on, with snowmelt from the mountain streams around the Snow Horse. (Photograph by Taylor Arave.)

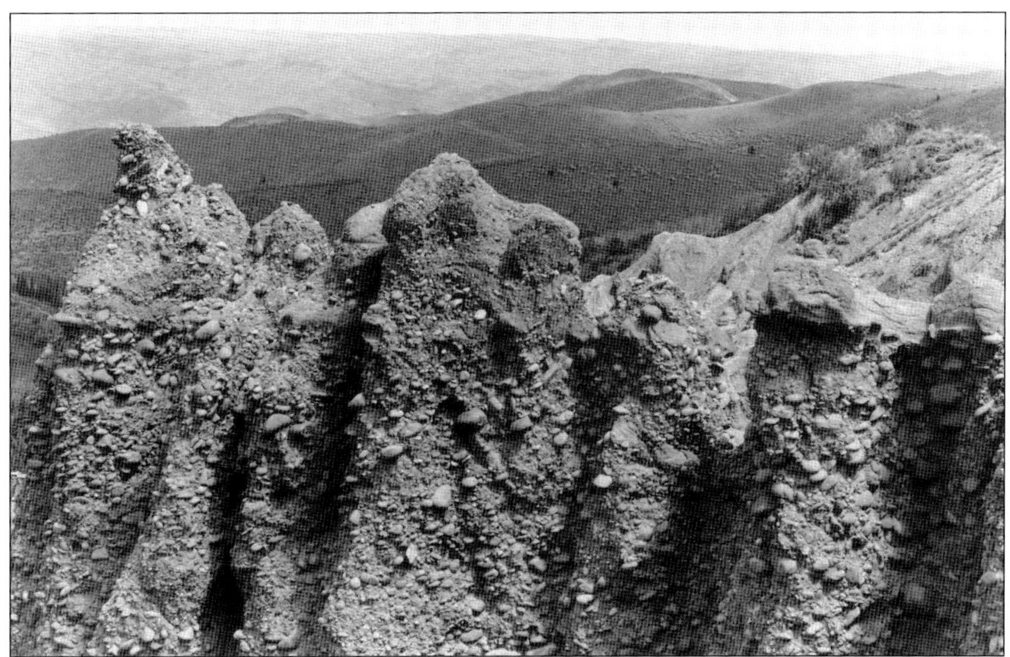

Chinatown, an unusual area of red rock and odd shapes, is located in the Morgan County area of the Wasatch Mountains, above the north slope of Weber Canyon, near Lost Creek. This is Chinatown's area of conglomerate rock shapes, in a 1988 photograph. (Photograph by author.)

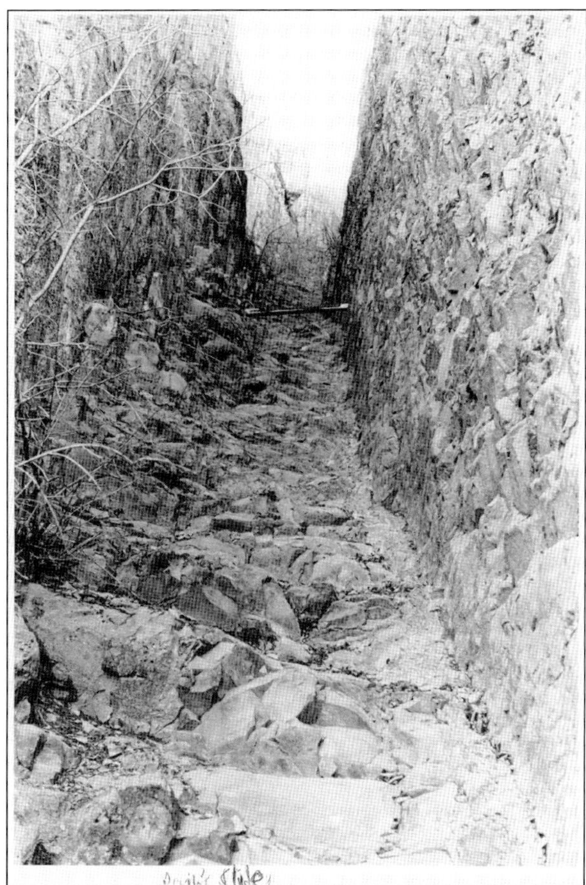

This is what the inside of Devil's Slide, Weber Canyon, looks like from partway up in a 2008 photograph. These vertical slabs of rock are 20 feet apart, about 40 feet high, and some 200 feet long. They are located across the Weber River from the Interstate 84 freeway. Strangely, in August 1911, some Shriners held initiations and ceremonies at the slide, and some members may have actually slid down it into the Weber River below. (Photograph by author.)

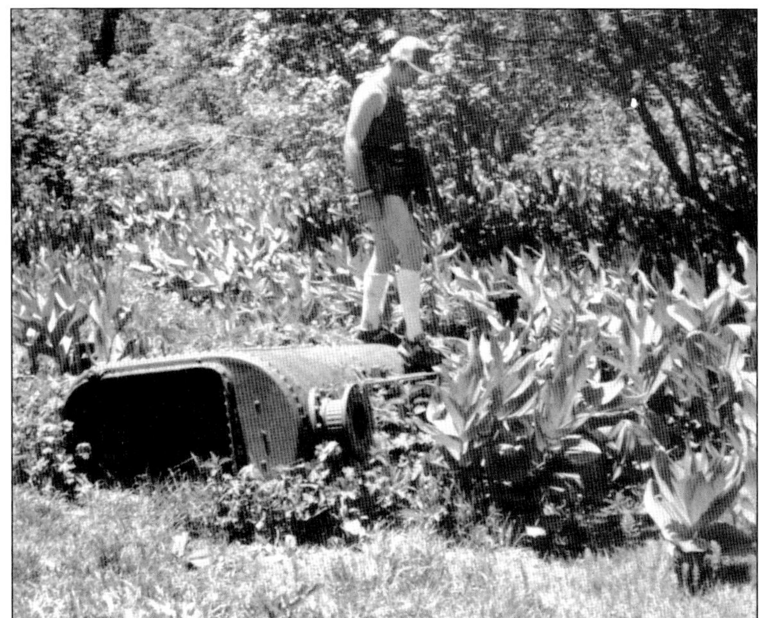

The author walks on top of an old boiler, one of the few remains of Malan's Basin, a late-19th-century mountain resort that existed in the Wasatch Mountains above Ogden City. Located at an elevation of 6,800 feet, the basin used to include a hotel and specialized in chicken dinners. A narrow wagon road, now just a hiking trail, leads there now. (Photograph by Wayne Arave.)

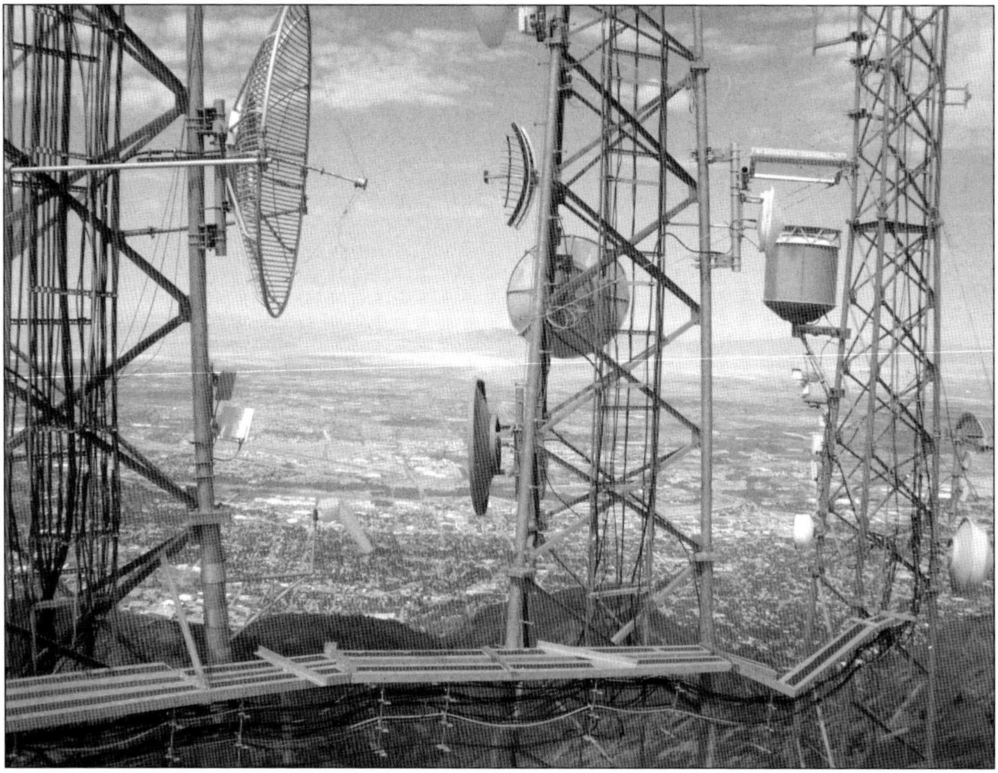

Modern technology has definitely transformed some Wasatch Mountain peaks, for good or bad. This is a portion of Mount Ogden Peak, elevation 9,572 feet, and all the high-tech communications equipment crammed on top. The apparatus here includes cell towers and emergency communication systems for the greater Ogden area. Note that downtown Ogden City is seen in the picture. (Photograph by author.)

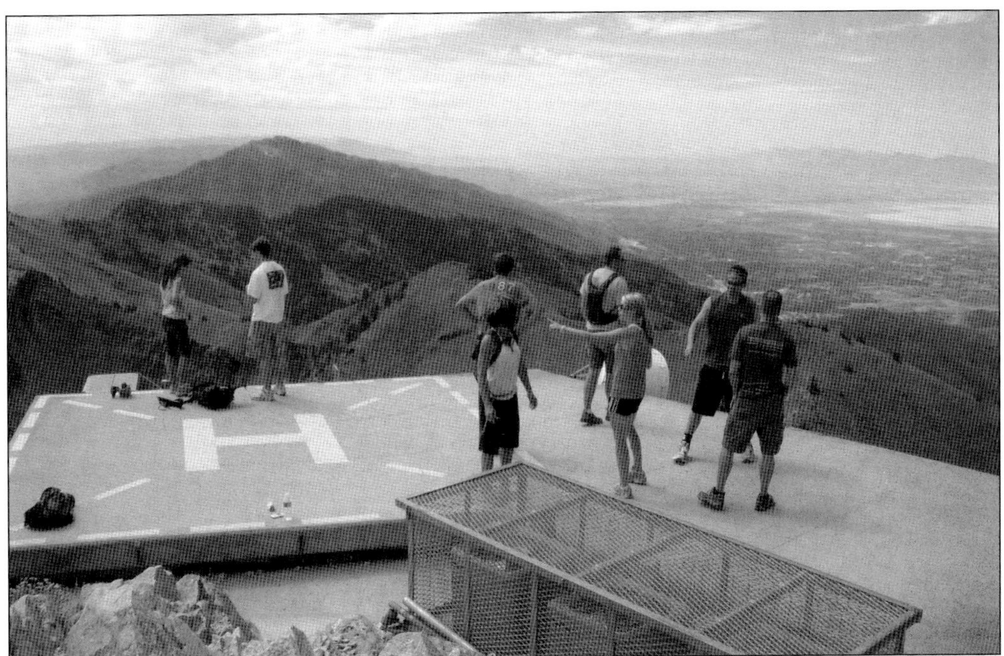

This is the helicopter pad atop Mount Ogden Peak. This all looms above Ogden City on its west side and with Ogden Valley and Snowbasin Ski Resort on the east side. Two groups of hikers enjoy the view in this July 2010 picture. Portions of the Great Salt Lake and Antelope Island can be seen in the distance to the southwest. (Photograph by author.)

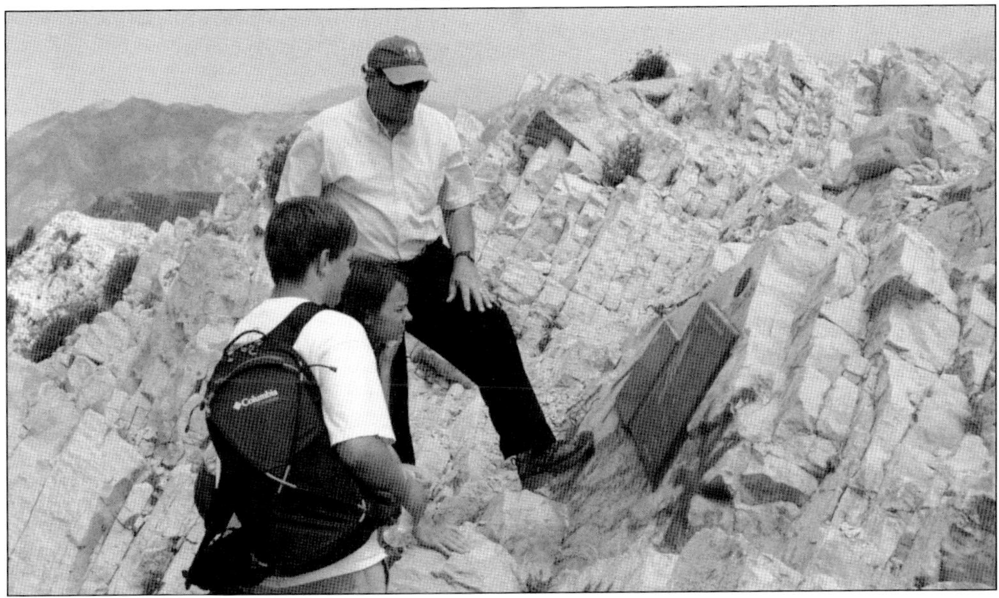

From left to right, Daniel Hafen, Liz Arave Hafen, and author Lynn Arave read the historical plaque atop Mount Ogden. Originally known as Observatory Peak, the summit was climbed regularly by Weber State University students in the 1920s. Starting around that time, there was a mass hiking event by the students, but it soon faded away. It was revived in 1987 by the late Gary D. Willden. Ever since, Weber State University students in large numbers hike Mount Ogden each fall. (Photograph by Roger Arave.)

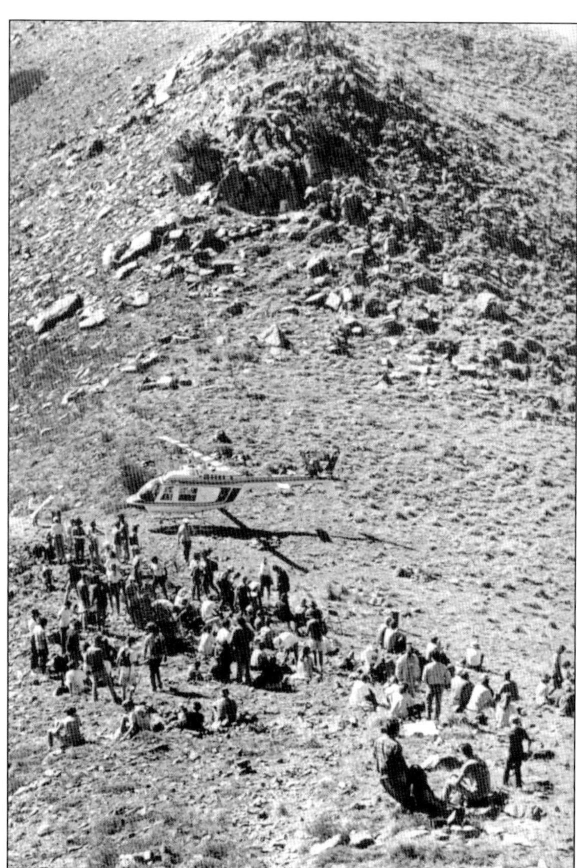

A helicopter sits on the mountain saddle above Ogden in a September 24, 1988, photograph. A special event was held that day, restarting the annual Weber State University mass hike to Mount Ogden, the highest peak near the university. The copter transported key area senior dignitaries who could not hike to the 9,572-foot summit. (Photograph by author.)

A group of six hikers, including then Weber State University president Stephen D. Nadauld (second from right), proceed upward and toward the Mount Ogden summit on September 24, 1988. In the original 1922 fall hike by the university, David O. McKay hiked to the summit. He was a former principal for Weber State and then a member of the board of trustees. He was later president of the LDS church. (Photograph by author.)

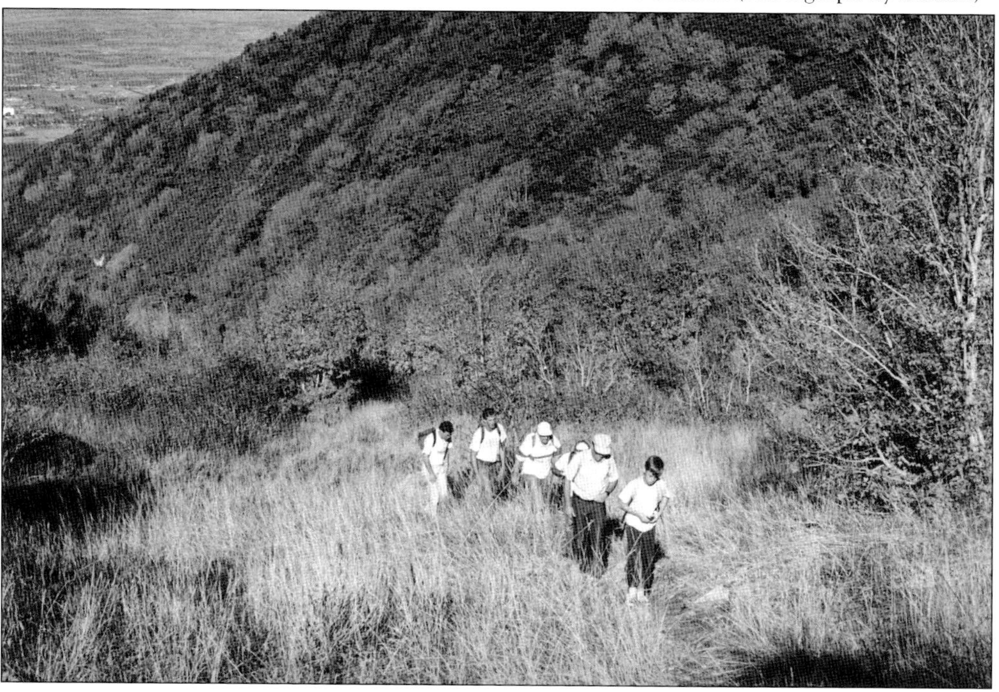

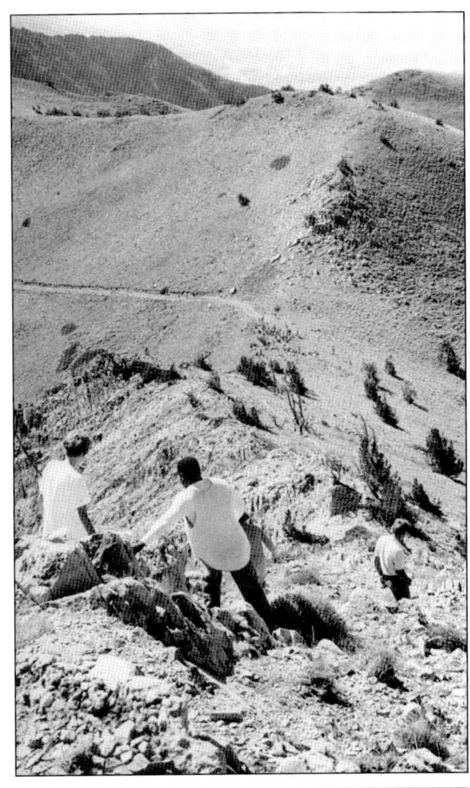

Some hikers slowly creep down the precarious south slope of Mount Ogden Peak on September 24, 1988, to join the group below. A special program, in the dip of the mountain saddle, was later held on the restart of the annual Weber State University hike and part of the celebration of Weber State's centennial birthday that year. (Photograph by author.)

This is a close-up of Ben Lomond Peak, elevation 9,712, the most majestic mountain in Weber County. In fact, it inspired the "Mountain of Dreams" logo that Paramount Pictures Corporation uses. The company's founder, William Wadsworth Hodkinson, grew up in Ogden and drew the logo out of his childhood memories. However, like Hollywood often does, the peak was exaggerated in the logo. Still, this makes Ben Lomond Peak perhaps the most famous of all peaks in the Wasatch Mountains. (Photograph by author.)

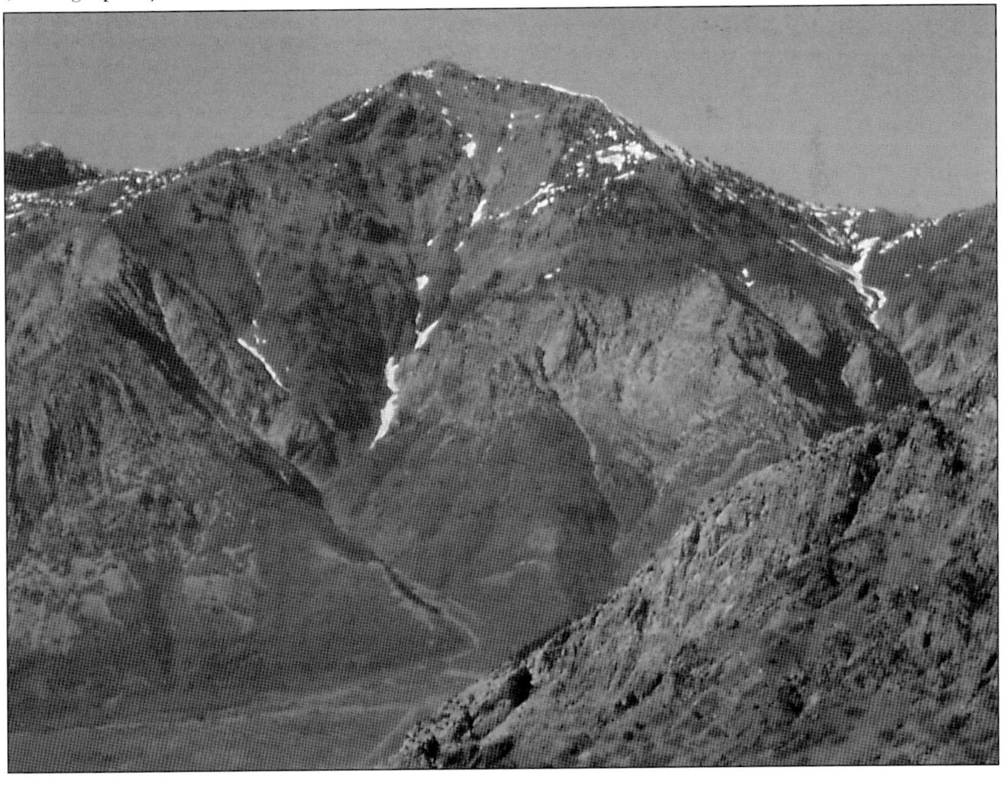

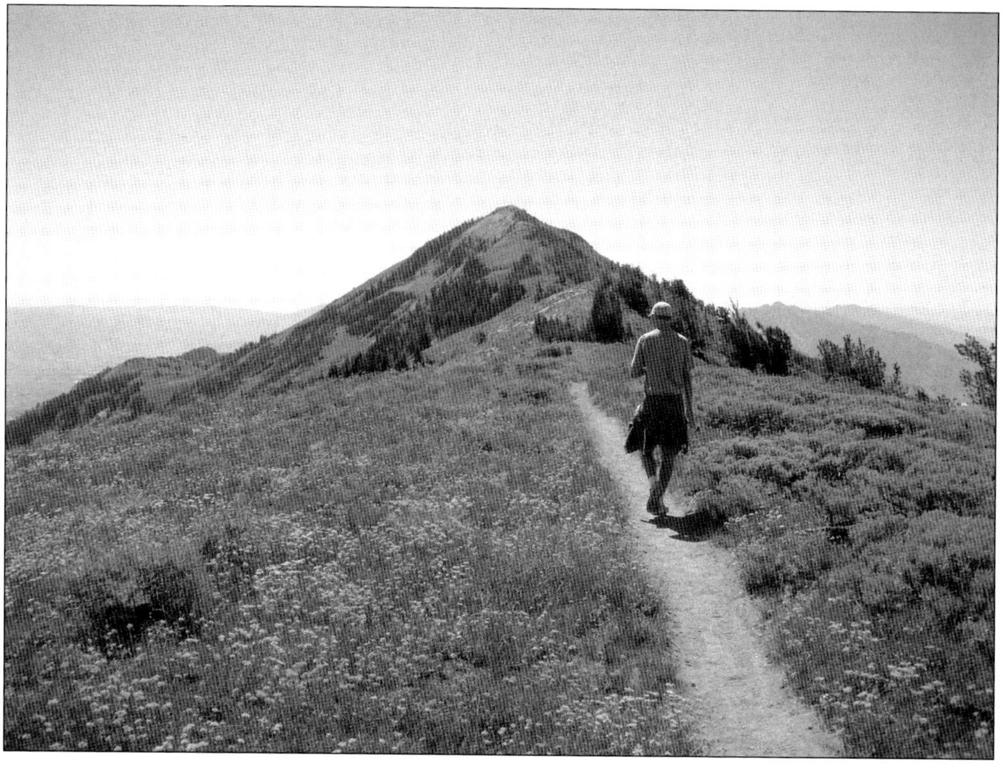

Taylor Arave hikes toward the summit of Ben Lomond Peak during an August 2010 visit. With wildflowers aplenty, summer is a great time to visit the area. This was a hike from Willard Basin to Willard Peak and then to Ben Lomond Peak and back. Since Willard Basin is some 9,000 feet in elevation, hiking from there requires much less elevation gain. (Photograph by author.)

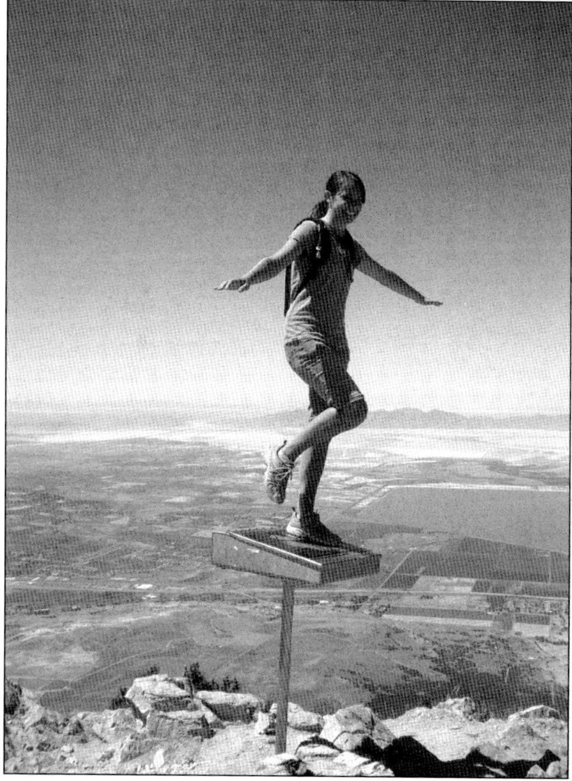

Liz Arave Hafen balances atop the metal pedestal on Ben Lomond Peak in August 2010. Such a marker has been on the summit since the early 1970s, but this one is the second version since the first pedestal only lasted a few decades. Willard Bay is the square body of water in the picture. (Photograph by author.)

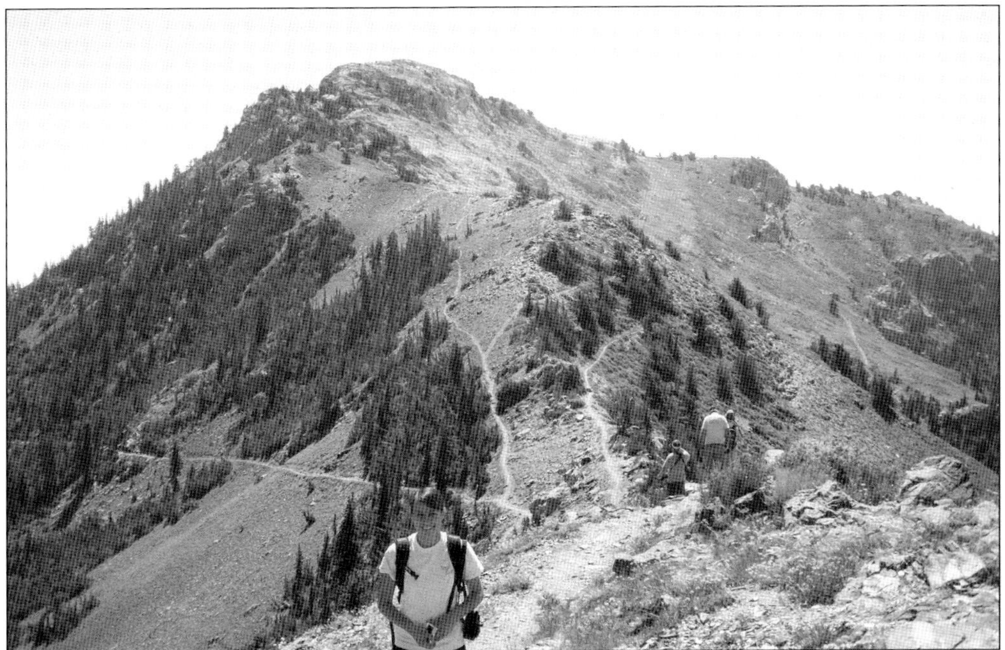

Liz Arave Hafen poses in front of Willard Peak during a July 2008 hike in the area. It rarely looks like it, but Willard Peak is actually taller than neighboring Ben Lomond Peak at 9,763 feet in elevation. Ben Lomond is 51 feet shorter, but about the only place it appears shorter than Willard, the tallest summit in Weber County, is to the north—on the east bench of Logan, Cache County. (Photograph by author.)

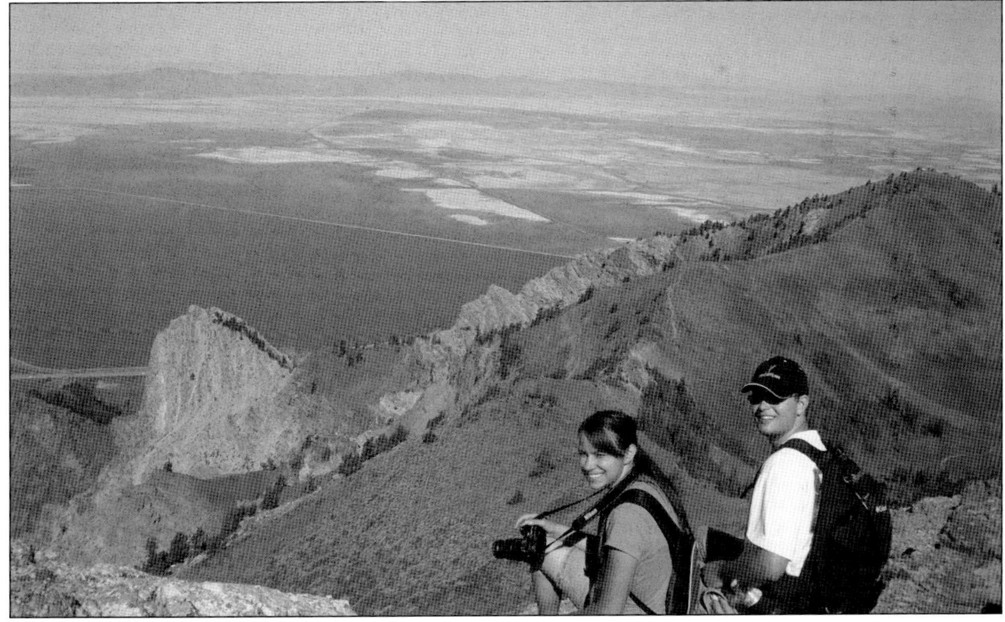

Liz Arave Hafen and Daniel Hafen enjoy the spectacular view from atop Willard Peak, on the Weber and Box Elder County line, in the summer of 2010. Note the massive rock fin sticking out of the Wasatch Mountains below. Willard Bay is also highlighted in the valley below, and the Great Salt Lake is beyond that. (Photograph by author.)

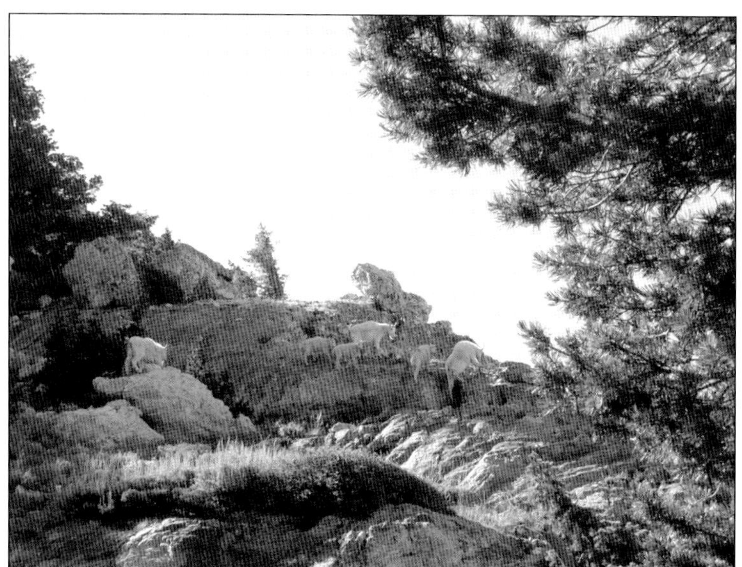

A large herd of mountain goats scurry about the rocky hillside below Willard Peak as a group of hikers intrude on their space. Mountain goats were reintroduced to the Willard Peak area starting in 1994. These mountain goats were transplanted from Wenatchee, Washington, and have been in the area ever since. (Photograph by author.)

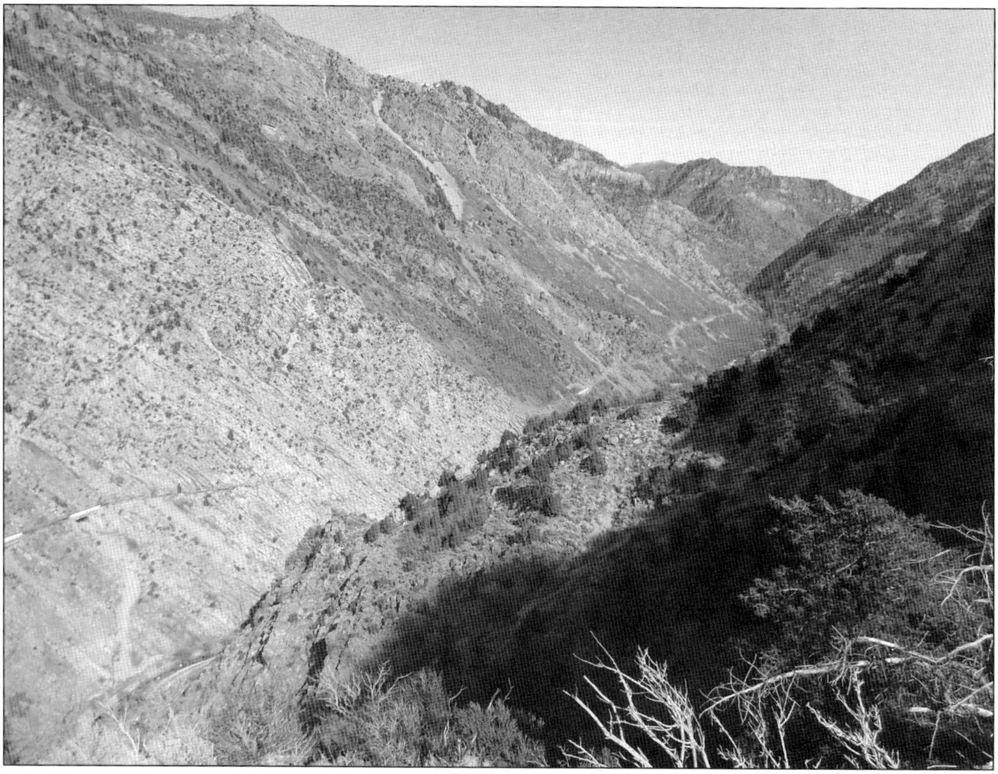

This is the view from the Indian Trail looking northeast down into one of the narrowest portions of Ogden Canyon, near the canyon mouth. In this 2015 picture, a slice of State Highway 39 is visible below as well as the large waterline coming from Pineview Reservoir. This ancient trail is how Native Americans used to access the canyon. (Photograph by author.)

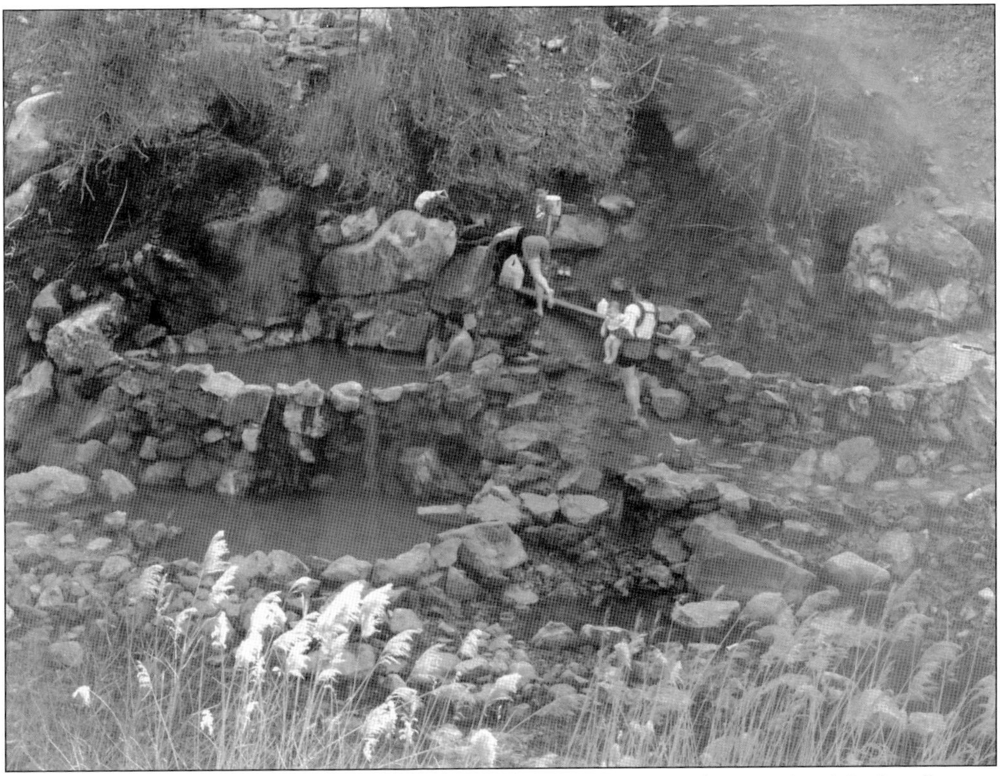

This is the natural hot springs located about 600 yards east from the mouth of Ogden Canyon on the south side. Although it is on private property (and has no trespassing signs posted), some enthusiasts, like those shown, still frequent the site year-round despite a crackdown on trespassers. This hot spring is also the source of the natural hot water that all versions of the resorts at the mouth of Ogden Canyon have used, from the original Ogden Canyon Sanitarium to today's Rainbow Gardens. (Photograph by author.)

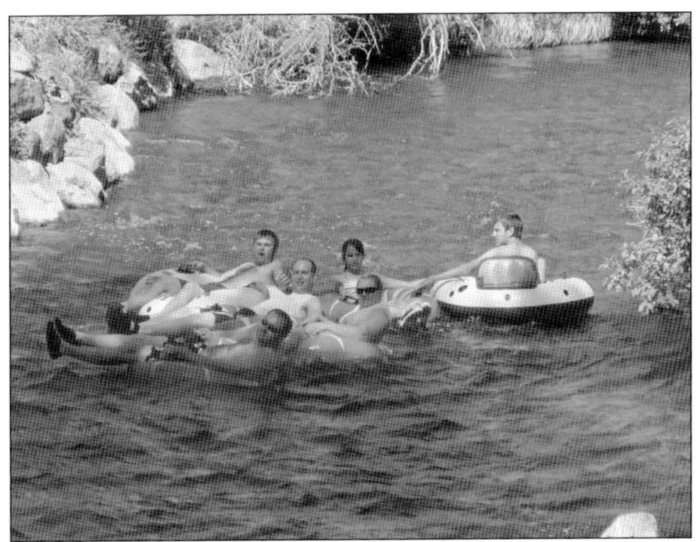

There is nothing more refreshing on a hot summer's day than tubing down a cold mountain river. This is the South Fork of the Ogden River, east of Huntsville, where a large group of the Lynn and LeAnn Arave family is tubing near the Perception Park Campground in late July 2012. A nearby return walking trail allows tubers to float 600 yards down the river, exit, and walk back to their starting point to repeat the float. (Photograph by author.)

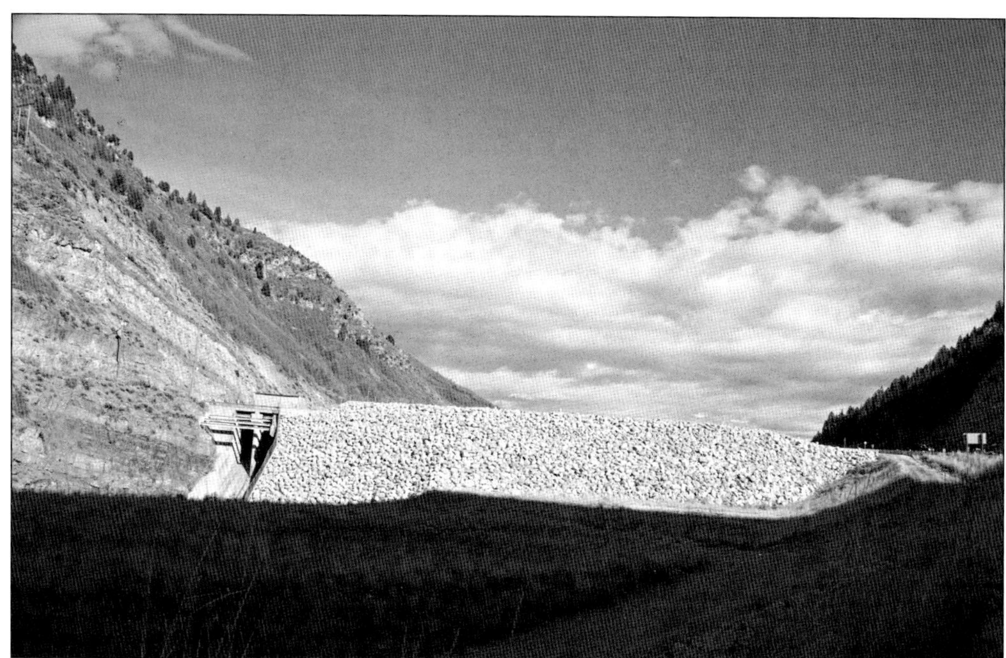

This is the rock and earthen-lined Pineview Dam in Ogden Valley. Pineview is one of many such reservoirs that store water in the Wasatch Mountains for later use in the warm and dry months of the year. Pineview was constructed in 1937. The dam was expanded in 1957 and is now 132 feet high and 600 feet wide. (Photograph by Whitney Arave.)

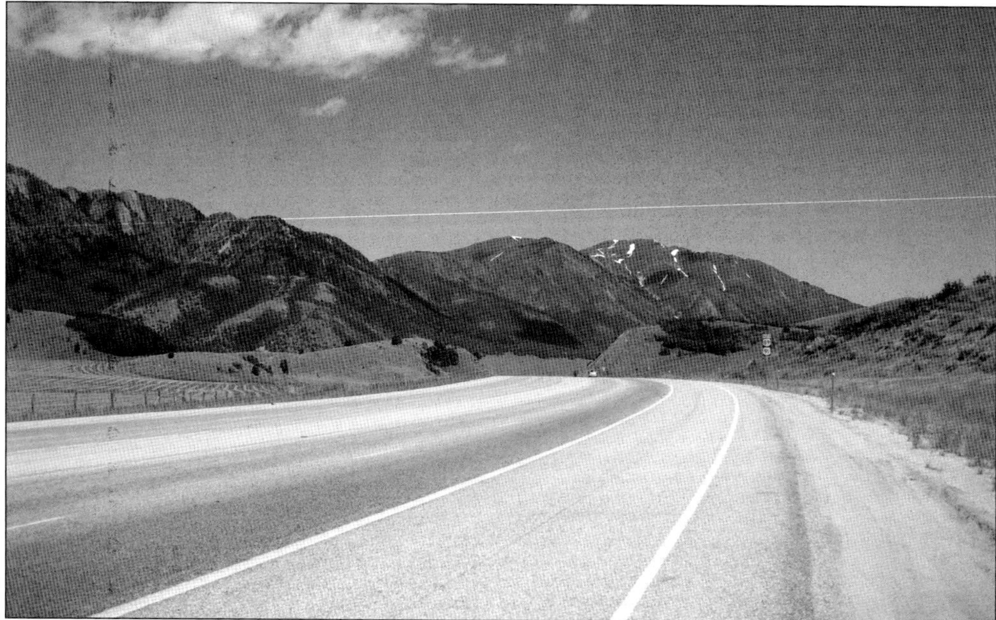

The Wellsville Mountains are a segment of the Wasatch Mountains, as seen in this 2012 photograph from Sardine Summit along Highway 89. These mountains are sometimes reputed to be among the steepest in the world, but in reality, there is no geographical formula for determining such a superlative. Notwithstanding, the Wellsville Mountains do indeed appear unusually steep and rugged. (Photograph by author.)

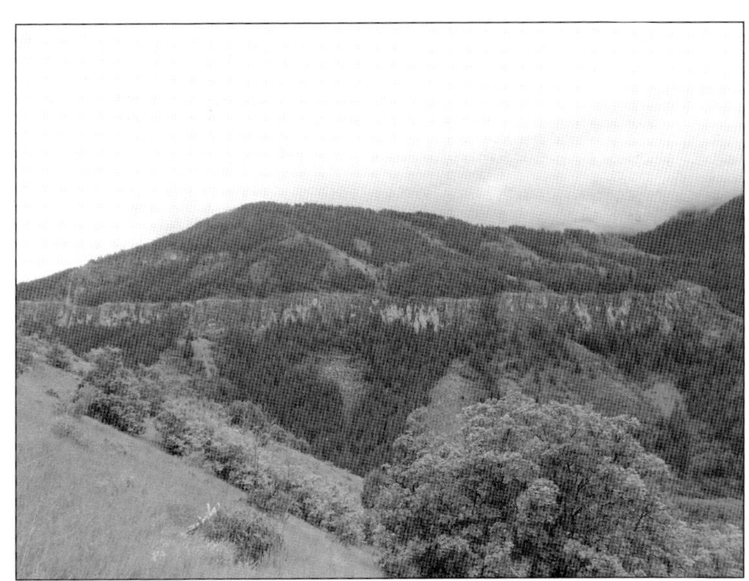

This is the China Wall on the south slope of Logan Canyon. This geological feature is highly visible and is composed of limestone. Its name comes from the formation resembling the Great Wall of China. This particular photograph was taken about five miles up the canyon from Logan, along the trail to the Wind Cave. (Photograph by author.)

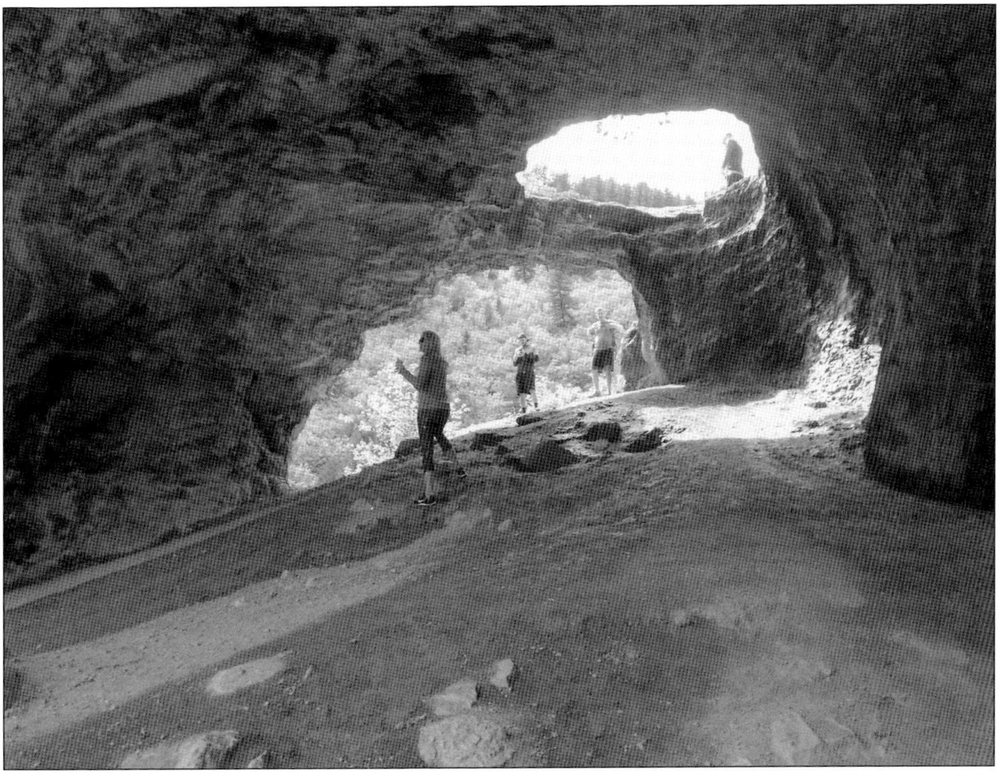

This is the inside of the Wind Cave in Logan Canyon. This geological delight has become a popular hiking destination in the Wasatch Mountains. This 2015 view is looking southward through the "cave." The trailhead to the Wind Cave is 5.1 miles up Logan Canyon, and the steep path leading up the mountain is 1.9 miles long. (Photograph by author.)

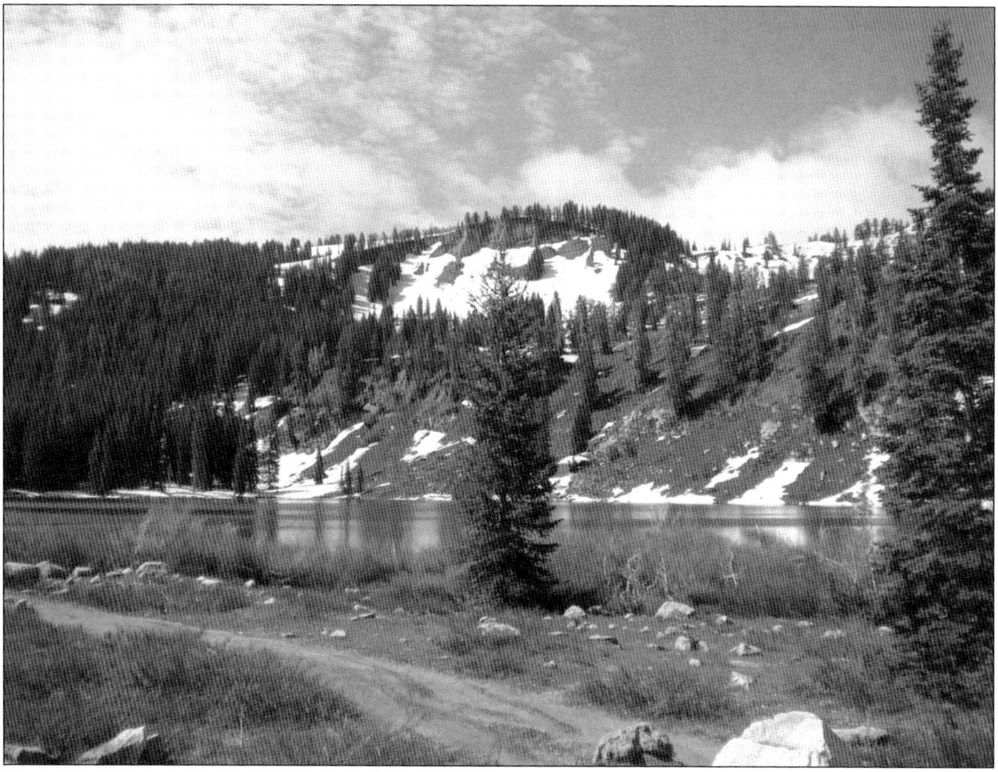

Tony Grove and its accompanying lake are shown in late spring, with lingering snow patches. Located at an elevation of 8,100 feet in the Wasatch Mountains, north of Logan Canyon, its name developed from the 1880s. That is when local ranchers and loggers first observed that the well-to-do crowd from Logan, then nicknamed the "Tony people," would congregate here every summer. Eventually, the "Tony" name took hold of the place. (Photograph by author.)

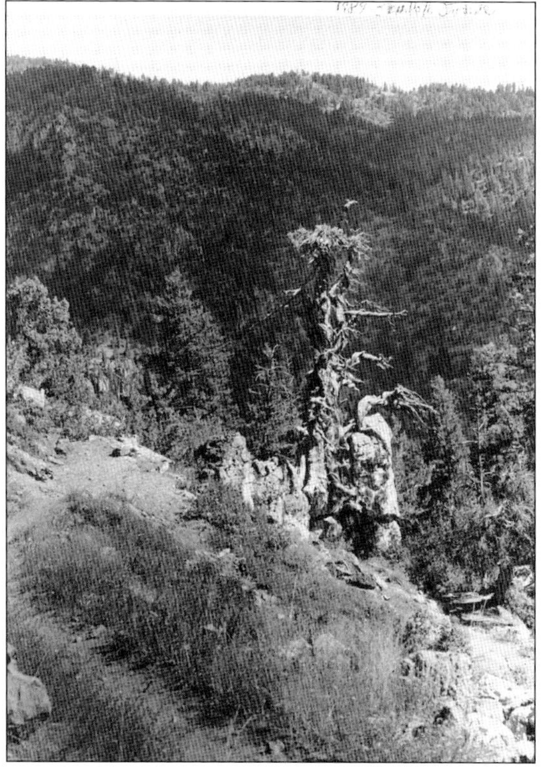

This is the Jardine Juniper Tree in Logan Canyon. This craggy old juniper tree is more than 1,500 years old and stands high, as a sort of a sentinel, above the north rim of the canyon. The 5.8-mile, one-way trailhead to the tree can be found 10.4 miles up Logan Canyon, near Wood Camp. (Photograph by author.)

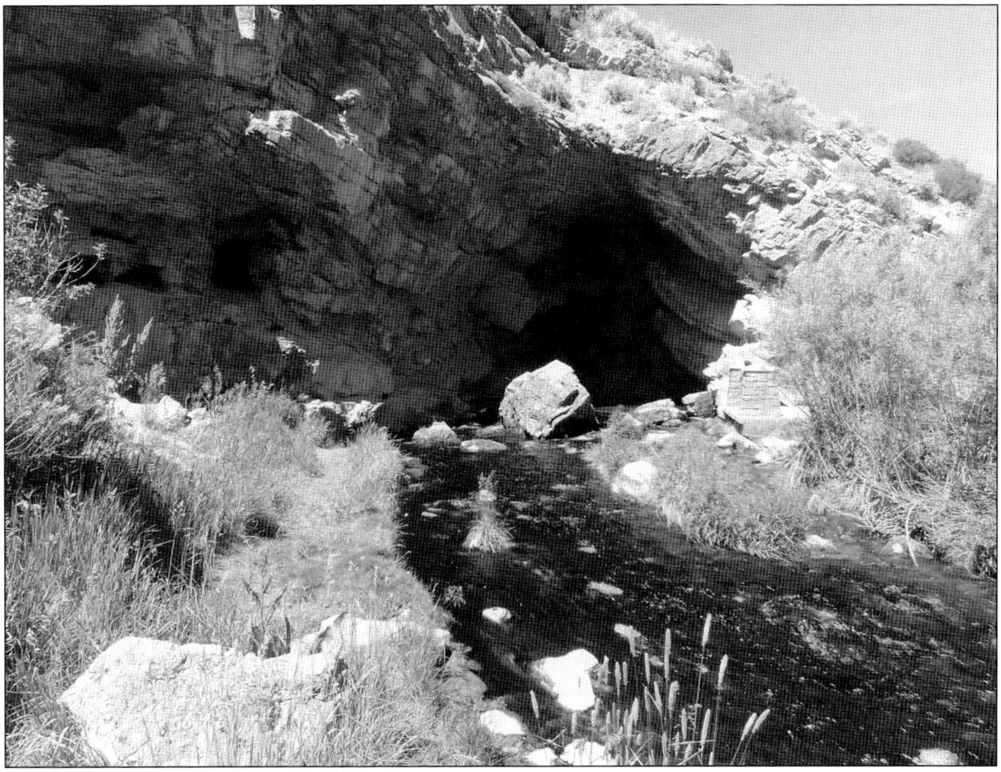

Ricks Springs has long been a way station in Logan Canyon since pioneer times. Located 15.7 miles up Logan Canyon, along US Highway 89, it is named for Thomas E. Ricks, who first discovered it. However, in 1972, scientists realized that Ricks Springs is actually both a spring and a diversion of part of the Logan River, so drinking the water coming from the cave there is no longer considered safe. (Photograph by author.)

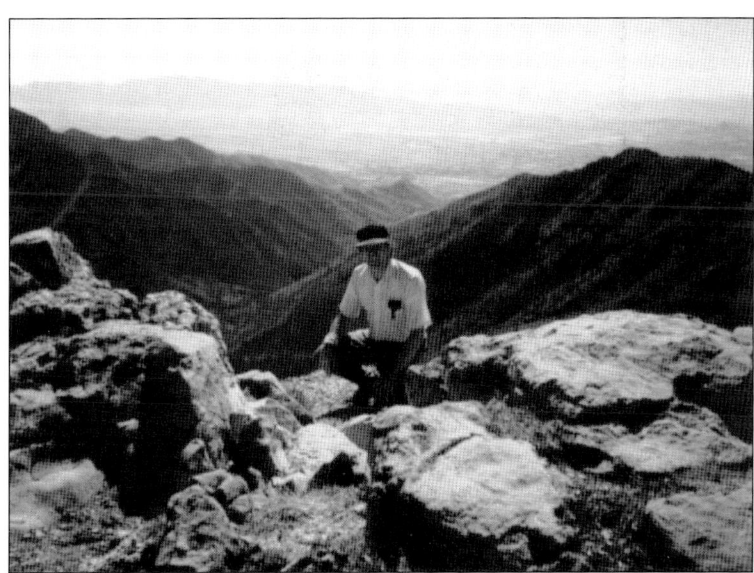

The author stands atop Mount Naomi in a 1995 photograph. This is the tallest peak in Cache County on the north end of the Wasatch Mountains, at 9,979 feet above sea level. The view is looking west into Cache Valley. The peak can be reached by a four-mile, one-way trail from Tony Grove that climbs 1,950 feet. (Photograph by Roger Arave.)

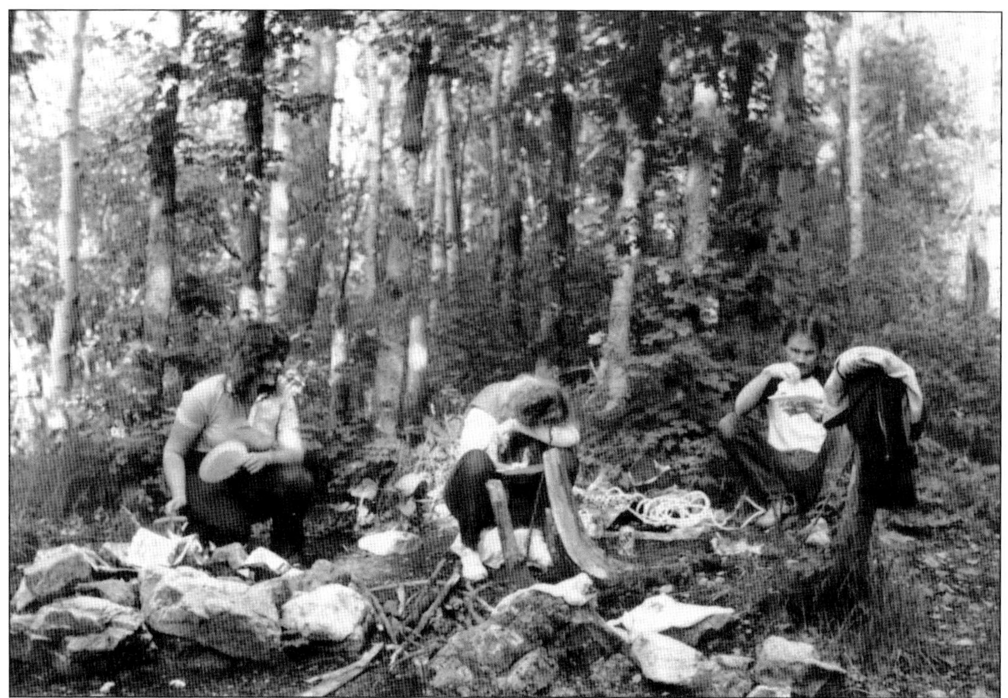

Three young adults enjoy a hot dog cookout deep in the Wasatch Mountains in the summer of 1984. Running more than 160 miles in length, these mountains offer countless recreational opportunities. However, more and more locations are instituting user fees because of high usage and even overcrowding. (Photograph by author.)

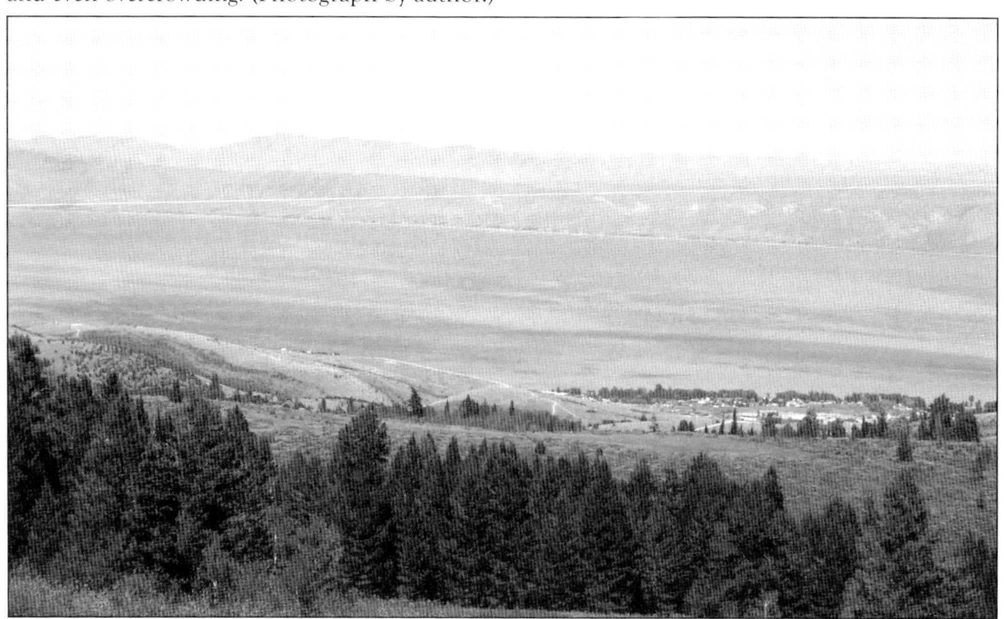

This is the overlook to Bear Lake, at the top of the Bear River/Wasatch Mountains in 2020. World-famous for its incredible turquoise blue color, black-and-white photographs do not do Bear Lake justice. This lake is more than 20 miles long and 8 miles wide. It is up to 208 feet deep and is a popular summer recreation area for both Utah and Idaho. (Photograph by author.)

The author stands behind an old weather station at the bottom of Peter Sinks, located south of the top of Logan Canyon, in July 1990. At the time, this extremely frigid spot in the Wasatch Mountains had not yet gained national attention for its hyper-cold temperatures. (Photograph by Wayne Arave.)

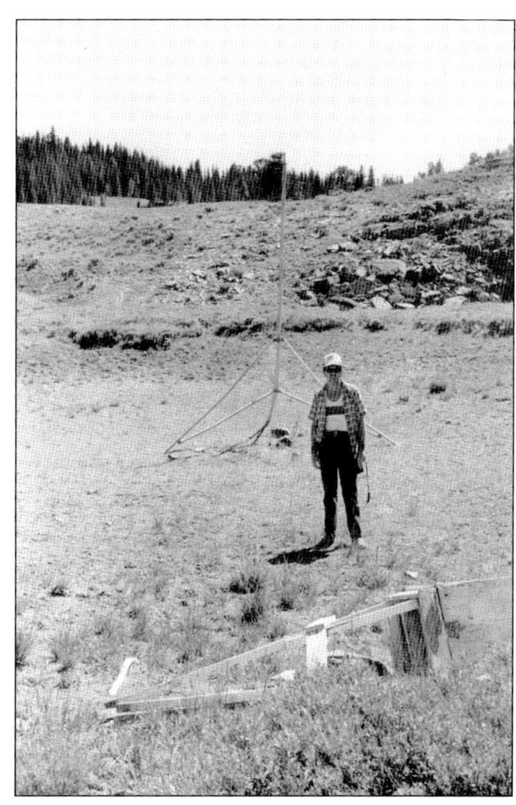

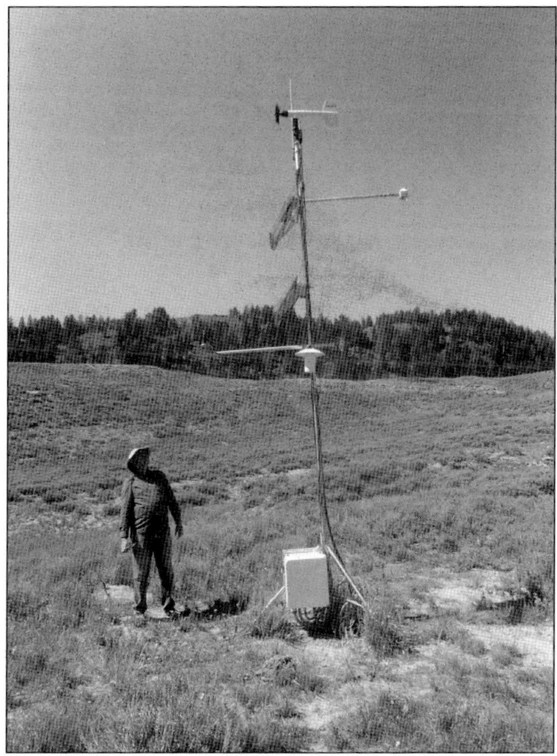

Scott Steele of Syracuse, Utah, examines the automated weather station at the bottom of Peter Sinks, south of Logan Canyon. Located in a limestone sinkhole at 8,100 feet above sea level, this area has dipped to some of the coldest temperatures in all of the United States, at 69.3 degrees below zero. A three-mile hike (or rugged jeep road) leads to the site off Sink Road at the top of Logan Canyon. (Photograph by author.)

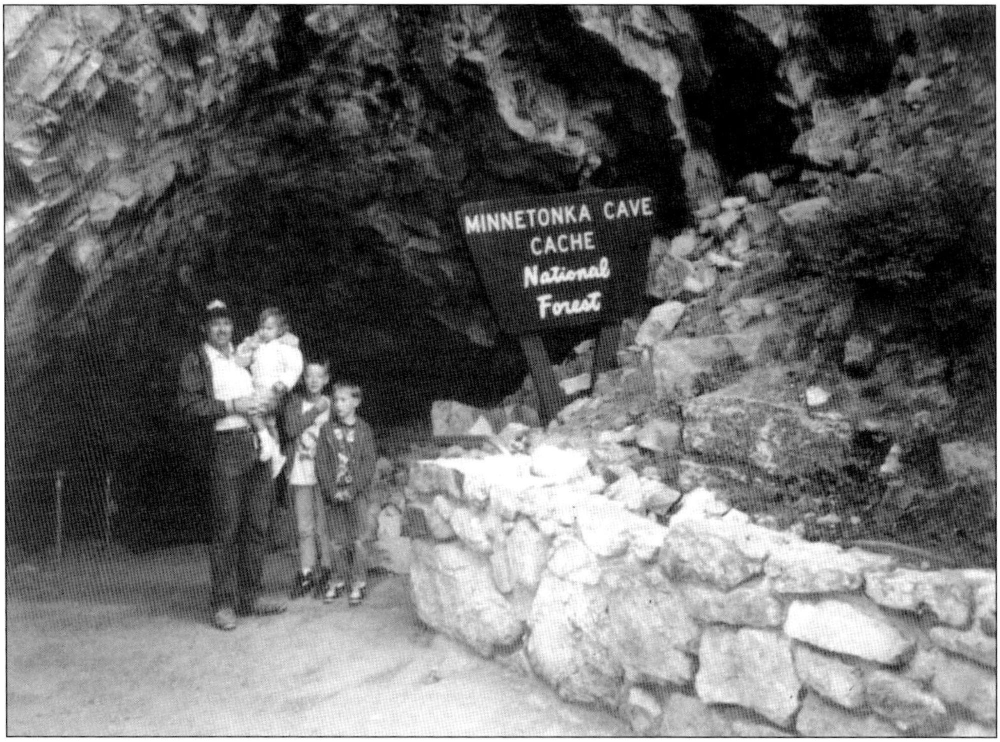

The author and three of his children pose next to the entrance of Minnetonka Cave, another significant, large cavernous formation in the Wasatch Mountains. Its interior was not vandalized as significantly as other such caves, so it still contains many intriguing formations. Minnetonka is only open in the summer season and is located eight miles west of St. Charles, Idaho. (Photograph by LeAnn Arave.)

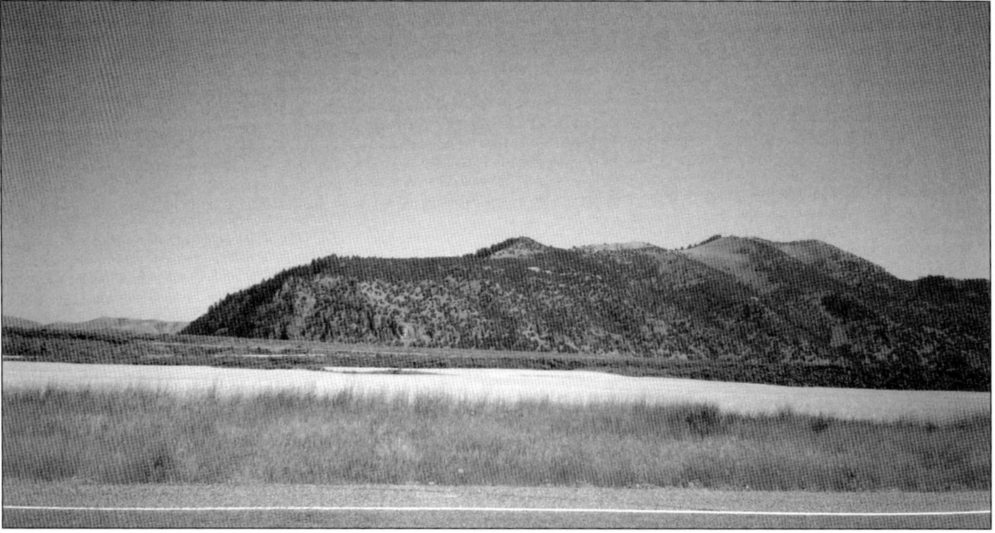

This is Soda Point/Sheep Rock, the northernmost end of the Wasatch Mountains. Located just north of the town of Grace, Idaho, and west of Soda Springs, this is also where the Bear River loops around the mountains and heads south toward the Great Salt Lake. Some Native American legends also involve Soda Point and its ancient history. (Photograph by author.)

Bibliography

Daughters of Utah Pioneers and Milton R. Hunter, ed. *Beneath Ben Lomond's Peak: A History of Weber County 1824–1900*. Salt Lake City, UT: Quality Press, 1995.
Deseret News Archives
digitalnewspapers.org
historytogo.utah.gov
Hunter, Milton R. *Brigham Young the Colonizer.* Salt Lake City, UT: Deseret News Press, 1940.
newspapers.com
Van Cott, John W. *Utah Place Names.* Salt Lake City, UT: University of Utah Press, 1990.
www.uen.org